THE UNBOUNDED HOME

Lee Anne Fennell

THE

**PROPERTY VALUES
BEYOND PROPERTY LINES**

UNBOUNDED

HOME

Yale University Press
New Haven & London

Published with assistance from the Louis Stern
Memorial Fund.

Printed in the United States of America.

Library of Congress Cataloging-in-Publication Data

Fennell, Lee Anne.
 The unbounded home : property values beyond property
lines / Lee Anne Fennell.
  p. cm.
 Includes bibliographical references and index.

 ISBN 978-0-300-12244-2 (pbk. : alk. paper) 1. Land
use—Law and legislation. 2. Right of property. 3. Commons. 4. Homeowners' associations—Law and legislation.
5. Home—Philosophy. I. Title.
 K3534.F46 2009
 343.73′025—dc22   2008054894

A catalogue record for this book is available from the British
Library.

This paper meets the requirements of ANSI/NISO Z39.48–
1992 (Permanence of Paper).

10 9 8 7 6 5 4 3 2 1

FOR CHRIS

CONTENTS

PART IV. RECONFIGURING HOMEOWNERSHIP

ACKNOWLEDGMENTS

This book grew out of ideas that I have been exploring for a number of years. In writing it, I have rethought, distilled, updated, and linked together many lines of analysis that have appeared in my past publications, interweaving past work with new elements. The book's chapters contain material drawn or adapted from my earlier scholarship, as indicated below. I thank the relevant publishers for their cooperation.

Chapter 1 covers some ground previously explored in "Property and Half-Torts," *Yale Law Journal* 116 (2007): 1400–1471.

Chapter 2 contains material adapted from "Exclusion's Attraction: Land Use Controls in Tieboutian Perspective," in *The Tiebout Model at Fifty: Essays in Public Economics in Honor of William Oates*, edited by William A. Fischel, 163–98 (Cambridge, MA: Lincoln Institute of Land Policy, 2006). It also contains some material derived from "Homes Rule," *Yale Law Journal* 112 (2002): 617–64 (book review of William A. Fischel, *The Homevoter Hypothesis: How Home Values Influence Local Government Taxation, School Finance, and Land-Use Policies* [2001]).

Much of Chapter 3 is drawn or adapted from "Common Interest Tragedies," *Northwestern University Law Review* 98 (2004): 907–90. A small portion of the chapter is drawn from "Slices and Lumps," University of Chicago Law and Economics, Olin Working Paper No. 395, March 2008, http://ssrn.com/abstract=1106421.

Portions of Chapter 4 were derived from "Contracting Communities," *University of Illinois Law Review* 2004 (2004): 829–98, and "Common

Interest Tragedies," *Northwestern University Law Review* 98 (2004): 907–90. In addition, some material in Chapter 4 was adapted from "Hard Bargains and Real Steals: Land Use Exactions Revisited," *Iowa Law Review* 86 (2000): 1–85, and from "Taking Eminent Domain Apart," *Michigan State Law Review* 2004 (2004): 957–1004.

Chapter 5 is derived in part from "Revealing Options," *Harvard Law Review* 118 (2005): 1399–488, and "Contracting Communities," *University of Illinois Law Review* 2004 (2004): 829–98.

Chapter 6 is derived in part from "Beyond Exit and Voice: User Participation in the Production of Local Public Goods," *Texas Law Review* 80 (2001): 1–87, and "Properties of Concentration," *University of Chicago Law Review* 73 (2006): 1227–97.

Much of Chapter 7 was drawn or adapted from "Properties of Concentration," *University of Chicago Law Review* 73 (2006): 1227–97.

Chapters 8 and 9 were drawn in significant part from "Homeownership 2.0," *Northwestern University Law Review* 102 (2008): 1047–1118.

I owe a great debt of gratitude to numerous colleagues and coparticipants in workshops and conferences who helped me refine and develop my ideas. For institutional support and intellectual community while work on this book and its antecedents was under way, I thank the University of Chicago Law School, whose faculty I joined in 2007; the University of Illinois College of Law, where I taught from 2004 to 2007; the University of Texas School of Law, where I taught from 2001 to 2004; and the New York University School of Law, the University of Virginia School of Law, and Yale Law School, each of which I visited for one semester. I have learned a great deal from the faculty and students at all of these institutions. Thanks also go to the Virginia Foundation for the Humanities, and to the University of Chicago Law School's Bernard G. Sang Faculty Research Fund.

It would be impossible to list all the individuals who have been generous with their time and advice in ways that have improved this book. Special thanks go to Benjamin Barros, David Callies, Nicole Garnett, Jonathan Nash, Robert Nelson, Daria Roithmayr, Richard Schragger, Lior Strahilevitz, and an anonymous reviewer for very helpful comments on earlier drafts. In addition, Ian Ayres, Vicki Been, Abraham Bell, Guido Calabresi, Robert Ellickson, Richard Epstein, William Fischel, Clayton Gillette,

Michael Heller, James Krier, Thomas Merrill, Gideon Parchomovsky, Eduardo Peñalver, Carol Rose, and Henry Smith have contributed immeasurably to my understanding of the topics taken up here, both through their own scholarship and through commentary and conversations relating to my work. The book has also benefited greatly from the input of everyone who provided comments on the prior works drawn on here. In addition to sending out another round of thanks to all the folks mentioned in the acknowledgment notes of those pieces, I would like to single out a few repeat players whose input has been especially valuable—Michael Abramowicz, Lynn Baker, Tom Ginsburg, Mark Gergen, Douglas Laycock, Leandra Lederman, Daryl Levinson, Saul Levmore, Richard McAdams, Eric Rasmusen, Warren Schwartz, and Thomas Ulen. My editor at Yale University Press, Michael O'Malley, provided excellent guidance throughout the publication process, and Otto Bohlmann improved the manuscript with his sharp copyediting skills. Catherine Kiwala and Eric Singer, both of the University of Chicago Law School's class of 2010, provided excellent research assistance. My greatest thanks go to my husband, Christopher Fennell, for his invaluable and tireless contributions to the book project and to all of the articles that preceded it. There are surely many others not listed who played important roles in making this book what it is; you know who you are, and I am grateful. Finally, lest thanking be mistaken for implicating, I remind readers that any errors in the book are entirely my own.

INTRODUCTION

What does property mean, here and now, in the early twenty-first-century United States? This book approaches the question by examining a set of problems surrounding our society's most familiar, important, and emotionally freighted manifestation of property—the home. That the home has evolved as a resource over the past two centuries should not surprise even the most casual observer of social history. In 1790, just over 5 percent of the U.S. population lived in urban areas; by 2000, the figure was 79 percent, and more than 80 percent of the population resided within metropolitan areas.[1] Homeownership rates have also grown significantly; about two thirds of metropolitan area householders are now homeowners.[2] The residential experience for most Americans thus uneasily combines the profound interdependence of metropolitan life with the promise of unbridled autonomy that homeownership connotes.

Property law has done surprisingly little to respond to these transformations in residential life or to address the resulting tension. Although land use controls attempt to counteract the spillovers that interdependence produces, they tend to operate in a blunt and categorical manner that introduces new difficulties. Meanwhile, our notion of home as a form of property remains mired in outdated concepts, dominated by fencelines and surveys, metes and bounds. My project here is to expose the increasingly poor fit between widespread property concepts and the home as it exists today, to isolate the problems caused by that divergence, and to suggest some ways of addressing it.

This book's analysis proceeds from a single, simple premise: the value of residential property in metropolitan areas has come unbound from the four corners of the owned parcel. As the realtor's mantra of "location, location, location" suggests, homebuyers are often much less interested in the on-site attributes of real estate than in the people, things, services, and conditions lying beyond what we continue to refer to as the property's boundaries. Residential property now serves not only as a resource in its own right but also as a placeholder for a quite different set of resources that are not, and cannot be, contained within the physical edges delineated by plat surveys. Yet, law and theory continue to apply boundary-focused templates to homes that bear a greater conceptual resemblance to Bluetooth than to Blackacre. This book uses a series of problems central to residential life in the United States to spotlight this disconnect and to consider what it would mean for law and policy to take seriously the increasingly diffuse nature of residential property's value.

To fix ideas, consider how property concepts surrounding the home might enter the consciousness of a fictitious household, the Middletons, over the course of a single month. The Middletons fret about a pending proposal to redraw elementary school attendance zones (even though their youngest is now in middle school). They speak out at a zoning meeting to oppose the introduction of townhouses in an area three blocks from their home that is currently zoned for single-family homes. They remark with approval on a news article about the planned condemnation of a "blighted" block eight miles from their home, to make way for a development that would offer convenient shopping. They are appalled by an inquiry from city officials about whether Maggie Middleton, who designs Web sites for dozens of clients and advertises her services in the yellow pages, is operating an unlicensed home business. They continue their long-standing dispute with their homeowners association about whether they can park their boat trailer in the driveway. And they register a complaint with the city authorities about their next-door neighbors, who seem to have rented out their basement to another family in violation of zoning law. And so on.

Socialized to view the home as a castle, the Middletons think it only natural that they should control what happens on their own property.[3] As a result, they vehemently resist any intrusion into their ownership prerogatives. But, like most Americans, the Middletons have another reason to be hypervigilant about their home: it represents the household's single largest asset, aside from human capital. For this reason, they feel fully justified in opposing activities beyond their parcel's borders that might devalue their most significant source of financial security.[+] What we have, then, is a nation of homeowners, largely concentrated in metropolitan areas, who act both as castle-keepers bent on controlling their own space and as community crusaders bent on controlling everyone else's. It would be easy to fault the Middletons for being inconsistent, but the real culprit lies in a popular notion of property that fails to square homeownership's promise of dominion and control with the realities of a complex, interdependent world.

Of course, spillovers that affect neighboring properties are nothing new, and law has long possessed tools for addressing them. But when enough of the value of a resource is found beyond the edges of the site we call "the property," we must ask whether we are looking in the right place when contemplating the resource. The question is not one of mere theoretical interest. I contend that the blunt mechanisms that have been used to deflect negative spillovers and to capture positive spillovers are not designed to bear the weight placed upon them by the outward shift in residential property's center of gravity. As a result, efforts to address overwhelming and pervasive off-site influences have created new dilemmas of their own.

Two overlapping sets of homebuyer concerns produce especially challenging interactions among neighbors, developers, and municipalities: neighborhood ambience and community composition. The strategic dilemmas that surround these issues reveal a central fact about property's unbounded nature: the physical exclusion of outsiders from individually owned parcels is a dramatically underprotective strategy for securing access to the resources that people mean to purchase when they buy a home. Unable to physically fence out unwanted impacts or fence in desired amenities, households collectively turn to property mechanisms like zoning and covenants to push control outward from the individual parcel. These mechanisms typically rely on categorical bans on particular land uses within a given neighborhood, zone, or jurisdiction.

The impulse to apply blunt principles of exclusion to a realm that extends beyond the individual parcel is comprehensible, but ultimately problematic. First, there is an obvious tension between the desire, grounded in traditional notions of property, to exercise dominion over one's own parcel and the desire, prompted by the realities of modern life, to control every aspect of the environment surrounding one's parcel. The result has been confusion about what property ownership means, and equal measures of outrage against intrusions on one's prerogatives as an owner and as an interested neighbor. Second, even if individual communities can reach internal agreement about excluding particular land uses from their midst, the overall pattern of land use choices within a larger metropolitan area can create additional negative effects. Because excluding land uses (such as multifamily homes) often amounts to excluding households (those who cannot afford single-family homes), associational patterns in metropolitan areas are deeply impacted by the use of these property tools.

This book considers how society might design alternatives to existing property instruments that would address both localized extraparcel impacts and the larger-scale dilemmas produced by efforts to control those localized impacts. In broad terms, these alternatives involve reconfiguring property so that it does a better job of aligning the homeowner's returns with the homeowner's choices. These reconfigurations require us to move beyond the binary choices that have dominated the metropolitan residential experience —banning or permitting uses, allowing or forbidding exclusion, renting or owning a home. Conceiving conflicts like those faced by the Middletons as resource dilemmas not entirely unlike those surrounding resources like clean air or a sustainable fishery allows us to expand the menu of policy options.

One reconfiguration approach involves developing new forms of alienable entitlements, rather than simply banning or allowing a particular activity. Drawing on innovations in environmental law, we can imagine devising tradable entitlements to engage in acts with aesthetic impacts, and even (in carefully delineated contexts) tradable entitlements relating to association with preferred neighbors and peers. These instruments would allow responsibility for inputs into common environments to be more precisely allocated and priced. Another, quite different, approach would attenuate homeowners' vulnerability to off-site impacts by scaling back their investment exposure so that it more closely aligns with their effective sphere of control. Here, building on an exciting line of work by Robert Shiller and his collaborators (among others), I examine the potential to reconfigure homeownership in a way that decouples the investment volatility associated with off-site factors from the homeowner's bundle.[5]

The analysis proceeds in four parts. Part I lays out the theoretical framework that will be employed throughout the balance of the book, working through and building on a set of concepts familiar to many academic readers—property rules and liability rules, competing models of property, the Tiebout Hypothesis, the tragedies of the commons and anticommons, and the strategic interactions captured in games like the Prisoner's Dilemma and Chicken. Part II examines problems of neighborhood aesthetics, assesses current attempts to address those problems, and proposes a new approach involving transferable entitlements in aesthetic impacts. Part III takes on the most ambitious and controversial implications of recasting residential property to account for off-site impacts. Here, I suggest that residential association itself constitutes a resource dilemma that can, in certain cases, benefit from the theoretical tools of property. Part IV steps back to consider whether some of the theoretical and practical problems surveyed in the book could be alleviated through a more fundamental alteration of the types of investment volatility included in the homeownership bundle.

While the book focuses on the home's theoretical place within the metropolis, my analytic method serves more generally to illustrate the interaction of collective action problems at different geographic scales. The commons, anticommons, and semicommons templates that I apply here to the metropolitan neighborhood context are general-purpose analytic tools that can be used to understand and respond to all manner of resource dilemmas. The unbounded home thus represents not only an especially pressing and important set of unresolved collective action problems but also a window into larger questions of property theory.

Before I continue, two stylistic matters bear mentioning. First, I follow the convention of using female and male pronouns, respectively, in alternating chapters. Second, the documentation style used in this book is much sparer than that which prevails in the law reviews. I employ endnotes rather than footnotes and, to avoid breaking the flow of the text, typically affix them to the ends of sentences or groups of sentences rather than tag them onto each individual proposition. The endnotes contain short-form citations to some of the most relevant sources as well as some explanatory notes; full citations appear in the bibliography. Readers desiring more background material may find the articles on which this book draws, which are listed in the Acknowledgments, to be useful sources of additional citations.

PART

I

PROPERTY OUT OF BOUNDS

1

BEYOND EXCLUSION

The institution of homeownership, despite its familiarity, produces conflicting and even incoherent attitudes. People are shocked to learn that acts like building a fence or painting a door can be prohibited on their own property, but they are equally appalled at the prospect of a high-density development down the block. They are terrified that their beloved home might be taken through eminent domain, yet they are aghast if the city allows local conditions to erode their property values. Homeowners want an ironclad sphere of privacy and autonomy, but they want it wrapped in an environment that they can control in every particular. They want a secure and lucrative investment vehicle that doubles as an inviolable repository for subjective value. In short, people try to wring a great deal more from their homes than any property system can deliver.

How should law respond to these incongruous demands on residential property? The fact that people want inconsistent things from their homes need not be interpreted as a sign of entrenched mental confusion or shortsighted selfishness. Property theory has offered people no coherent vision of what it means to own a home that might be reconciled in even a loose way with lived experience. Homeowners have been given no tools for perceiving—much less making—the relevant trade-offs between individual and collective control. Rather, they oscillate in an unreflective way between asserting individual control over their own parcels and protecting their stakes in off-site occurrences.

Resolving this tension requires more than merely bringing people's thinking about property up to date or increasing the sophistication with which they view the institution of homeownership. People already understand that the home's value comprises more than the parcel contains. Rather, the poor fit of existing property models corresponds to substantive shortcomings in property law. Land use controls, as they exist today, operate mainly in a binary manner—either a use is banned, or it is allowed. There is almost never the openly acknowledged possibility that households could pay for the privilege of engaging in an unusual but especially valued use, such as adding a garage apartment, or that governing bodies could be required to pay for the privilege of banning a particular land use, such as multifamily dwellings. Moreover, few have thought creatively about the set of risks that the standard homeownership bundle should and should not contain as a default matter. For example, must homeowners be exposed to housing market risks that they have no power to control, or might these risks be more efficiently held by investors within diversified portfolios?[1] By failing to probe such questions, property law has developed without a coherent understanding of the home as a resource.

In this book, I hope to advance a new understanding of residential property. In doing so, I chart the relevant trade-offs between household and community control and propose mechanisms to assist people and communities in making them. This task requires first stepping back to rethink the meaning of property. Above all, property represents a societal response to resource dilemmas. But property is also an inherently sticky institution that carries forward the forms and shapes that worked best in resolving resource dilemmas in the past. The adaptation of old property forms to new conditions presents familiar difficulties for property theory. Should we update property incrementally, expand it to include more legal interests, hold firm to our past understanding of it, or simply declare it dead as a distinct idea?[2] Here, I approach property from a functional perspective by asking what property is meant to *do*.

In the balance of the chapter, I consider the function of property in a quite general way. This discussion sets the stage for the next chapter, in which I examine the special characteristics of the home as a resource. Chapter 3 will then introduce the commons and anticommons templates that are used throughout the book to understand and devise solutions to a broad range of residential property dilemmas.

Property's Work

Writing more than two hundred and forty years ago (and using a fair degree of hyperbole even then), William Blackstone articulated an ideal of property as "that sole and despotic dominion that one man claims and exercises over the external things of the world, in total exclusion of the right of any other individual in the universe."[3] Legal thinkers have always recognized that property as it actually exists does not square with this model. Indeed, Blackstone himself did not endorse such an absolute view of property, as his writings make clear.[4] But idealized visions of dominion and exclusion live on in the popular imagination as representing the true core of property.[5] This model has worked less and less well as the spectrum of privileges conveyed by property ownership has narrowed and the percentage of value represented by factors lying outside the subject parcel has grown. Yet, no satisfactory model has emerged to replace it.

To be sure, many legal scholars (from the legal realists onward) have gravitated toward the metaphor of property as a "bundle of rights" or "bundle of sticks."[6] This approach has the advantage of permitting property to mean as much or as little as the situation requires—"sticks" can be added, subtracted, combined, and recombined in limitless ways, all without ever moving outside the category of property. But this theoretical strength is also a weakness. The sticks idea suggests that property lacks any stable core of meaning around which expectations might form; as such, it cannot help laypeople reconcile the shortcomings of the exclusion-based model. While the notion of a bundle of sticks may be helpful in understanding that property rights can be diminished without being extinguished, it is of little help in understanding why or how this diminution might occur.

Consider a simple dispute between Angus, who wishes to add a "granny flat" to his home to generate rental income,[7] and his neighbor, Beth, who strongly opposes this use. Angus might argue that what happens on his property is subject to his own personal dominion and is simply none of Beth's business. This argument, of course, proves too much. Even at common law, Angus could not defend his maintenance of a nuisance on his property using this logic. Beth, for her part, might invoke her own idea of exclusion by asserting that her dominion over her own property is compromised by the presence of granny flats within her viewshed. Abstract principles of exclusion on their own offer no way of choosing between Angus's position and Beth's. The bundle-of-sticks approach provides no determinacy either, as it would simply lead Angus and Beth to wrangle over who should be allotted the granny-flat stick associated with Angus's property.

Neither the bundle-of-sticks metaphor nor the model of Blackstonian exclusion offers useful normative guidance in resolving land use disputes, because neither approach focuses on the appropriate function of property. One might say that property is meant to exclude. But exclusion is pointless on its own; it only becomes valuable when it enables property owners to do something—or some set of things. Modern advocates of an exclusion-based understanding of property indeed emphasize that exclusion is instrumental to performing any of a broad and indeterminate set of uses on one's land.[8] Moreover, these scholars suggest that exclusion is an attractive core approach to property precisely because it can be enforced without any inquiry into the specific uses that might be made of the owner's exclusive realm.[9] On this account, property's job is to clear a space where diverse endeavors can be undertaken by an owner without interference.

By pushing a bit on this idea, we can see both the ways in which exclusion operates as advertised and the ways in which it falls short. Exclusion's advantage lies in its ability to strengthen the relationship between an owner's inputs and the outcomes that she enjoys or suffers. The idea is intuitive. Keeping others off the property safeguards one's own inputs (for example, by keeping carefully distributed fertilizer from being displaced) while keeping out extraneous and potentially harmful inputs (such as crop-damaging cows). Exclusion also protects positive outcomes from being carried away—outsiders cannot simply show up and fill their knapsacks with ears of corn that have been painstakingly cultivated over a series of months. More generally, exclusion is a broad-gauge strategy for protecting from interference whatever (unknown and perhaps unknowable) activities may be going on inside the property boundaries.[10] A culture of exclusion-based property ownership also encourages owners to fence in factors (such as unruly dogs) that might produce unwanted impacts for neighbors.

Intuitive as a boundary-focused approach seems when discussing crops and animals, it appears somewhat anachronistic when applied to homes. Although boundaries remain unquestionably important (especially for protecting interior space), fortifying and defending the parcel's boundaries is both an underinclusive and an overinclusive strategy for securing the home's value. Today, most of the threats to the value of one's home come not from marauding cattle or vegetable thieves, but rather from events and conditions that lie outside the parcel's boundaries and never cross those boundaries in a physical sense. Larger economic and social factors determine the demand for, and supply of, housing in a particular location. For example, changes in local labor markets can influence both the costs of home construction and the demand for housing. Local governmental decisions about matters like transportation, land use, education, and policing can have dramatic effects on the home's value. The aggregate actions of one's neighbors also produce effects without manifesting themselves in physical intrusions. For such reasons, a homeowner's defense of her boundaries is a radically underinclusive strategy for protecting and enhancing the value of her property.

Boundary exclusion is also an overinclusive strategy for safeguarding home values. While homeowners may be quite vigilant about exclusion when it comes to the dwelling itself and its private fenced areas, strong exclusion from the parcel's edges would be unworkable, even ludicrous. For example, only the most curmudgeonly homeowner would try to keep neighborhood children from making reasonable use of the front lawn to retrieve wayward toys or pets. Pedestrians are typically allowed to use the edges of front yards as walkways in areas lacking sidewalks, especially where traffic makes walking in the roadway unsafe. Likewise, homeowners routinely allow motorists to use their driveways to execute K-turns; they also allow uninvited individuals to approach the front door under most circumstances.[11] And although one's ownership interest rises "to the sky," airplanes, satellites, and spacecraft are legally allowed to enter one's airspace.[12]

In addition to such obvious physical invasions, innumerable lesser boundary crossings occur at the molecular level. Fumes, odors, sound, and light cross freely over property boundaries. Even if banning all activities producing such cross-boundary impacts were possible, it would not be desirable—at least if we understand exclusion not as an end in itself but rather as a means to the end of safeguarding meaningful land uses. Because virtually any activity on one's property will generate some extra-boundary effects, such a rule would render property worthless as a practical matter. For example, simply walking across one's own front yard stirs air molecules and doubtless causes some of them to cross the boundary line. Nor can we assume that these moving molecules will have no impact on a neighbor's enterprises. For all we know, the neighbor is engaged in a sensitive weather experiment that will be grievously disrupted by even the slightest stirring of air across the boundaries.[13]

The point is a simple one: some degree of exclusion helps property do its job of pairing inputs and outputs, but too much exclusion can be harmful to property's ultimate ends. As exclusion rights become more and more categorical, they erode some of the use-content that exclusion was meant to protect in the first place.[14] Hence, property law cannot simply adopt a rigid, categorical rule of exclusion but rather must decide on the strength and content of exclusion rights. Moreover, exclusion is not sufficient to deliver all of the protection that homeowners seek. Thus, the law must also decide what else it will do—or allow homeowners acting collectively to do—to influence events and conditions occurring outside individually owned parcels.

Traditionally, law has responded to the shortcomings of boundaries by deciding whether to permit various activities with extraboundary impacts or to prohibit them outright. As greater numbers of people live and work in close proximity and as activities with extraboundary impacts proliferate, so too does the number of required societal judgments about those activities. The bundle-of-sticks metaphor initially seems well suited to handle these adjustments. Disaggregating property into separate sticks representing different uses or different powers suggests that we can decide in an endlessly precise and customized manner what property should mean in any given instance. As legal theorists have noted, however, this decomposition threatens to destroy property as a distinct subfield of legal entitlements.[15] Because the sticks metaphor is not tethered to a functional understanding of property, it contains no stopping point in breaking down familiar property forms and, as noted above, cannot provide any guidance in deciding how the various sticks should be distributed among owners.

I argue that property's essential nature resides in the institution's capacity to pool together inputs and outputs. It need not do so perfectly, of course. Routine spillovers across boundaries can be identified and readily controlled through standard legal instruments: regulation, tort law, contractual arrangements, or special-purpose property instruments like easements. But as the volume and proportion of extraboundary effects arising from activities undertaken on property grows, the property form itself (as it is currently conceived) becomes increasingly incapable of collecting together inputs and outputs and charging them to the account of the owner. The bundle-of-rights model never registers this problem—the bundle is simply split into ever more sticks. On a functional account, however, pervasive and uncontrollable off-site effects signal a fundamental failure in property's configuration.

A Leaky Bucket of Gambles

A functional look at property suggests that a new metaphor is in order, one that focuses on property's job of pairing together inputs and their (often quite uncertain) effects or outcomes. Taking a page from Henry Smith, who recently adopted an image William Markby employed more than a century ago, I suggest that a bucket offers the best working model of property.[16] Smith finds Markby's "bucket of water" metaphor compelling because it suggests that property is made up not of distinct, well-articulated sticks but rather of a unified and undifferentiated whole representing all the things that one might do with one's property.[17] I find the metaphor fitting for a second reason—buckets are not pristine, airtight containers but rather rough-and-ready catchments that are notoriously prone to leaks and sloshes.

Property, true to its bucketlike form, can at best capture most of the outcomes associated with an owner's inputs most of the time. Meanwhile, other sources of law (tort, regulation, and so on) stand ready to clean up routine spills and sloshes. When the sloshes start to overwhelm the system so that more is spilling out than is staying in, however, it is time to reconfigure the bucket—whether by making it larger, nesting it within other buckets, or devising special-purpose beakers and pails that can address identifiable sources of spillage. In later chapters, I suggest in a more concrete way how these possibilities might play out. For now, it is worth taking a moment to flesh out the metaphor.

What, exactly, is collected in the bucket? On one view, the bucket arrives prefilled with all the conceivable things that an owner might do with the property. The owner can then selectively dip out and transfer specific uses to others, or see particular use privileges siphoned away politically.[18] While this way of thinking about the bucket vividly suggests that the initial set of use privileges represents an undifferentiated whole rather than discrete, enumerated entitlement sticks that have been stacked together, it does no better than the sticks analogy in offering intuitions about when subsets of the overall entitlement should be shifted to another party, or indeed about how large the bucket should be and what its contents should originally include.

A better way of understanding the bucket's contents follows from a functional understanding of property. On this view, the bucket itself represents the conceptual boundaries of a particular property form, which is ideally capable of holding and amassing value for an owner over time. The owner puts content into the bucket by engaging in any of a wide variety of endeavors on or with the property; these endeavors will involve inputs of materials, time, effort, and skill. The associated choices represent gambles that will play out within the domain of the owner's holding.[19] The institution of property aspires to pair together, with some regularity, control over inputs and ownership of outcomes.

Of course, owners are not free to plunk all kinds of inputs into their property buckets willy-nilly. The law rules out some activities because they run afoul of normative constraints on action quite independent of property law (for example, murder is prohibited, even if an individual owns the place in which the murder would occur and the weapon for carrying it out).[20] In other cases, law places constraints on what can be done with the property even though the activity in question carries social value, because of its tendency to produce harmful side effects. But property allows owners significant choice among inputs on the expectation that the results will be charged back against that same owner.

This picture of property suggests that the bucket (that is, the conceptual boundaries of the property) should be scaled in a manner that renders it generally capable of containing the outcomes, whether positive or negative, of the gambles that are typically undertaken by the person designated as owner. The task of appropriately scaling property is a dynamic one; changes in the way that owners use property may yield outcomes that are captured less well (or more well) by existing property forms. For example, in times and places where owners commonly used property for agriculture with only incidental residential uses, the recreational music-making of one family was unlikely to disturb a neighbor's activities. As property holdings grew smaller, residences became more tightly spaced, and technologies for amplifying music became available, the inputs into the endeavor of merrymaking in one's home became increasingly likely to yield outcomes that would interfere with the endeavors undertaken by neighboring property owners. In short, the scale of the activities that owners undertake on their property may fall out of alignment with the scale of the outcomes of those activities.[21]

What should the law do about inputs that have a demonstrated or suspected tendency to generate negative effects beyond the property's boundaries? There are many possible responses—some that are well recognized and others that have not been as carefully explored.

Four Rules

A standard starting point for analyzing society's slate of choices for resolving land use conflicts is found in Guido Calabresi and Douglas Melamed's groundbreaking 1972 *Harvard Law Review* article.[22] Calabresi and Melamed offer a systematic look at the alternatives available to a court adjudicating a conflict between two neighboring parties, such as a factory spewing smoke and a homeowner suffering nearby. Their framework broke the court's choice into two parts: which party holds the entitlement at issue (here, over what happens to the air shared by the factory and the homeowner) and how that entitlement is protected by the law.

As Ronald Coase emphasizes, it takes two parties to create a land use conflict.[23] The law must therefore choose which party's interests will receive priority. In a world of zero transaction costs, the Coase Theorem holds, the parties could bargain their way to an efficient solution regardless of the initial legal rule (although they might not reach the same solution from every starting point).[24] But because transaction costs are often significant, the law's choice about whom to entitle can matter a great deal.

Table 1-1 Calabresi and Melamed's four rules

	Homeowner holds entitlement	*Factory holds entitlement*
Protected by a property rule	Factory is enjoined (Rule 1)	No relief (Rule 3)
Protected by a liability rule	Factory can pollute and pay damages (Rule 2)	Homeowner can stop pollution by paying stopping costs (Rule 4)

Once that decision has been made, a second decision becomes necessary—how the entitlement will be protected. Calabresi and Melamed distinguish between two alternative protection regimes—property rules and liability rules. What they term "property rule" protection is exemplified by the sorts of injunctive relief typically available to property owners to prevent trespasses, although it would also encompass other, supercompensatory forms of relief, such as punitive damages. In contrast, "liability rule" protection, which provides only for compensatory damages, effectively sets a price at which an entitlement belonging to one party may be unilaterally obtained by another party without the original entitlement-holder's consent. Combining the choice of initial entitlement assignment with the choice of entitlement protection yields a two-by-two grid, as shown in Table 1-1.[25]

Rules 1 and 3 represent the opposite poles of categorically allowing or prohibiting the factory's operations. In each case, the party disfavored by the legal rule would be stuck with it unless she could successfully negotiate a change with the other party (that is, a move from a regime in which the factory's operations were prohibited to one in which they were permitted, or vice versa). Rules 2 and 4 introduce the possibility that one party might begin with the right to control what happens to the air, but the other would be able to buy up that right unilaterally, over any objections of the original entitlement holder, at a price set by a third party. That the court's choice set included not three possibilities but four was an important insight of the piece. Not only could the court (by setting damages) effectively establish a price at which the factory could emit over the objections of the homeowner, the court could also establish a price at which the *homeowner* could shut down the factory's operations over the factory's objections.[26] As it happened, this unusual fourth alternative was independently approximated in a case decided by the Arizona Supreme Court around the time that Calabresi and Melamed published their article.[27]

Although Calabresi and Melamed's four-rule grid has not gone uncriticized, it has served as a crucial catalyst in thinking broadly and creatively about the many possible ways society might structure legal rules. Numerous scholars have used the Calabresi and Melamed framework as a springboard for exploring additional applications of the four rules originally outlined, as well as for adding new combinations and permutations to the choice list.[28] Taken in combination with the insights of Coase, the Calabresi and Melamed framework leads to two observations that are foundational to the analysis here. First, at least where normative side constraints do not rule out the possibility, the law's initial assignment of entitlements need not be the final assignment—instead, entitlements can be transferred between parties. Second, the law can choose how to structure those transfers. Thus, not only can entitlements be designed to permit movement from a given legal starting point upon mutual consent, they can also be formulated to give one party or the other the option of making a unilateral shift to a different legal regime at a particular price.

Scholarship building on the work of Calabresi and Melamed offers additional insights into the many ways that control over conflicting land uses might be structured.[29] For purposes of the arguments in this book, one refinement is especially significant. In discussing pricing mechanisms in land use contexts, we can distinguish the pricing of *inputs* that generate a risk of harm from the assignment of liability for harmful *outcomes*.[30] The next section explains.

Inputs and Outcomes

Suppose Edison runs over Ferris's foot with his Land Rover. A court puts a dollar figure on the costs of the foot damage and makes Edison pay that amount to Ferris. On the popular scholarly understanding, this is a classic example of a liability rule in action, one in which Edison has "bought out" Ferris's entitlement not to have his foot crushed by paying for the damage caused. For many, this account grates against moral sensibilities.[31] Beyond that, it is simply an odd way to describe what has happened. As Carol Rose has noted, participants in an accident are thrust into an interaction that was neither desired nor contemplated in advance, making it inapt to suggest, as the scholarly literature does, that the injurer has engaged in a purchase transaction or exercised an "option."[32] Normally, when one buys something, one learns the price in advance and makes a conscious decision to enter into the purchase transaction. Edison, the injurer in our story, did neither of these things; instead, he merely selected an input (the activity of driving at a particular level of inattentiveness) that triggered his liability for any resulting harmful outcome.

Entitlement transfer mechanisms may involve liability payments triggered by accidental outcomes (such as a crushed foot), or may instead involve pricing inputs that create a risk of unwanted results (such as driving in a certain manner). While advance input-based payments to potential victims are hard to imagine in the accident context, they are much more plausible in land use settings. Land use conflicts do not present one-off chance encounters among strangers; they produce ongoing interactions among neighbors. The explicit pricing of privileges to undertake particular endeavors on land (such as keeping pets or making particular aesthetic choices) therefore forms a viable alternative to an outright ban on the activity or a rule allocating liability for harmful outcomes.

Pricing inputs has some underappreciated advantages. First, because the price term is not tied to the actual manifestation of harm, it can be consciously adjusted to meet distributive or other goals. The amount might be set equal to an objective projection of the expected harm, but it might also be keyed to the subjective value placed on the exercise (or nonexercise) of the input by one party or the other. The explicit pricing of an entitlement to engage in an otherwise legitimate input activity also avoids the implication (commonplace where liability for actual harm is characterized as a mere "price") that a party is buying the right to harm another person. Instead, input pricing makes clear that the payment is being made only for the privilege of engaging in the legitimate activity itself.

Another closely related point involves incentives for the "victim" in the interaction. Suppose Jack pays Jill a lump sum in advance for the entitlement to throw boulders down his hill toward Jill's property. If the rolling boulders create a risk of harm for Jill, she has no less incentive than she did before the payment to engage in efficient self-help or mitigation efforts (such as staying out of the rolling boulders' path).[33] Not so, if Jack will have to pay Jill for the damage actually caused. Although we can assume that Jill has her own reasons for not wanting to be crushed by a boulder (even if she—or her estate—were compensated for it), it is not implausible that she would be at least marginally less careful about keeping her personal property out of harm's way if payments were based on realized harm.[34]

One disadvantage of paying for an input in advance is that it leaves any luck-based risk to fall on the victim. If random factors determine whether a given boulder rolls in a straight (and hence avoidable) path or instead careens crazily through Jill's property, and if we assume that Jill is less able to insure against risk than is Jack, then making Jack liable for the actual harm may have advantages. Improving Jill's access to insurance would be another alternative, of course. To the extent we can identify the factors that influence outcomes and isolate their impacts—perhaps boulders roll crazily in snowy or muddy conditions but in a predictable path when the ground is dry—the risk associated with the occurrence of those factors can be alienated to some third party who is well positioned to bear it. Precisely such slicing and dicing of risks can be seen in innovations like weather derivatives—financial instruments that pay off only if certain weather conditions obtain, permitting weather-sensitive businesses to hedge against bad weather luck.[35]

Another problem with prepaying for inputs involves Jack's future incentives to make use of innovative new technologies to reduce harm. Having already prepaid to roll boulders, Jack might not seem to have any reason to employ a newly invented boulder-removal machine that would cost less to buy and operate than the expected value of the harm to Jill. The dissenting judge in *Boomer v. Atlantic Cement* made precisely such an argument against allowing a factory to proceed with its operations upon payment of a preset amount in "permanent damages" to neighbors harmed by those operations.[36] Making payment for inputs iterative (rather than once and for all) offers a solution, but one that may be administratively cumbersome. Alternatively, we might devise mechanisms whereby

Jill can buy back Jack's boulder-rolling privileges in accordance with specified protocols at some point in the future. We would expect Jack to give up his boulder-rolling privileges if Jill offered him enough money to purchase the boulder-removal machine and still come out ahead, but negotiations may be difficult. Giving Jill the right to require Jack to adopt new externality-reducing technologies, provided she pays for them, could offer a more streamlined solution.

Pricing and Property's Function

It is helpful at this point to step back and examine how the notion of pricing inputs connects to the functional understanding of property introduced earlier. If property is understood as a reservoir for containing inputs and their outcomes, enforcement of property boundaries represents only one way of accomplishing the containment function. There are a number of other possibilities. First, activities that have a propensity to generate too many harmful outcomes can simply be banned. For example, the law might forbid the Jacks of the world from heaving boulders across the landscape. Alternatively, prohibitions could be stated in terms of outcomes—Jack could be forbidden to roll boulders that cross within ten feet of Jill's dwelling—with supercompensatory penalties attached to violations. It would also be possible to charge harmful outcomes back to the actor whose actions produced those outcomes. Here, Jack could compensate Jill for the harm she suffered as a result of his boulder-rolling activities. Finally, inputs that produce a risk of harmful outcomes for others might be priced, as discussed above.

Although remedies for nuisance have included damages as well as injunctive relief, spillovers have primarily been managed through prohibitions on particular land uses. Because nuisance covers only a limited spectrum of impacts, zoning or covenants are typically at issue when homeowners attempt to expand the envelope of control beyond their individual parcels. These land use controls tend to rely on bans that can be enforced injunctively. As the volume and extent of these input-based prohibitions grows, almost unbearable pressure is placed on the understanding of ownership as a realm of relative autonomy. The relief valves that exist tend to be political in nature.

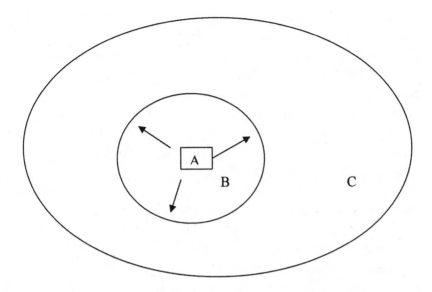

Figure 1-1. The expanding envelope

Explicitly pricing inputs may offer a better way to reconcile the prerogatives of land ownership with the realities of community interdependence. Where a multitude of activities undertaken on property are central to a landowner's own legitimate ends and at the same time potentially detrimental to the legitimate ends of neighboring landowners, blunt categorical bans fall short— they either underprotect owners or overregulate them. More nuanced solutions are possible through pricing mechanisms. In Parts II and III, I flesh out how such mechanisms could operate to resolve two distinct sets of conflicts in neighborhoods that are schematically represented in Figure 1-1.

The letter A in Figure 1-1 represents a single residential parcel of land. As the next chapter discusses in more detail, Parcel A is a porous resource that both impacts and is impacted by its neighbors. Zoning or covenants might be employed to establish a larger envelope of control, represented by the oval labeled B. This outward expansion of control indeed helps to address the problem of spillovers, but it can generate problems of its own. Difficult trade-offs must be made between the rights vouchsafed to the community falling within the expanded area of control and those left with individual parcel-holders. The sorts of relatively inalienable, categorical rules that are most often used to govern realm B may not work especially well at striking that balance. Moreover, even if all of the interests within B could be perfectly addressed through a governance regime that shifted an optimal amount of control to the community, the policies enacted by B might create inefficiencies within the larger community of which B is a subset, represented by the larger oval labeled C in Figure I-I.[37] In Parts II and III, respectively, I explore mechanisms that can be used in conjunction with the traditional homeownership paradigm to address these two sets of problems.

Part IV, in contrast, challenges the traditional homeownership paradigm directly. Increasingly refined mechanisms for pricing inputs into common environments can make headway in reducing the divergence between the choices made by homeowners and the impacts that the homeowner suffers or enjoys. However, not all inputs into home price volatility can be captured through such mechanisms, and not all inputs that can be captured in this manner are most efficiently managed by individual homeowners. Rather than focus on ways to extend control to match exposure, the final part of the book considers ways to scale back the homeowner's exposure so that it aligns more closely with the homeowner's effective sphere of control. In other words, I examine whether the home should be turned into a less porous entity, at least as far as investment risk is concerned, through institutional mechanisms that absorb some of the shocks to home values.

To set the stage for the analysis that follows in Parts II, III, and IV, two additional pieces of groundwork are necessary. The next chapter discusses more concretely the unbounded nature of residential property in metropolitan areas. Doing so requires considering the many components of the home that go beyond its physical structure. Although I refer to the whole as a "bundle" and the home purchase as a "bundled" one, I do so not to invoke the bundle-of-rights or bundle-of-sticks metaphor for property, but rather to draw attention to the elements that constitute the home as a resource and that account for its value. Many of these elements are shaped by the choices that other actors, whether neighboring homeowners or local governments, make. Chapter 3 concludes this part with a game-theoretic discussion of the dilemmas arising from those interdependent decisions, which are more fully explored in Parts II and III.

2

CONSTRUCTING THE HOME

Consider the residence selection task of a typical homebuyer, Homeria. In evaluating a home, she cares about its layout, construction, curb appeal, square footage, and other physical attributes. But these concerns are hardly primary. Before she even begins house hunting, she has likely narrowed her choices to a particular geographic area based on a complex set of factors usually lumped under the heading of "location." Buying a home means buying much more than a structure—it also means buying a set of near neighbors, a neighborhood living environment, a particular degree of proximity to points of interest such as one's workplace, a bundle of services and amenities provided by the local jurisdiction and by other jurisdictions to which one has regular access, and a political and social address.[1]

The elements in this bundle make a home "unbounded" in two respects. First, homeowners recognize that in terms of both consumption and resale value, the "home" is not confined to the assigned lot but rather comprises a constellation of factors, many of which are off site. Second, any given parcel of residential property plays a role in the diffuse bundle identified as "home" by neighboring landowners. The home, thus conceived, is an amorphous resource that overflows parcel boundaries. It is both porous and ambient, vulnerable to outside influences while generating influences of its own. To merely say, as we often do, that a piece of property generates and suffers from spillovers does not fully capture this point. The notion of a "spillover" suggests that most of the value exists within the designated resource, with only a relatively small proportion of effects sloshing over the edges. Where the home is concerned, a great deal of the relevant action, including much of what infuses the home with meaning and value, occurs beyond the parcel's borders. Closer in spirit is M. A. Qadeer's view of urban land parcels not as autonomous units but rather as mere "anchors" in a contiguous, interdependent system.[2] The term "spillover" remains intuitively useful, but I use it here with an eye to whether the overflowing impacts, in the aggregate, make redefining the resource worthwhile.

The unbounded nature of the home presents two competing sets of concerns. First is the concern that the home's value will be eroded by actions off site. Clearly, the home cannot serve as a stable repository of value unless some controls are established that reach beyond the individual parcel's borders. Second, however, is the concern that efforts to extend control beyond the parcel's borders will generate negative effects of their own. As I will show, the unbounded nature of the home gives residents strong incentives to employ exclusionary tactics to keep away unwanted uses and people. These tactics, which often introduce inequities, can be quite costly in efficiency terms as well.

The Homeowner's Bundled Choice

That homeowners are buying more than just a home has long been recognized. Indeed, perhaps the most influential existing model of residential choice, the Tiebout Hypothesis, focuses attention on a set of factors that lie outside the parcel boundaries—the basket of local goods and services provided by the jurisdiction in which the homebuyer chooses to locate.[3] A simple model of Tieboutian choice is depicted in Figure 2-1.

Suppose our house hunter, Homeria, confronts this choice set. The outer boundary of the large oval shown in Figure 2-1 represents the greater metropolitan area in which our protagonist wishes to live. To keep things simple, assume that she must live somewhere within this area in order to enjoy what economists term "agglomeration benefits"—the gains that come from the interactions that spatial clustering facilitates.[4] The lettered squares within that oval represent the different jurisdictions within that metropolitan area that she may choose among. Charles Tiebout observed

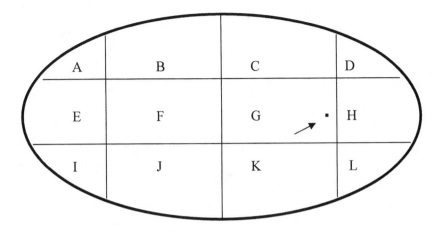

Figure 2-1. Tiebout shopping

that homebuyers (or, in his phrasing, "consumer-voters") make a choice among jurisdictions that can be analogized to a shopper's selection among products.[5] On this account, when Homeria chooses a home within a particular jurisdiction, such as jurisdiction G in Figure 2-1, she does so because she prefers the specific basket of local governmental goods and services that jurisdiction G offers over those available in the competing jurisdictions. While this vision of the Tieboutian choice offers a helpful entry point into an examination of the bundled residential decision, it is incomplete.

Significantly, Homeria can purchase the goods and services of a selected jurisdiction only indirectly, by buying (or leasing) one of the containers in which they are delivered—physical residential structures within the chosen jurisdiction.[6] If all housing sizes and types were available in all jurisdictions, this observation would be of little moment; she could select any combination of structure and governance she desired, just as if she were able to purchase the components separately. Because controls on land use limit the type and style of housing in some jurisdictions, however, homebuyers may be unable to find a right-sized container for their consumption of local government in all jurisdictions. Entire categories of housing stock may be excluded outright from certain jurisdictions by zoning restrictions. The availability of some kinds of housing may also be limited in less drastic ways

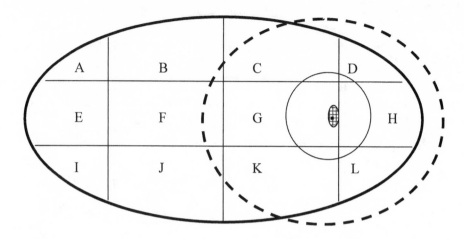

Figure 2-2. Complex shopping

by regulations, market forces, or some combination of the two. Such limits on housing stock complicate Homeria's shopping task considerably.

Figure 2-2 depicts a few more sources of complexity.[7] Assume that one of the small squares in the innermost ring in Figure 2-2 represents the home Homeria is contemplating buying. Not only must she consider the suitability of the physical structure and the local governmental services and facilities provided by the jurisdiction (G) in which the home is located, she must also consider several other components of the overall housing package.

Homeria will, of course, acquire a set of neighbors along with the home.[8] The near neighbors that share the small checkerboard area inside Figure 2-2's inner ring occupy what we might view as the "direct spillover zone." Each of the neighbors in this zone is in a position to make decisions that impact Homeria, whether positively or negatively. Likewise, Homeria's activities can generate spillovers for each of these neighbors. In addition, these neighbors can influence the quality and cost of some of the local public goods provided by jurisdiction G, such as public safety and education, and will also participate in the production of additional local public goods in the area, such as the neighborhood's ambience or status.[9]

Homeria will also receive a daily living environment as part of her package, represented in Figure 2-2 by the next-largest ring. This daily living environment comprises not only the physical elements that affect her quality of life (stores, parks, roads, schools, spas, gyms, walking paths, libraries, museums, places of worship, and so on), but also the many sets of people with whom she will interact in these places.

Homeria's prospective home also occupies a unique location within the metropolitan area. This location determines the ease with which she and other members of her household can reach important points of interest, notably their workplaces.[10] The outer dashed circle in Figure 2-2 attempts to capture this element of the housing package by suggesting a rough approximation of the feasible daily commuting range from the selected home. Very often, both the commuting range and the daily living environment will extend into jurisdictions other than the one in which the home is located. As Figure 2-2 suggests, Homeria's quality of life will be influenced not only by the spending patterns and policies of jurisdiction G but also by those of jurisdictions B, C, D, F, H, J, K, and L, all of which lie within her commuting range, and most of which contain parts of her daily living environment as well.

Finally, Homeria will obtain a political and social address when she selects a home. As a matter of politics, she will become a member not only of jurisdiction G but also of any other local or regional political jurisdictions, such as a county, that encompass her home.[11] In addition, she may become involved in the politics of neighboring jurisdictions, even though she cannot vote in them. Also important is the home's "social address"—the reputation of the place name with which the home is most closely associated. In central cities, neighborhoods often carry their own familiar brand names, such as the Castro in San Francisco, Hyde Park in Chicago, and Georgetown in Washington, D.C.[12] In the suburbs, the jurisdiction name is more likely to be the brand name identifier, although smaller subsets of the jurisdiction, such as private neighborhoods, may become known by their own names.

These social addresses have real consequences. Empirical work shows that job prospects may be enhanced—or torpedoed—by the neighborhood in which one lives.[13] Resale value can also be deeply impacted, given that prospective homebuyers use place names as heuristics in their searches. And it is a matter of common observation that place names are capable of winning the approval or attracting the disdain of friends, family members, and coworkers. Thus, in choosing a home, Homeria will be cognizant of the place name that comes with it, and of the signals that the name might send to others. She will also be concerned about the likely trajectory of the place name's fate throughout the foreseeable future and about anticipated land uses that might impact that fate.[14] Homeria might, for example, demand a heavy discount before she would purchase a home that will soon share a social address with a maximum security prison.

In theory, all of the portions of the housing bundle just described would be priced (or "capitalized") into the value of the home itself.[15] Such capitalization is evidenced by the fact that, for example, homebuyers will pay more for an otherwise identical home if it is located in a desirable school district or if the taxes are a bargain, relative to the benefits offered by the community.[16] Likewise, a house that is located near a noisy or smelly industrial site will command a lower price than a physically equivalent house located near a beautiful, well-tended park. While there is debate about the extent to which capitalization actually occurs, there is little doubt that predictable features in the surrounding environment are largely captured in home prices.[17]

Suppose, however, that one or more of the factors important to Homeria were subject to change. For example, imagine that the state was considering radically redrawing school district boundaries or disconnecting school assignments from residential location altogether. Or perhaps Homeria learns that the row of neatly kept single-family homes near her prospective abode is likely to be replaced by a sewage treatment plant within the next few years. In these cases, the homebuyer's assessment of the home's value would be adjusted to incorporate information about the changes that might transpire in the surrounding environment and the projected probabilities of them occurring. If Homeria is risk averse (and we have reason to believe that most homeowners are), she will deduct more from the price she is willing to pay than the expected value equivalent of any potential detrimental changes.[18]

Shoppers, Diners, and Residents

The complexity and potential uncertainty of the house hunting task call into question the simple shopping metaphor introduced by Tiebout. A consumption experience that evolves over time and is shaped by other consumers would offer significantly more analytic and descriptive power. In place of a shopper on a quest for breakfast cereal or electronic gadgetry, let us consider the problems faced by Dino, who is in the market for a dining experience (or, if you like, an evening of drinking or dancing). The stakes are lower for him than they are for Homeria in the home-buying setting, and the time horizon over which events can alter value differs considerably. But the concerns are largely parallel. There are at least two important ways in which a dining bundle, like a housing bundle, differs from a typical private good, such as a toaster or a shirt. The next sections explain.

Implicit Pricing

Dino, like Homeria, is buying a bundled good that includes not only a concrete, explicitly priced component (food) but also a number of other goods and services that contribute to or detract from the overall dining package. When Dino pays for menu items, he will receive along with them other elements of the dining experience that are not explicitly priced—wait service, an eating space and its decor, short-term use of furniture, utensils, glasses, and dishes, and largely unrationed access to extras like ice water, condiments, and bread.[19] Additional services complementary to the dining experience, such as a cloakroom, restroom facilities, and parking facilities, are often provided on an unpriced or subsidized basis. The political jurisdiction in which the restaurant is located supplies additional services relevant to the dining experience, such as fire and police protection, sidewalk maintenance and lighting, and municipal water, garbage, and sewage service. The restaurant Dino chooses also occupies a physical location that may be more or less desirable on dimensions such as neighborhood character, the travel time from Dino's home or workplace, and the quality of the views available from the windows.

True, the tax and tip that Dino will pay address some of the unpriced portions of the bundle. But consider the basis on which those charges are levied. Just as homeowners pay property taxes based on their property's value, diners pay taxes and tips that are based on the value of the priced menu items they purchase. The use of priced items to allocate the cost of unpriced items opens up the possibility that customers will attempt to consume the unpriced items without paying for a "fair share" of them via the priced items. Dino, for example, could enjoy a fine restaurant's wonderful ambience, gorgeous views, and delightful service for a pittance if he could occupy a choice table for hours while consuming nothing but coffee. Likewise, Homeria could obtain local public goods funded by a property tax for a bargain if she could live in an inexpensive home in a high-service area.[20] Such bargains are only possible, however, if there are other consumers around to pick up the slack by purchasing, and being taxed on, higher-priced items.

Indeed, Dino and Homeria may well worry that they will wind up cross-subsidizing the coffee-sipping or small-house crowd. Of course, Dino knows that food prices will not increase unexpectedly during his meal, but he cannot be certain that chiseling will not occur on quality or quantity grounds as a way of recouping lost overhead. Homeria faces a longer time horizon and the possibility of tax rate changes that will place heavier burdens on her than she could readily predict upon entry into the community. There are responses to these concerns, as we will see, some of which involve directly or indirectly excluding certain would-be customers (thereby triggering a variety of new concerns). Significantly, these responses also alter the product under consideration insofar as they change the mix of diners or residents. As the next section explains, other customers profoundly influence the bundled products that Dino and Homeria seek to purchase. These influences occur not only through the potential free-riding behaviors just discussed but also through the sets of characteristics and behaviors the other customers bring to the environment.

The Role of Other Customers

Most private goods do not morph in our hands after we purchase them, nor does their value change radically depending on who else is using them. This is not to deny that in some instances the identity, number, characteristics, or practices of those who are consuming a particular private good can influence whether we consume it as well, and perhaps influence our level of product satisfaction. But a distinction can be drawn between goods that have relatively fixed attributes and need not be consumed in the immediate presence of one's co-consumers, and consumption experiences that evolve over time and for which the co-consumers themselves represent a crucial input.[21]

Like a residential experience (and unlike ordinary private goods, such as toasters or shirts), a restaurant meal must be consumed on site and in the presence of others who can influence its value.[22] The environment that is part of Dino's dining bundle is likely to depend in significant part on the behaviors of the other consumers. These other diners are the co-producers of one of the most important elements in the dining bundle—its ambience. A slovenly, loud, drunken, chain-smoking cohort will produce a brand of ambience decidedly different from that produced by a collection of well-dressed, well-groomed, quiet, sober, nonsmoking patrons.

Residents of a local jurisdiction similarly influence the cost and quality of local services. It has been well noted that goods like education and public safety depend not just on exogenous inputs (teachers, school buildings, police officers, patrol cars) but also on the characteristics and behavior of people who are ostensibly "receiving" the services—an elementary school's students, or a neighborhood's residents.[23] Such goods involve what Charles Clotfelter has termed "participation effects."[24] Other things being equal, the same dollars will produce a better education in a school attended by more fully prepared, better-nourished, and more highly motivated students, just as a fixed sum will produce higher-quality public safety in a neighborhood populated by a larger proportion of concerned, law-abiding, safety-minded citizens.

The number of other consumers matters as well. Too few customers may diminish the liveliness of the experience of dining out, while crowding can produce a suboptimally harried and noisy dining experience. Likewise, communities have an optimum size, as Tiebout recognized.[25] As in a restaurant, some critical mass of community members is necessary to produce the desired agglomeration benefits, but the potential for congestion limits the number of new entrants who can be accommodated without raising costs or reducing the quality of services and amenities.[26] To be sure, a restaurant may benefit when more people are clamoring to get in than the establishment can accommodate, and a community may likewise enjoy a boost when it becomes highly sought after by throngs of would-be residents.[27] But these benefits crucially depend on the ability of the proprietor or local governmental body to ration actual entry. Thus, it is entirely possible for restaurants and communities to have too many as well as too few customers.

An additional way in which customers matter in both contexts involves their ability to shape the product they are collectively consuming through the exercise of "voice."[28] Residents in a municipality are both market and political actors—consumers and voters.[29] As consumers, they choose a product, but as voters, they participate in shaping that product. They may do so by voting, or through more or less organized pressure against political leaders and service providers. In a restaurant, customers may informally petition the wait staff and management for changes in temperature levels, lighting, music, television channels, and the like; in the case of conflicts, well-regarded "regulars" may receive greater deference. In the residential context, where formal voting carries the potential to change the overall package, mere residence in the jurisdiction equates with the franchise—although certain citizens may, for whatever reason, have more "pull."

Significantly, the cohort of other diners—like the collection of neighbors—is dynamic over time. A diner can scan the restaurant upon arrival to see whether the currently assembled clientele seems appealing in terms of quantity and characteristics, but the mix and number of people are subject to change over the course of an evening. Likewise, a homebuyer can observe the set of neighbors present at the time of the purchase decision but cannot foresee who will move in or out over the ensuing years. Moves in and out of the environment—such as those made by an entering Dino or Homeria—may set in motion chain reactions of entry or exit.[30] The behaviors of a new entrant, or the behaviors lost when someone exits, can also influence the behaviors of others in restaurant or neighborhood.

In sum, choosing a restaurant or a home means both selecting an environment and contributing to it. The environment is constructed from the interdependent choices made by those within it, whose presence and relative influence within the environment is itself the product of interdependent choices about entry and exit.

Packaging Predictability

However complex the bundled decisions faced by Homeria and Dino may be, homebuyers and restaurant-goers are not, as a rule, paralyzed by indecision or consigned to suffer radical uncertainty about the products they are buying. That is because consumers seek, and jurisdictions and managers provide, a variety of mechanisms that operate to stabilize the products under consideration.

Rules Plus Sorting

Consider first the choices faced by people like Dino who are selecting among quite localized environments that they will occupy for very limited periods of time. In these contexts (which include not only restaurants but also bars, theaters, sporting events, and so on) two factors help to minimize difficulties associated with implicit pricing structures and interdependent customer inputs: (1) the ability of individuals to sort themselves among environments, entering and exiting as they choose; and (2) the ability of proprietors to set and enforce binding rules, some of which double as signals that assist individuals in the self-sorting task.

To take the second point first, restaurants commonly employ rules to address the risk of free-riding that a pricing structure based on food and drink alone might generate. Would-be free riders can be driven away or made to pay a fair share for the ambience and services they consume by tactics such as enforcing minimum drink purchase requirements, increasing the prices of the cheapest menu items, limiting free refills and other extras, limiting tables only to those ordering meals, adding charges for splitting dishes, and so on. For example, chips and salsa, that staple of Tex-Mex dining, may be made less than freely available in some restaurants to deter overconsumption by patrons who purchase little or no food.

Restaurants and bars may also adopt rules that are designed either to change the behavior of patrons or to screen out certain patrons. Dress codes may be imposed. Smoking may be banned. A bouncer or maitre d' may ration entry, picking and choosing among would-be patrons. Large parties may be discouraged (say, through lack of adequate contiguous seating or a failure to provide bus parking) or may be charged mandatory minimum service fees. Children may not be accommodated, or at least not cheerfully. In these and many other ways ranging from the overt to the subtle, proprietors practice de facto exclusion or send what Lior Strahilevitz has termed "exclusionary vibes" to would-be patrons.[31] Aided by rules, observable cues, and word-of-mouth buzz, people generally do a reasonably good job of sorting themselves into agreeable short-term environments. Mistakes may occasionally happen, but they can be easily corrected; exit is cheap and readily available, and it is usually easy to enter a different environment that is a better fit.

The multiplex movie theater offers another useful illustration of how signals facilitate self-sorting. Different people wish to see different movies, yet everyone in a given auditorium must view the same movie. It is efficient for people who wish to see the same movie to cluster together in the same room, rather than disperse themselves randomly among the auditoriums and, once there, agitate for the movie of their choice. With signs posted above each auditorium door indicating the movie to be shown within, self-sorting proceeds smoothly. Of course, the quality of the moviegoing experience also depends to some extent on the actions of the people present. Therefore, theaters may set rules about such matters as throwing popcorn or talking during the feature presentation, and these can vary from theater to theater, or even from showing to showing. For example, the Alamo Drafthouse Theater in Austin, Texas, offers special "baby day" matinees at which infants and young children are welcome, but the theater will not admit children under the age of six to its regular shows.[32] Such rules assist people in sorting themselves into the showings that will best match their desired moviegoing experience, obviating (in most cases) the need for direct enforcement by management.

Special Features of Residential Housing

Can the same combination of "sorting plus rules" yield equally agreeable results in the residential context? If so, then Tiebout's shopping metaphor requires only modest refinements. If the customer interdependencies and pricing structures discussed above serve only to make the consumer choice more like one among restaurants than among toasters, the core notion of "voting with one's feet" remains valid. Unfortunately, matters are not so simple. While some rule-like mechanisms operate to stabilize environments in neighborhoods, and sorting plays an important role in matching people to places, some additional features complicate the problem of residential choice.

First, product control in the residential context is highly fragmented, both temporally and spatially. One reason that self-sorting plus rules works well in settings like restaurants is that the "selves" doing the sorting and the proprietor setting the rules together have almost complete control over the resulting product. It is true that lapses in municipal services (blackouts or water main breaks) or surrounding events or conditions (traffic accidents, strikes, poor weather, or heavy smog) can influence the quality of the overall dining bundle. But the odds of these outside factors negatively impacting the dining environment during the course of a given meal are low. In contrast, Homeria will regularly face impacts emanating from many sources within her own jurisdiction and surrounding jurisdictions. Moreover, because she is likely to stay in the home for years (if not decades), there is much more time for these impacts to unfold. In addition, Homeria's own preferences may also change in the interim, making her initial self-sort less suitable as time passes.

Second, exit is very costly in the residential setting. Aside from the often substantial out-of-pocket costs associated with moving to a new home, Homeria cannot stop buying the jurisdiction's bundle of goods and services through tax payments until she sells her house. Ronald Oakerson has usefully observed that departing homeowners are effectively required to recruit a "replacement customer."[33] If Homeria wants to move for relatively idiosyncratic reasons, and if market conditions are right, she may not find this requirement too challenging. But if her move is prompted by unwanted changes in the area that many or most other people would also find undesirable, a replacement may be harder to come by. Any buyer that Homeria does manage to attract will demand a reduced price in order to accept a housing bundle that has now become less valuable.[34] Under conditions of full capitalization, the negative factors behind Homeria's desire to flee the jurisdiction, including expectations about future value drops, have already been incorporated into her home's (now-lowered) value. This makes exit an incomplete and painful response to unsatisfactory conditions that affect the home.

Third, and closely related to the problem of costly exit, houses deliver both a consumption stream and an investment return that will be realized on resale.[35] In this respect, the housing bundle Homeria is choosing differs markedly from the dining bundle that Dino seeks. Homeria, unlike Dino, cannot simply consider her own consumption preferences in selecting a particular environment. Instead, she must take into account the likely preferences of the future homebuyers to whom she will someday need to sell. As we will see, the prospect of resale increases the incentive to find ways to stabilize the overall product, through exclusion if necessary.

Fourth, self-sorting can only take place on a limited number of dimensions when one is purchasing a single, long-lasting, bundled product. Because choosing a restaurant is a short-term commitment, a diner can afford to give priority to one aspect of the overall dining bundle (such as good food) on some occasions and another aspect of that bundle (such as an artsy atmosphere) on others. A house, in contrast, must be selected for the attributes that will be most important over the long haul. People lack the computational capacity to optimize on every dimension, and market selections are not numerous enough to give everyone his first choice on every component even if such computations were possible.[36] Consequently, only the most important criteria, such as price and location, will "do the work" in determining which bundle will be chosen. Some parts of the bundle will represent compromises or the results of mental shortcuts rather than deliberately chosen elements. These unchosen portions of the bundle can lead to conflict among neighbors, as we will see.

Finally, the stakes are much higher in the residential context, not only because the purchase is larger and longer-lasting but also because it so pervasively and unavoidably impacts quality of life for members of the household. While measures that have the purpose and effect of excluding certain patrons occur both in residential contexts and in shorter-term settings like restaurants and bars, the former kind of exclusion has a great deal more bite for the simple reason that everyone must live somewhere. Dino can react to direct or indirect exclusion from restaurants and bars by opting out of those domains altogether; he can eat a self-prepared or carry-out meal at home. Those who are turned away by bouncers and maitre d's are not forced by virtue of that exclusion to mingle together in the Outcasts Café. But if Homeria is excluded from a given community or set of communities in a metropolitan area, yet still must live somewhere within that metropolitan area in order to take advantage of agglomeration benefits associated with metropolitan life, exclusion from her preferred communities amounts to forced inclusion in a residential community that she did not choose.[37]

The implications of these special residential features are explored at length later in the book. For now, it is sufficient to observe that homebuyers have a tremendous incentive to seek products whose value has been "stabilized" in some fashion, and that the stabilizing measures undertaken by local governments and private developments have their own impacts on the formation of communities.

Land Use Controls as Product Stabilizers

Land use controls, both public and private, work as "product stabilizers," reducing the uncertainty associated with lengthy time horizons and fragmented, interdependent influences.[38] True to their name, they control what can be done with land, but they can also have the effect, or even the overt purpose, of restricting entry into the jurisdiction. Because there are a variety of motives for wanting to control land uses as well as for wishing to restrict entry, land use controls can serve any of a number of functions.[39] As outlined below, land use controls can stabilize (or augment) tax collections, control spillover-producing actions, facilitate self-sorting, or screen out segments of the population. It will often be unclear which purpose or purposes a given restriction is meant to serve, or is in fact serving.[40]

Collecting

If we assume a system of local government funding that is based on a property tax, and if we further posit that the value of the public goods and services actually consumed by residents bears no particularly tight relationship to property value, then the potential exists for free-riding on premium services by occupying less valuable housing. As Bruce Hamilton explains, we might expect to see a game of "musical suburbs" in which the poor chase the rich from community to community, occupying small homes and paying small amounts of taxes until their better-off counterparts flee to another jurisdiction.[41] Because such a prospect would dramatically destabilize the value of the bundle that Homeria is purchasing, we would expect her to seek ways to prevent it. Unlike a restaurant proprietor who can respond to the risk of free-riding by raising prices on its cheapest menu items, a local government cannot unilaterally raise the price of cheaper homes in the community to eliminate free-riding. But it can use its zoning powers to do other things that have the same effect.

Most straightforwardly, a local government can set minimum lot sizes or require particular housing types, thus keeping property values within a relatively narrow band of variance. Anyone locating in the community must consume at least a minimum amount of housing and, by extension, must contribute at least a certain amount of property tax to the municipality's coffers.[42] Such a zoning restriction is analogous to a nightclub imposing a two-drink minimum in lieu of a cover charge. Alternatively, the local jurisdiction could cap the overall amount of housing stock at a particular level and allow the market to bid up the prices of those smaller housing units that are property tax bargains, through capitalization.[43] Under conditions of full capitalization, a Susie Smallhouse living in such a jurisdiction will end up paying just as much for local services as a Bentley Bighouse. Only part of Smallhouse's payments take the form of property taxes, however; the rest is built into a higher home price.

The latter alternative shows that heterogeneity in housing need not produce fiscal instability. But this does not mean that current homeowners will welcome a loosening of zoning restrictions to let in the Smallhouses. Neither the Bighouses nor the jurisdiction will benefit from the higher home prices that the Smallhouses must pay; that money flows to the party—typically a developer—who owned the land at the time the zoning regime was relaxed to permit the entry of smaller homes.[44] Meanwhile, the Bighouses are stuck with higher tax bills for as long as they live in the community, and with a lower sales price (due to the capitalization of this tax burden into the home's value) when they leave. This dynamic explains why moves from homogeneity to heterogeneity may be difficult, especially in the absence of open-ended bargaining opportunities between developers and the communities affected by development.

The potential for such fiscally detrimental zoning changes will not only capture the interest of current residents but may also appear on the radar screens of prospective buyers. Regardless of Homeria's aesthetic preferences about living near larger or smaller homes, we would expect her to prefer a jurisdiction that will preserve over time the relationship between the taxes she pays and the services she receives.[45] Moreover, once in the community, Homeria and her neighbors may contrive to do more than merely ensure that newcomers bear a proportionate share of costs. They may press the local zoning authorities to apply more stringent housing consumption requirements to new residents than they themselves faced—what Michelle White has termed "fiscal squeeze zoning"—or they may attempt to extract large impact fees or other fiscal advantages from the newcomers.[46] Likewise, if the incumbents enjoy unique advantages based on the location, services, or amenities that come packaged with their homes, they may even try to freeze the housing supply to monopolize those advantages and cause their own homes' values to be bid up.[47] Thus, Homeria will be interested not only in the zoning constraints already in place but also in those that she foresees may be enacted in the future.

Controlling

Land use controls are not always about manipulating fiscal contributions, however. They are often designed to do just what they advertise—control how land can be used. Because land uses frequently generate spillovers for neighboring parcels, property ownership has never entailed the right to use one's property any way one pleases. Common-law nuisance doctrines, as well as the finer-grained devices of zoning and private covenants, operate to shift control over some aspects of land usage from the individual parcel owner to the larger community. Up to a point, this shift from individual control to community control can increase the aggregate value of the individual parcels. While each such shift constrains a landowner with respect to uses on his own property, it also generates benefits for him by similarly constraining his neighbors.[48]

As the next chapter explores, land use controls can solve "tragedies of the commons" and produce community-wide gains by reciprocally restraining each parcel-holder. In the absence of such a collective arrangement, self-interest might lead owners to undertake land use choices that, while individually beneficial, would produce net social harm. Significantly, this motivation for land use controls exists even in settings where a community's population is stably fixed and the desire to attract or repel particular residents plays no role. These controls work not by pushing people away or drawing them in but rather by altering what they do while in the community. Of course, the fact that a land use control addresses a dilemma that can be characterized as a commons tragedy does not rule out the possibility that the control will also have effects on the population that deserve independent normative analysis.

Sorting

Land use controls can also facilitate self-sorting into mutually agreeable residential communities. Consider a simple prohibition on parking boats in the driveway. This rule might seem to induce efficient sorting: people who valued a boat-free environment more than they valued the option to park a boat could choose this community, while those bent on boat parking could choose a different community that allows the practice. Likewise, a community that places a premium on low-density living might ban apartment complexes, while another community might welcome such complexes. On this account, the set of rules in a given community operates a bit like the movie marquees at the multiplex theater: announcing what will go on inside induces people to sort themselves into different environments based on their tastes and preferences.

This idea is at the heart of the Tiebout Hypothesis, and it carries an obvious efficiency rationale: it is easier to provide the right quality and quantity of goods and services to a group with homogeneous tastes. Moreover, residential groupings are involved in co-producing certain goods and services, like local ambience and safety. We might expect those who have similar tastes in these matters to be more efficient co-producers and co-consumers of these goods and services.[49] Given the bundled nature of the housing product, however, most households cannot realistically self-sort on all the dimensions that matter to them. Moreover, land use controls that limit certain types and sizes of housing do more than provide signals to assist in self-sorting—they effectively screen out those who cannot afford the permissible kinds of housing. Thus, some households may lack the financial capability to select homes in communities that exhibit the qualities that they find important. As Gerald Frug has observed, people locate in neighborhoods with high crime rates and subpar schools not because they have a "taste" for these attributes but rather because they lack better choices.[50]

When Homeria searches for housing, then, she may be attracted by certain kinds of land use controls because they suggest a community of like-minded others. At the same time, however, land use controls in some of the jurisdictions may operate to keep her out altogether. The entrances to communities are outfitted not only with marquee signs, as it were, but also with filters or screens that sift among those who attempt to enter the community. Making matters more interesting, the shape and size of the intake filters—that is, the content of land use controls, and their capacity to exclude—may attract those who are capable of making it through the screen.

Screening

The discussion above suggests that the exclusion of people may sometimes be a side effect of land use controls that are directed at collecting contributions from residents, controlling their behavior, and providing information to would-be residents about community rules. But it is well known that land use controls are often undertaken with the intention of excluding people. We have already considered how land use controls might consciously exclude people who will not (or cannot) pay what is deemed to be their fair share or who are not inclined to follow community rules. But that is only part of the story.

The consumers of some of the most important local public goods, such as education and public safety, contribute directly to the production and cost of these goods through peer and neighborhood effects. Heterogeneity in the pool of potential co-consumers can, therefore, provide another motive for exclusion. Suppose that some co-consumers—call them "quality-enhancing users"—make positive contributions, whereas others—"quality-detracting users"—do the opposite.[51] Jurisdictions have an incentive to attract the former and exclude the latter. Because the propensity to be a quality-enhancing user is not observable, communities might fall back on a highly imperfect proxy, such as the financial wherewithal to purchase a home of a particular type or size.[52] Of course, outright prejudices of community members (or the prejudices that those members predict future homebuyers will have) may also explain screening on income or wealth.

That entrants to a community will also become voters capable of politically shaping the community's offerings provides yet another motive for exclusion. Models of local government politics often assume that control over outcomes lies in the hands of an abstraction known as "the median voter"—the fictional person who occupies the middle of the spectrum of views and, in close cases, supplies the critical swing vote.[53] If transformations in the composition of the community's voters alter the preference profile of the median voter, outcomes can change.[54] By controlling entry, current residents control the political apparatus for making decisions about local public goods.[55] Land use restrictions can be used to increase the chances that the new entrants will resemble current residents along dimensions like age, family size, and socioeconomic status. Such demographically similar entrants will be less likely to vote for dramatic alterations in public services or create unexpected pressures on the fisc. Zoning regulations can thus become self-replicating—sustaining political processes that continue to produce the zoning regulations that, in turn, perpetuate those same political processes.[56]

There are a number of additional reasons why existing residents might want to screen incoming residents, and these considerations can cut in varying and even conflicting directions. Residents might want the agglomeration benefits, such as the ability to attract better stores, that would come from certain kinds of growth, but such growth might also produce spillovers in traffic or noise that would not be welcome. Incumbents attracted to the tax money that wealthy newcomers would bring might simultaneously fear the impact of such an influx on their own relative social standing. If choosing a community amounts to "choosing the right pond" (to use Robert Frank's expression), then incumbent households may be deeply invested in keeping the pond "right."[57] Similarly, just as some communities strive to keep out smaller homes and their lower-income owners, others fight to keep gentrification at bay or to outlaw houses that are deemed too large. For example, a number of communities have recently made the news with their efforts to curtail the spread of "McMansions."[58]

Whatever their motivations and effects, land use restrictions are pervasive responses to the unbounded nature of the home. While such mechanisms effectively extend control beyond the four corners of the owner's parcel and remove some of the uncertainty associated with the dynamic bundle that makes up the home, they also present difficulties that require attention. In the next chapter, I step back to frame the problem of the unbounded home in game-theoretic terms. Doing so illuminates the potential benefits and risks of typical land use controls, and sets the stage for a broader exploration of alternatives.

3

THE COMMONS AND THE ANTICOMMONS

In 1967, Ezra Mishan used the example of gasoline-powered lawn-mowers to argue for an "amenity rights" approach to neighborhood spillovers. Mishan observed that the noise produced by a single power mower could disrupt the peace and quiet of dozens of neighbors. Mishan's solution shifted the balance of power from the oblivious mower operator to the suffering neighbors by granting each of those neighbors the right to be free of the disturbance. If a homeowner wanted to operate a gas-powered mower, she would first have to purchase amenity rights from everyone within earshot. Under such an arrangement, "no man could be forced against his will to absorb these noxious by-products of the activity of others."[1]

Mishan expressed little concern that the person who wished to run the power mower might not succeed in collecting the necessary amenity rights, noting only that in such a case the person "would have to make do with a hand lawn-mower until the manufacturer discovered means of effectively silencing the din."[2] James Buchanan, in contrast, found this "possible tendency toward the underproduction of the valuable externality-generating good or service" to be the "central flaw" in amenity rights schemes like Mishan's.[3] The problem to which Mishan's idea responded and the flaw that Buchanan identified with that solution illustrate the twin dilemmas that are the subject of this chapter. If unconstrained, members of a community may act in ways that fail to take into account the interests of others. But if all of those others are given veto power, some efficient actions will be blocked.

Two templates drawn from property theory—the commons and the anti-commons—will help to frame these difficulties.

The Tragedy of the Commons

Garrett Hardin popularized the phrase "tragedy of the commons" to refer to a set of problems typified by the tendency of ranchers acting in their own self-interest to overgraze a common field.[4] Such problems are characterized by a payoff structure that leads people to take actions that are individually rational but collectively harmful—whether drawing too many resource units out of a common pool or doing so too quickly, degrading a commons through the introduction of negatives like litter or pollution, or investing too little effort in upgrading, maintaining, or cultivating a shared resource.[5] These actions are inefficient—their total costs exceed their benefits.[6] Because they make the users of a resource collectively worse off than necessary, they are deemed "tragic."

In these scenarios, externalities—costs or benefits imposed or bestowed on others that an actor does not take into account in deciding how to act—skew decisions toward suboptimal outcomes.[7] For example, a homeowner might invest too little in lawn maintenance, given that she must bear all of the costs of a well-kept lawn, while many of the benefits accrue to her neighbors. Or, put differently, the homeowner enjoys all the benefits of leisure time associated with not tending the lawn, while her neighbors bear many of the costs of the unsightly yard. Considered more generally, we might understand a neat, well-kept neighborhood as a common pool resource that individual parcel-holders may invest too little in maintaining or make too many draws upon (by, say, neglecting lawn care or leaving rubbish in plain view).

When Is a Commons Tragic?

The fact that people may not take their neighbors' interests into account in choosing levels of lawn maintenance or rubbish removal does not mean that they will always make the wrong decisions on such matters. Externalities are indeed an important prerequisite to the commons tragedy, because they lead actors to make "blindered" decisions that do not take into account all of the socially relevant costs and benefits. But this disregard for external costs and benefits will not always produce tragic outcomes that reduce the overall value of the common resource for the collectivity as a whole.[8] For example, a small group of people fishing from a large, remote lake may pay no heed to the costs their catches impose on others in the group. But this heedless fishing may not cause the group to suffer any net losses; if the fish population is large enough, the catches will pose no threat to its sustainability.[9]

In other words, an actor's self-interested choice might be no different from the one she would have made had she been forced to internalize all of the relevant costs and benefits. Suppose Alma is deciding whether to leave unsightly rubbish piled in front of her garage door, where it generates aesthetic discomfort for herself as well as for her neighbors. If Alma's internalized share of visual unease outweighs her costs in moving the rubbish, she will move it even if she completely ignores the impacts on her neighbors. Alternatively, suppose the cost of moving the rubbish is extraordinarily high—a freak blizzard has mired the rubbish in sticky snow and made it impossible for Alma to work outside. Alma may ignore her neighbors' interests when she chooses to leave the rubbish in place, but she would make exactly the same choice if she were forced to take their interests into account; under these circumstances, the cost of rubbish removal (at least in the short run) outweighs the aggregate benefits to the entire neighborhood. In both of these situations, externalities are irrelevant to efficiency; Alma makes the efficient choice even though she is wearing blinders.[10] Nonetheless, externalities make inefficient choices more likely.

Actions are only "tragic" in the sense used here when they diminish the total social value available to the group. Decisions that frictionlessly shift value among parties are not tragic in this sense, although they may be unfair; if the game is truly zero-sum, no inefficiency results.[11] Yet, self-interested choices with respect to a resource can produce tragic consequences even without altering the total amount of the resource itself. When parties compete over a resource that is nonreplenishing and in fixed supply, like a cache of gold or a plate of cookies, the total amount of the resource remains the same after the competition as before. Our ultimate concern, however, is not with the resource as such but with the total social value or utility that the resource produces, and this value can change depending on the outcome of the resource struggle.

First, if some individuals value the resource more highly than others do, it can matter a great deal who ends up with how much. Even if everyone had identical utility schedules, most resources (including money itself) are believed to deliver diminishing marginal utility.[12] Alternatively, a resource may be less valuable when fragmented into pieces held by different people than when assembled into a larger whole. This might be because boundary problems or coordination problems are exacerbated by fragmentation, because economies of scale or other complementarities among resources cannot be realized, or because additional transactions are necessary to aggregate a usable physical quantity of the resource.[13]

Second, the actions parties take in competing over a fixed stash can dissipate social value. For example, imagine that competing miners learn of a newly discovered deposit of gold and race to extract it. Even though their haste does not alter the total amount of gold available for extraction, it can impose other costs on them—overinvestment in mining equipment, mining accidents, fights over claims, and so on.[14] These costs reduce the net benefit that the miners obtain from the fixed supply of gold. We might think of these situations as involving not only the common resource (here, a set quantity of gold) but also another "commons" that is relevant to the participants' total payouts—the resource-gathering environment. When the two commons are considered together, we see that the appropriation choices that the parties make can reduce the total returns to the group, even if the underlying resource does not shrink.

This problem of wasteful competition for resources can emerge in any common resource setting, not just those involving a fixed supply of the underlying resource. Hence, in considering the potential for tragedy in a particular common resource setting, it is important to examine not only the possibility that actors will dissipate the underlying asset through noncooperative choices (extracting too much or investing too little) but also the possibility that they will act in a costly manner in the resource-gathering environment.[15] People engage in a form of "overgrazing" when they fight over resources: they take resource-appropriation actions that provide them with benefits (a larger share of resources) without bearing all the costs of those actions (a more difficult and dangerous resource-gathering milieu). Likewise, people may underinvest in the resource-gathering commons by, for example, dispensing with pleasantries and civilities that would be socially valuable on balance, if they do not personally internalize a large enough share of the resulting benefits.

Translating these ideas into the metropolitan setting, the total amount of resources that are available to a group of communities may be capable of growing or shrinking, depending on how those resources are distributed among the communities. But even if we were certain that moving resources from community Alpha to community Beta would be a complete wash (Beta gains precisely what Alpha loses), we still must consider the social costs of the mechanisms that Beta employed to bring about that move (and that Alpha employed to resist it).

Payoff Structures and Norms

Although the tragedy of the commons involves many actors, the basic problem can be understood through the lens of a two-player Prisoner's Dilemma.[16] The Prisoner's Dilemma game structure takes its name from a scenario in which two partners in crime are taken into custody and questioned separately. Each player must decide whether to "cooperate" (with the other prisoner) by remaining silent or to "defect" by squealing. Each player gets the best payoff if she defects while her partner cooperates, the next best payoff if both cooperate, the third best payoff if both defect, and the worst payoff if she cooperates while her partner defects. This creates a payoff structure in which each player is better off defecting, no matter what her partner does.[17]

To translate this same dilemma into a neighborhood context, consider the plight of Rowan and Colleen, who own adjacent property and must decide whether to invest in maintaining the fence between them or, instead, to let it deteriorate.[18] For simplicity, assume that each party is deciding whether to purchase one additional increment of maintenance that will cost him or her ten dollars but will generate total benefits of fourteen for the pair. Table 3-1 depicts the payoffs the players face.

Each person must choose between the cooperative action (here, maintaining the fence) and the defecting action (letting the fence deteriorate). Rowan must choose between the two rows, and Colleen must choose between the two columns. Their payoffs are shown by the parentheticals at the intersection of their two choices. If both choose to maintain the fence (Cell I in Table 3-1), each will enjoy a net gain of four dollars. Each party's

Table 3-1 A Prisoner's Dilemma

	Payoffs for (Rowan, Colleen)	
	Colleen maintains the fence	*Colleen lets the fence deteriorate*
Rowan maintains the fence	I. (4, 4)	II. (-3, 7)
Rowan lets the fence deteriorate	III. (7, -3)	IV. (0, 0)

expenditure of ten will produce a gain of fourteen, half of which will be internalized by the spending party, and half of which will accrue to the neighbor. If both parties do this, each will receive the seven-dollar share associated with his or her own fence-mending action, plus seven from the neighbor's parallel action, for a net gain of four. The result for the pair, eight, is better than any other alternative. Yet we would not expect this outcome to occur if the parties act independently to maximize their own payoffs.

First, look at things from Rowan's point of view. He recognizes that if Colleen works on the fence, he can maximize his position by neglecting fence maintenance. He will enjoy a seven-dollar improvement, courtesy of his neighbor, without lifting a finger. Colleen in this instance would receive the "sucker's payoff"—a loss of three dollars. She bears all of the cost of fence maintenance but captures only half of the benefits. Of course, Rowan must consider the possibility that Colleen will refuse to be a sucker and will also defect by refusing to fix the fence. By comparing his payoffs in Cell II and Cell IV, however, Rowan can see that he does best shirking on fence maintenance in this case as well. If Colleen shirks while Rowan mends, he will get stuck with the sucker's payoff of negative three. If he also shirks, then his payoff rises to zero. He is better off not bothering with fence maintenance, no matter what Colleen does.

Colleen can be expected to reach the same conclusion. She faces precisely the same structure of payoffs as does Rowan, and will rationally choose to shirk on the grounds that it will maximize her payoff, regard-less of what Rowan does. Shirking, then, is each player's dominant strat-egy; these dominant strategies combine to produce a Nash equilibrium in Cell IV.[19] The game works the same way in the case of many players.[20] In place of fence maintenance, consider a common greenbelt running through a neighborhood, the landscaping of which is capable of produc-ing net benefits for the group. If each party's cooperative action would cost her more than she would personally internalize, then she would be ex-pected to play the dominant strategy of defecting. The result is a tragedy of the commons.[21]

We will soon discuss some legal mechanisms for resolving the tragedy. Before doing so, however, it is helpful to consider the potential role of so-cial norms and similar informal mechanisms in averting tragedy. The strat-egy selected by a party may be influenced not only by pecuniary payoffs and legal rules but also by de facto arrangements, norms, and other so-cial factors.[22] One way to think about these influences is to understand them as modifying the payoff structure shown in Table 3-1.[23] Suppose Colleen and Rowan are friends, so that each would derive pleasure from seeing the other made better off, as long as the other reciprocates. In-deed, they may enjoy positive utility from the project of working together on the fence.[24] If this is so, then the true payoff for mutually maintaining the fence (Cell I) may be higher than is reflected in Table 3-1. Suppose, for example, that each will derive an additional four dollars' worth of util-ity from fence maintenance if—but only if—the other party also engages in fence maintenance. This additional source of utility thus changes the payoffs in Cell I from (4, 4) to (8, 8).

This change in payoffs alters the game so that it no longer constitutes a Prisoner's Dilemma but rather becomes an "Assurance Game" or "Stag Hunt." Taking its name from a passage by Jean-Jacques Rousseau, the Stag Hunt is a situation in which two players acting together can achieve the outcome that is best from both of their perspectives (bringing down a stag for dinner).[25] Because neither of the parties can bag a stag single-handedly, however, a party that chases a stag without the cooperation of the other will go hungry; she would be better off working independently to obtain the less-desired meal of a rabbit.[26] The Assurance Game likewise refers to a setting in which the best outcome can be achieved through cooperation; each actor merely requires assurance that the other actor will co-operate as well.[27]

In these cases, there is no tension between the best individual payoff and the best joint payoff—each player does best individually and collectively by cooperating, as long as the other player does the same. Unlike in the Prisoner's Dilemma, where one does better by defecting regardless of what the other player does, playing one's best strategy in the Assurance Game or Stag Hunt depends on learning the other player's intentions. If both players are confident that the other will engage in fence maintenance, each does best sticking to that plan. There is no temptation to cheat by defecting when the other player cooperates (again, unlike in the Prisoner's Dilemma) because the best individual payoff is found in Cell I with mutual cooperation.

There are many other ways that the payoffs in Table 3-1 might be modified to change the nature of the game. Suppose instead that Colleen and Rowan have a very tense relationship, such that each can expect an escalation of unpleasantness from the other for any act or omission that is perceived as unneighborly. Or perhaps the pair are part of a larger social network in which norms dictate certain standards of fence maintenance and informal sanctions (such as glares or fewer dinner invitations) are imposed on those who fall short. Either of these possibilities might attach some negative utility to the choice not to maintain the fence. Informal sanctions that penalize players who fail to cooperate would amount to deductions from the "defection" payoffs in Table 3-1. If these sanctions are large enough, cooperation becomes a dominant strategy; each player is better off maintaining the fence, regardless of what the other does.

As these examples show, the payoffs in a given game are not fixed by nature but rather depend crucially on all of the factors that impact utility. Relatively small changes in our assumptions about what people get out of a given action can dramatically alter the game that we understand them to be playing. Thus, it not unusual for situations that might appear to outsiders to be tragedies in the making to resolve themselves agreeably without the need for any formal intervention at all. This is especially likely to be the case in close-knit communities whose members are bound together in enduring relationships that crosscut many facets of life.[28] As residential mobility and the relative anonymity of residential life have increased, however, the kinds of collective action problems that emerge in neighborhood settings have increasingly required resort to formal legal mechanisms. While this book focuses on situations in which such mechanisms are deemed necessary, it is important to bear in mind the interplay between informal social norms and formal legal alternatives, and the potential that the former could, at times, successfully substitute for the latter.

Devising Solutions

As Elinor Ostrom has observed, scholars often focus on two divergent approaches to the tragedy of the commons, both of which attempt to make the individual's choice align more closely with the social optimum.[29] First, individually maximizing behavior with socially undesirable consequences might be coercively constrained by government mandate. Hardin alluded to this "Leviathan" solution when he recommended "mutual coercion, mutually agreed upon" as a solution to the tragedy of the commons.[30] A competing possibility is to convert the resource into private property and place it under the exclusive control of owners who will reap both the positive and the negative consequences of their resource-related actions.[31] For example, a common grazing land might be broken up into separate parcels to be allotted to individual households. (It is worth noting, however, that the actual history of the enclosure movement does not follow this simple story of tragedy resolution, in part because medieval villages were sufficiently close-knit to govern resource use through informal means).[32]

The amorphous and anonymous set of potential players who can access a commons that is truly "open to all"[33] makes it difficult to fathom solutions that depart from the polar alternatives of government action and privatization. Scholars responding to Hardin's piece, however, were quick to distinguish between an "open-access" resource that literally anyone can use, and a "limited-access" commons to which only certain actors are granted admission.[34] Where access to a commons is limited, the prospects are much brighter for additional, group-initiated solutions—whether through contract, internal governance mechanisms, or the informal operation of norms. Ostrom has explored the empirical potential for such alternatives by studying communities that have successfully managed common-pool resources.[35]

While these group-initiated arrangements can indeed be understood as alternatives to governmental and privatization solutions, they incorporate elements of both of those standard approaches. To see why, it is helpful to begin with Carol Rose's insight that a limited-access commons only looks and feels like a "commons on the inside," to those who have been granted access; because such a commons excludes the rest of the world, it works like private "property on the outside."[36] A limited-access commons thus necessarily incorporates an element of privatization inasmuch as the privileged commoners collectively hold the resource in common, to the exclusion of the outside world. Of course, excluding outsiders only solves part of the problem. Those inside the limited-access commons are in a position to engage in self-interested behavior that would be damaging for the collectivity, unless some mechanism is devised to align their interests with those of the group as a whole. Whatever solutions the group conjures up will involve either establishing an internal governance regime (that is, a mini-Leviathan) or dividing up and allocating specific entitlements among the commoners for at least certain periods of time (that is, microproperty). These group-devised alternatives may be quite informal, enforced with norms rather than with legal sanctions. In addition, internal solutions can combine property and governance in a customized manner that incorporates valuable local knowledge.[37] Nonetheless, each component of the resulting arrangement must either direct action through some form of centralized decision-making or parcel out, in some manner, the right to make decisions affecting the common-pool resource.

The same choice set applies in the neighborhood context, with a few qualifications. Neighborhoods fall closer to the limited-access end of the spectrum than the open-access end, although the nature and degree of the limitation on access varies somewhat among neighborhoods. The exclusion of outsiders is perhaps most obvious where a gated community physically fences nonresidents out, but most other metropolitan neighborhoods place some limits, whether through zoning or covenants, on the introduction of new land uses and housing stock into a neighborhood. Because one must be physically present in (or at least proximate to) a neighborhood to influence it, most of the world is excluded from any given neighborhood by distance alone.[38] Further, the high opportunity cost of hanging around a neighborhood for no reason binds individuals' physical presence in the neighborhood to the existence of permanent physical structures in which they reside, work, shop, dine, visit friends, and so on. Street design can further raise the costs to outsiders of entering a particular neighborhood. The neighborhood's residents are thus uniquely positioned to access the commons that the neighborhood comprises and to make decisions that enhance or degrade its quality.

While the partial privatization that occurs through the exclusion of outsiders limits some of the unwanted impacts on the neighborhood, the insiders still must be reckoned with. The fact that homes are unbounded, constituting both ambient and porous resources, presents challenges for a private property solution. While property within a neighborhood can be (and usually is) divided into separate physical chunks owned by individual households, other aspects of life within the neighborhood are held in common and cannot be as easily parceled out. For example, the noise level, aesthetic appeal, and overall ambience of the neighborhood cannot be divided up among homeowners in a manner akin to slicing up the landscape into tracts of land. While a science fiction world might allow households to individually customize their residential surroundings, physical reality requires proximate households to share overlapping environments. In this sense, the neighborhood is not a resource amenable to full parcelization; it must instead be held in common.

Nonetheless, both governance and property solutions can be employed to control spillovers within the neighborhood. Zoning operates not only to control entry into the commons but also to specify what those living in a given area may do while they are there. Private neighborhoods embody a hybrid approach. These neighborhoods typically feature a web of reciprocally binding covenants that place limits—often quite specific ones—on what parcel owners may do with their property, as well as a governance structure that is capable of altering the rules applicable within the community. In other words, private neighborhoods combine the mini-Leviathan and microproperty regimes by giving owners both a voice in a regulatory body that wields coercive power and a property right in the restrictions that are placed on others.

These approaches to neighborhood controls will be explored at length later in the book. For now, it is sufficient to observe that these devices, as they have operated on the ground, have relied almost entirely on prohibitions, whether embodied in restrictive covenants, private community rules, or zoning restrictions. These prohibitions can threaten to create another sort of tragedy.

The Anticommons

The anticommons began as a thought experiment introduced by Frank Michelman.[39] Envisioning a regime that would be the opposite of a commons open to all, Michelman posited an imaginary world in which everyone has the power to exclude all others from a resource, but nobody has the power to enter or use that resource without the permission of everyone else.[40] While it is never the case that literally everyone holds veto power over the use of a resource, it is not unusual to encounter a resource over which some limited number of people have independent veto powers.[41] Michael Heller developed the idea of the anticommons by finding real-world examples that exhibit this structure.[42] For example, he posited that the persistence of empty storefronts in postsocialist Moscow could be attributed to the number of permits that were required from different actors in order to set up shop.[43]

The same structural problem exists whenever multiple parties hold veto rights that must be assembled before an actor can use a resource in a particular way. The term "anticommons" has thus become a shorthand way of referencing a broad class of entitlement assembly problems—whether the entitlements at issue are pieces of land, biotech patents, layers of permission, or covenant releases.[44] Of course, the difficulties associated with assembling entitlements for resource use were recognized well before the anticommons terminology came into vogue. In a 1973 article, for example, Buchanan observed that the bargaining dynamics produced by an amenity rights approach could inefficiently curtail externality-producing activities.[45] Likewise, Kenneth Arrow noted in 1979 the difficulties that a factory owner might face in attempting to buy the rights to clean air held by a number of nearby landowners.[46] And Harold Demsetz's groundbreaking 1967 article noted the holdout problem that can accompany the most fundamental assembly problem of all—getting people to agree to a property regime in the first place.[47] But the anticommons literature has made the problem of entitlement assembly much more salient. Both public and private land use controls can present anticommons-like dynamics under some circumstances, whether by erecting a series of administrative hurdles or by conferring veto power on a number of neighbors. Consider again Mishan's amenity rights proposal, which would entitle neighbors to be free from the noise of gas-powered lawnmowers. If a homeowner, Mildred, finds the costs of employing a push mower very high, it might be efficient for her to use a power mower instead. In theory, she could buy a release from each of her neighbors to run the mower, but in practice this may be impossible. Administrative difficulties aside, each of her neighbors might try to hold out for a large share of the surplus that will be produced by the exchange. Control over Mildred's mowing choice has been fragmented among multiple neighbors, creating very high transaction costs. The result can be characterized as an anticommons.

The anticommons problem has generally been identified with inefficient resource "underuse" arising from the fragmentation of exclusion rights over a resource.[48] This characterization allows the tragedy of the anticommons to be readily contrasted with the tragedy of the commons, at least insofar as the latter is associated with the prototypical "overgrazing" situation. While some of the anticommons problems that have received the most attention indeed involve problems of underuse, the anticommons problem is structural in nature: it stems from the need to assemble rights from a number of other individuals in order to make a desired use of a resource. In some cases, the would-be assembler of entitlements wishes to make a less intensive use of the resource than the current set of entitlement-holders. Think, for example, of an environmental rights group that seeks to buy up land slated for commercial or industrial use in order to assemble a large open area that will be restored to its natural state. We might well attribute the group's difficulty in achieving its objective to an anticommons dynamic, but it would be odd to characterize the problem as "underuse."

When Is an Anticommons Tragic?

It is intuitive that assembling fragmented entitlements in order to use a given resource in a desired manner can be difficult, perhaps prohibitively so. Yet this result is only "tragic" in an efficiency sense if the resource is more valuable when assembled together in one party's hands than it is when dispersed among many hands—and this will not always be so.[49] Whether or not it is the case in a given instance depends crucially on the valuations placed on the fragments by their (many) current owners as well as the valuation that the would-be assembler places on the assembled collection of fragments. There may or may not be an "assembly surplus" in which the whole is greater than the sum of its parts. In short, fragmented resource entitlements are not always a bad thing. The problem, which the anticommons analysis underscores, is that it can be very hard to tell whether a given failure to assemble entitlements stems from the fact that the entitlements are actually worth more as fragments or whether it is instead a tragic case of strategic behavior blocking an efficient assembly.

To illustrate, suppose that an assembly effort seems doomed to failure because Fran, who holds one of the essential fragments, refuses to sell—even when Arnie, the would-be assembler, raises his offer to three and even four times the fair market value of Fran's fragment. Fran's resistance could be an entirely honest expression of the fragment's value to her. If so, and if Arnie is unwilling to pay a price Fran will accept, then assembly would not have been efficient, and no inefficiency results when it fails to materialize. In other words, instead of being a holdout, Fran may be what Gideon Parchomovsky and Peter Siegelman have dubbed a "holdin"—someone whose refusal to sell is based on an honest subjective valuation.[50] Even if Fran is a holdin, we might still have reason to complain. Perhaps her tastes seem so idiosyncratic or selfish as to make her refusal to deal appear unfair. Or we might question the allocative process that gave her the fragment in the first place and, with it, the power to veto the desired assembly. But these objections are distributive in nature; they do not speak to the efficiency of the arrangement.

On the other hand, perhaps Fran really is a holdout, and her price resistance merely a ploy designed to garner a larger share of the surplus that will be generated by the assembly of the fragments.[51] She may be bluffing when she turns down offer after offer from Arnie. If the bluff works, she may be able to extract a great deal of the surplus that Arnie would otherwise enjoy from assembling the entitlements. If Fran is a perfect bluffer who can costlessly and convincingly force Arnie to take a smaller share of surplus, the resulting realignment of surplus is a distributive matter, not a source of inefficiency.[52] We might argue about whether Fran deserves that much surplus, but the surplus must be divided up in some fashion.[53]

If Fran's bluff doesn't work, however, her artificially high reservation price (or strategic refusals to deal) may prevent assembly of the interests in the hands of the higher-valuing Arnie. Even if she and Arnie ultimately make a deal, value may be dissipated as she and Arnie wrangle over prices. Moreover, Arnie's fears of facing a phalanx of strategic Frans may discourage him from even attempting an assembly that would represent a much more valuable use of the resource.[54] Because of these possibilities, holdout behavior is socially costly. It is obviously costly for the holdout herself: Fran's strategic posturing and wrangling consumes energy, and she risks losing out on a deal that would actually make her better off. But the holdout also inflicts losses on others interested in the deal, who must suffer transaction costs or, possibly, the complete loss of a value-enhancing assembly.[55]

The holdout is well aware of this dynamic; indeed, it is the holdout's knowledge of the pain that others will suffer if the deal collapses that gives her strategic leverage. But if she miscalculates and pushes too hard, a deal that would have generated surplus for everyone falls apart. The tragedy of the anticommons, then, can be understood as an extremely wasteful version of the fixed-pot resource game described earlier. In the case of a fixed-pot resource like a deposit of gold, parties' attempts to gain larger shares of the surplus can reduce the value available for all of the parties to carry away from the interaction. What is remarkable about the anticommons situation is the possibility that strategic posturing and wrangling may sink a deal altogether, so that the entire surplus that might have been shared among the parties vanishes outright. In that case, everyone walks away empty-handed. Each party would have been better off taking a sucker's payoff—a smaller than average share of the surplus—rather than destroying the entire surplus. The basic strategic interaction fits into the well-known game template of "Chicken."

The Anticommons as a Game of Chicken

In the familiar game of roadway Chicken, two drivers proceed on a collision course toward each other. The one to swerve first is called "Chicken" and loses the game. The best outcome for each player is for the other party to swerve first so that she can drive straight ahead in victory while yelling "Chicken" out the window. The worst possible outcome occurs, of course, if nobody swerves and a crash ensues. When both parties swerve, both parties enjoy a second-best outcome—it is better than swerving while the other party drives straight ahead, and better than crashing, but worse than being the one to drive straight ahead while the other party swerves.

The Chicken Game has been explicitly invoked to describe land assembly problems that involve an anticommons-like structure.[56] The link between the Chicken Game and the anticommons is also implicit in the focus on holdouts in the anticommons literature.[57] While land assembly problems and other anticommons dilemmas typically involve multiple parties, the basic strategic interaction can be captured by a two-player game of Chicken. Regardless of the number of parties involved, the essential difficulty is that overreaching in an attempt to capture a larger share of surplus can keep a mutually beneficial transaction from going through. Indeed, the potential for this problem exists in any bargaining interaction. For example, two parties to a real estate transaction might each attempt to capture more than a proportionate share of the surplus that the deal will generate. If one or both back down, then a deal will occur. If neither backs down, no deal will occur—the worst outcome for both.[58]

Consider again the plight of Rowan and Colleen, neighbors who share a fence and must make maintenance decisions concerning it. We saw already how they might fall victim to a Prisoner's Dilemma, which equates structurally to a tragedy of the commons. Suppose, however, that Rowan decides to address the problem by hiring a fence repair company that will provide optimal maintenance of the fence. Naturally, he wants Colleen to kick in a share of the cost, since she will benefit as well. In our earlier discussion, we established that fence maintenance performed by the parties would cost each party ten dollars, or a total of twenty dollars for the contributions of both parties. We will assume that the fence company can maintain the fence optimally for this same price of twenty dollars. We also know that each party will enjoy benefits worth fourteen dollars from a properly maintained fence, for a total of twenty-eight dollars. Thus, the pair will enjoy a total surplus of eight if the fence is properly tended, as compared to a world in which it is allowed to deteriorate.

Table 3-2 Chicken Game

	Payoffs for (Rowan, Colleen)	
	Colleen cooperates *(accepts less surplus)*	*Colleen defects* *(demands more surplus)*
Rowan cooperates (accepts less surplus)	I. (4, 4)	II. (1, 7)
Rowan defects (demands more surplus)	III. (7, 1)	IV. (0, 0)

Rowan and Colleen have the opportunity to strike a deal with each other that will generate this surplus, but there is no guarantee that their efforts at bargaining will be successful. Each may attempt to capture a disproportionately large share of the eight-dollar surplus that a bargain over fence maintenance will provide. Their bargaining interaction can be captured by Table 3-2, which sets out a payoff structure that corresponds to "Chicken."

Each party must decide whether to cooperate or swerve by accepting a smaller share of the available surplus or whether instead to defect by demanding a larger share of the available surplus. While the parties might decide to split up the surplus in any number of ways, Table 3-2 illustrates the basic choice between accepting a proportionate (or smaller) share of the surplus and demanding a disproportionately large share. If both parties swerve, then the surplus can be shared equitably and the deal will occur (Cell I in Table 3-2). But the best outcome for each player is for that player to garner a disproportionately large share of the surplus—Cell II for Colleen and Cell III for Rowan. Obtaining that result is, of course, only possible if the other party agrees to accept a smaller-than-proportionate share of the surplus (that is, agrees to swerve). If both parties demand a disproportionately large share of the surplus, no deal will occur. This is the worst outcome for both parties, as shown in Cell IV; there, both parties receive a payoff of zero.

What is most significant about this game structure is the fact that there is no dominant strategy for either player. Rowan's best move depends on what he expects Colleen to do, and vice versa. If Colleen is not going to swerve, Rowan does best by swerving. Capturing a disproportionately small share of the surplus is an unattractive outcome, but it is still better than the situation in which the deal fails to occur at all. But if Colleen can be bluffed into swerving, Rowan does best by holding out for a larger share of the surplus. Here we see the critical difference between the Prisoner's Dilemma structure and the Chicken Game structure—a distinction that can also be used to differentiate commons tragedies from anticommons tragedies. In the Prisoner's Dilemma, one always does better by defecting (failing to cooperate) regardless of what others do. In Chicken, defecting yields better results only if the other party can be bluffed into cooperating; otherwise, one does better cooperating.

Just as social norms and other nonpecuniary factors can influence payoffs and alter the Prisoner's Dilemma game, so too can they operate to alter the game of Chicken. For example, parties typically have a strong aversion to being "suckered" in a transaction, and are often willing to bear pecuniary costs in order to punish another player who is viewed as having acted unfairly. In the well-known "ultimatum game" experiments, one player is asked to propose a split of an amount of money (such as ten dollars) with another player. If the responding player agrees to the proposal, each gets the money, but if not, neither receives anything. Proposed splits that give the responder less than 20 percent are routinely rejected, even though the party rejecting such an offer is made worse off in pecuniary terms than if she simply accepted the paltry split.[59] Clearly, the responder perceives the payoff as involving more than just money.

It is entirely possible, then, that the payoffs that actually drive Rowan's and Colleen's choices are different from the ones that appear in Table 3-2. For example, suppose that the anger and humiliation Rowan would feel from being suckered would subtract three dollars from his payoff in Cell II. The no-deal outcome in Cell IV would then dominate the sucker's payoff in Cell II for him. Yet, even if Rowan avoids what is (to him) the worst outcome—being suckered—a "crash" in Cell IV would still be tragic, because it would mean forgoing the surplus of eight that could have been enjoyed in Cell I had both parties cooperated. The next part of the book will introduce some mechanisms for avoiding this undesirable outcome. Devising solutions, however, requires taking account of the interactions between the commons and anticommons tragedies.

Linking the Commons and Anticommons Tragedies

As the pair of examples involving Rowan and Colleen suggests, commons and anticommons tragedies are, in an important sense, two sides of the same coin. Thus, we can see a tragedy of the commons (the tendency to shirk on fence maintenance) morph before our eyes into a tragedy of the anticommons once we take note of the fragmented interests involved and the difficulty of assembling them to produce an efficient result. Indeed, a potential anticommons problem stands between every garden-variety commons tragedy and its solution. In short, the tragedy of the commons explains why things are likely to fall apart, while the tragedy of the anticommons explains why it is often so hard to get them back together.

We can also see the links between commons and anticommons problems in neighborhood settings involving many parties. Suppose Alma lives in a community bound by covenants that grant each of her neighbors the right to enforce a rubbish-removal rule against her. Those covenants, of course, were established to prevent a tragedy of the commons from developing. But suppose that the enforcement of the covenants against Alma is inefficient in a given set of circumstances (she values not removing the rubbish more highly than all of her neighbors, combined, value having it removed). Reaching the efficient result would require Alma to "buy up" the entitlements held by every neighbor. It is easy to see how this might present an anticommons dilemma.

But simply eliminating the covenants so that Alma can keep her rubbish in place is not necessarily a superior solution. A commons tragedy might well develop in the absence of such covenants. While we have stipulated that Alma's rubbish heap is efficient, there will likely be many instances in which leaving out rubbish will impose net social costs on the neighborhood. Moreover, if antirubbish covenants were repealed and people began to "overgraze" the commons by letting trash pile up, efforts to address the dilemma anew could present a new anticommons dilemma.

Establishing a new set of covenants in an existing neighborhood would require all of the neighbors to agree to the curtailment of their property rights. This is likely to be quite difficult if the neighbors are already in place and each one has the power to withhold her consent from the covenant scheme.[60]

The diffuse, unbounded nature of the home as a resource can produce both commons and anticommons tragedies. Moreover, as Parts II and III of the book explain in more detail, these tragedies can occur at multiple scales. We might think of a neighborhood setting as a semicommons that contains both privately owned elements (individual parcels and structures) and commonly owned elements (golf courses, greenbelts, sidewalks, and "atmosphere").[61] The neighborhood is itself nested within larger groupings (jurisdictions and metropolitan areas). The goods produced at each scale are influenced by—and call for the collective action of—the households or entities that are contained within them. In each case, too much or too little control over the actions of individual actors can generate difficulties.

The discussion of commons and anticommons problems in this chapter has been intentionally abstract in order to focus attention on the structure of the problems and the sticking points they present. The balance of the book explores how these kinds of problems might be addressed in the semicommons-like atmosphere of metropolitan neighborhoods. Part II explores a set of simple yet confounding problems involving ambient aspects of the residential experience that cannot be reduced to individual ownership or control—"the neighborhood commons."[62] Part III drops back to examine potential collective action problems that play out at a larger scale—those between individual jurisdictions or neighborhoods and the larger metropolitan areas of which they are a part. Part IV revisits the semicommons template and asks whether the pattern of risk-holding associated with traditional homeownership bundles is optimal.

4

MANAGING THE NEIGHBORHOOD COMMONS

In any community, control over resources must be divided some-how between the individual members and the group as a whole. This holds true even in the smallest of communities, the household, as Robert El-lickson's work has shown.[1] Although household members may share many resources, specific individuals typically have proprietary control over pri-vatized areas, such as particular bedrooms. Even within these spaces, how-ever, the household's "management" has veto rights over activities that produce spillovers. Thus, a child may correctly assert that a particular bed-room is "his," even though he lacks the authority to set a fire within it, to crank the stereo to an earsplitting level, or to admit unapproved guests through its windows.

Similarly, land use rights must be divided up between households (who own particular parcels of land) and the community that those households constitute. Property law must respond to the fact that the neighborhood environment experienced by each homeowner—an integral part of his housing bundle—is deeply influenced by the acts of nearby property own-ers. The previous chapter framed the problem by explaining that goods such as local ambience that are shared among neighbors can be under-stood as common-pool resources. Scores of commonplace residential ac-tivities—lawn maintenance, rubbish control, yard art, external painting, on-site car repairs, and pet keeping, to name just a few—can constitute draws against, or investments in, the neighborhood commons.[2] Moreover, absent some constraint, owners might shift residential parcels into more intensive and lucrative uses that would have pronounced effects on the local environment.

Public land use regulation (zoning) and private land use regulation (covenants) both attempt to manage the common resource of the local environment. These two approaches line up with the two dominant approaches that are usually prescribed for resolving commons dilemmas—governmental regulation (or "Leviathan") and private property.[3] At another level, each can be understood as a version of the group-initiated arrangements that have often emerged within limited-access commons. Both sorts of land use controls are premised on the idea that property owners can be made better off as a group if each of them cedes some property rights to the community. While each owner gives up something in the process, he gains something that is at least potentially more valuable—his neighbors' reciprocal concessions. Although land use controls can be quite effective in shutting down certain kinds of resource dilemmas, these devices can introduce problems of their own. One set of concerns—the effects that controls have on who locates within a given community—will be deferred to Part III. Here, I focus not on such "membership effects" but rather on what we might call "compliance effects"—the impacts of land use controls on what people do while living within the community.[4]

Ideally, we want households to be constrained from engaging in behavior on their property when, but only when, that behavior generates net social costs. Because both public and private land use controls operate primarily by banning inputs outright, they are relatively insensitive to differences in the balance of costs and benefits within categories of uses. While both types of land use controls contain political interfaces for toggling between permission and prohibition, neither offers a pricing mechanism or a bargaining platform capable of facilitating market interactions. The result is that prohibitions may inefficiently block behavior that would produce net social gains. Yet, lifting a prohibition across the board, even if politically possible, may produce net social losses. In other words, land use controls generally present communities with binary choices, and neither choice may produce efficient results. What is needed are mechanisms that will facilitate efficient bargains while protecting the parties against unwanted draws on the neighborhood environment.

In this chapter, I consider in a general way how traditional land use controls work to preserve local environments and how these mechanisms can fall short. I start by examining zoning, which remains the dominant method of land use control in the United States. I then turn to private covenants, which are rapidly gaining ground as a primary mode of land use control due to the proliferation of private neighborhoods. The balance of the chapter explores concerns common to both forms of land use control.

Zoning

Robert Nelson aptly describes zoning as a set of collective property rights held by the community.[5] Unlike most property rights, however, zoning restrictions are not freely alienable. This does not mean that zoning patterns are carved in stone. On the contrary, changes are commonplace; money and politics combine in well-established ways to surmount regulatory hurdles.[6] But limits on such deals exist, and the resulting inflexibility of the bargaining process can produce suboptimal results.

An Overview of Zoning

Upheld by the Supreme Court's 1926 decision in *Euclid v. Ambler Realty*, zoning has become an accepted part of the police powers of local governments, and is almost universally employed in populous cities (Houston, Texas, is a notable, long-standing exception).[7] Zoning's justification, however, remains rather ambiguous. At times it is justified as a means of controlling spillovers, in a manner analogous to (though more proactive and protective than) nuisance law, while at other times it is justified on "planning" grounds or on the supposed incompatibility of the separated uses.[8] Whatever the precise justification, there is no question that zoning can limit spillovers. But notice how it does so.

First, zoning controls inputs (particular uses) rather than outcomes (effects of those uses). Zoning classifications typically declare large categories of uses off-limits within particular spatial bounds without regard to whether those prohibited uses would actually produce any appreciable negative spillovers for other properties within the designated zone. While there has been some interest in "performance zoning," which makes uses permissible or impermissible based on their measured impacts (such as decibels of sound), zoning schemes almost invariably target classes of uses.[9] A zoning ordinance may specify an exhaustive list of uses for each zone ("noncumulative zoning"), or it may make the uses cumulative, so that each "lower" (more intensive) classification allows the uses in all of the "higher" (less intensive) zones, plus an additional set of uses.[10] A landowner cannot proceed with a forbidden use, even if he can establish that it would have no negative impact on his neighbors. Zoning can also allow results that seem inconsistent with its own rationales. For example, cumulative zoning would allow single-family homes and heavy industry to exist side by side in the zones at the bottom of the land use hierarchy, a result that seems hard to square with either a planning rationale or the idea that these uses are wholly incompatible.[11]

Second, zoning bans disfavored uses outright—violations are enjoined, and violators can even be subject to criminal penalties—rather than "pricing" those uses through fines or fees.[12] While zoning changes are frequently negotiated, the process bears little resemblance to an ordinary market transaction. Notably, a pair of Supreme Court cases decided in 1987 and 1994 placed limits on public land use bargains. *Nollan v. California Coastal Commission* required a "nexus" between the purposes served by the landowner's concession and the purposes served by the land use restriction to be lifted. *Dolan v. City of Tigard* added a requirement of "rough proportionality" between the concession and the impacts controlled by the lifted restriction.[13] As I have explored elsewhere, these bargaining limits are ill suited to the purpose that seems to have motivated their formulation—protecting landowners from governmental overreaching.[14] My concern here is with the costs these limits impose by constricting potential bargains over zoning classifications. Developers can often work around the *Nollan* and *Dolan* limits, whether through impact fees, development agreements, or the kind of repeat play that makes a lawsuit over bargaining terms unlikely.[15] The opportunities for individual landowners to strike bargains with their local governments to change zoning classifications, however, are much more limited.

Optimal Zoning?

If zoning were perfectly calibrated to counteract spillovers and thereby produced an optimal state of affairs with respect to land use, we would not worry about its categorical nature or about barriers to bar-

Figure 4-1. Public land use controls

gaining. Concerns about the structural characteristics of zoning only become interesting and important if we believe that politically derived land use restrictions will fail to align in at least some circumstances with the social optimum. Such shortfalls introduce the possibility of mutually advantageous bargains between landowners and the community.

What would optimal zoning look like, and how can we tell whether a community has achieved it? To start, imagine a community made up entirely of landowners with identical preferences about land use. Because every landowner in this fictional regime is identical, the preferences of one individual, Lena, can stand in for the preferences of all. Assume further that this community decides to eschew traditional "zoning" (which would imply different restrictions in different zones) in favor of a single set of land use restrictions that will apply jurisdiction-wide. Each restriction takes away some of the land use choice that would otherwise fall to the individual parcel-holders. Although land use restrictions usually operate to preclude more intensive uses, they could work in the opposite direction as well by, for example, prohibiting low-intensity uses that would not generate enough foot traffic for local shops. Figure 4-1, adapted from William Fischel's "restriction index," depicts the choice that a community must make.[16]

In this simple diagram, control over every aspect of land use is held either by individual households or by the community. As restrictions expand, so too does community control over land use; the control of individual parcel-holders like Lena shrinks accordingly. Lena, and those like her, will be happy with this constriction so long as the gains that come from controlling an incipient tragedy of the commons outweigh the individual costs that come from ceding personal authority over the land. If the political process works smoothly to translate the (by assumption, identical) preferences of the constituents into policy, the constriction will be an optimal one. This does not mean that Lena's desires with regard to land use will never be thwarted—like any commoner with access to a common-pool resource, she will be prone to private calculations that are at odds with the social optimum. But, importantly, she will only be thwarted when she "should" be thwarted—that is, where taking the interests of the other (identical) members of the community into account would cause her to choose otherwise.

Back to Reality

Even the most public-minded regulatory body will encounter severe informational difficulties in discerning and aggregating the preferences of the population.[17] Once heterogeneity among households and imperfections in the political process are introduced, the picture changes even more dramatically. It becomes not only possible but very likely that an across-the-board restriction will diverge from the social optimum with respect to at least some parcels. Local communities attempt to deal with these difficulties through the introduction of different zones allowing different uses, as well as through a variety of mechanisms, both formal and informal, for adjusting land use rights. But none of these mechanisms offers a market-like interface for carrying out mutually beneficial trades. Thus, while zoning rights are not wholly inalienable, they are not freely salable either.[18] Critics of zoning have long noted that it fails to serve consumer demand. For example, Nelson analogizes the zoning of available land to governmentally imposed automobile production quotas mandating high proportions of luxury cars.[19] It is one thing to establish that certain kinds of vehicles produce larger externalities and to tax them accordingly, and quite another to keep them from being sold at all.

To return to the classification scheme of Calabresi and Melamed, the local community does not hold an ordinary, property-rule-protected entitlement that it can alienate to any willing buyer on mutually agreeable terms.[20] Instead, there are strains of inalienability wrapped around zoning entitlements, owing perhaps to zoning's historical justification as an exercise of the government's police power.[21] Inalienability makes sense for some exercises of the police power—we don't want people to be able to buy a favorable health inspection, to use an example offered by William Fischel. Most zoning restrictions are far removed from such concerns, however, and blocking their sale can introduce inefficiencies.[22] Zoning entitlements can be bargained over pursuant to an arcane amalgam of legal rules, entrenched local practices, social norms, and political influence, but they cannot be sold outright.[23]

Some efficient adjustments to zoning restrictions may be blocked, as a simple example illustrates. Suppose Ambrose would like to construct a premier dog boarding facility on his property—a use that is currently prohibited by the applicable zoning regulations. Building the kennel would increase the land's value to him by $800,000. Ambrose's extensive knowledge of kennel acoustics and canine psychology will enable him to make the facility significantly quieter than the typical kennel, and his architectural skills will enable the facility to blend beautifully into the surrounding landscape. Thus, although the community would ordinarily suffer aggregate losses of $1 million or more from a large dog kennel on Ambrose's property, Ambrose's kennel will only cause the community to incur losses of about $300,000.

Because Ambrose's marginal gains from the kennel exceed the community's marginal losses, building the kennel would be efficient in the Kaldor-Hicks sense—Ambrose could compensate the community for its losses and still come out ahead.[24] The difference between Ambrose's gains and the community's losses ($500,000) represents a surplus that could be divided between the parties in a multitude of different ways. If zoning rights could be freely sold, we would expect Ambrose to strike a deal with the community and build his kennel—although the division of the surplus could be the subject of some aggressive wrangling.[25] Even though zoning rights cannot be openly sold, the existence of such a surplus generates pressure to strike some kind of bargain. One extreme (although far from hypothetical) possibility is outright corruption.[26] But other forms of barter can also emerge—the landowner trades something (often a piece of his own land) for the entitlement to use the balance of his land in a particular way.

For example, perhaps Ambrose's community would be willing to permit the zoning change if Ambrose would agree to construct a public swimming pool on a portion of his land. Ambrose will agree to the deal because he can install the pool for $400,000 (counting the lost value of the land); he will still net a gain of $400,000. While this "barter" deal may create less of a social surplus than the cash payment would (if, as is likely, the community values the pool less than it will cost Ambrose), it still allows Ambrose's efficient kennel to be built.[27] The Supreme Court placed limits on these types of transactions in the *Nollan* and *Dolan* cases.[28] Indeed, the swimming pool deal just described would be impermissible under *Nollan* because of the lack of nexus between the reason for the original land use regulation (spillovers from a kennel) and the condition placed on lifting it (a swimming pool). Yet blocking this bargain impedes efficiency.

To be sure, there are some instances in which barter arrangements might justifiably give rise to suspicion, as a variation on the kennel example will show. Suppose that Ambrose's kennel will not manifest any of the aesthetic and acoustic advantages mentioned before and will therefore impose aggregate costs of $1 million on the community. As before, Ambrose will enjoy gains of only $800,000, making the conversion of the land to kennel use inefficient. But Ambrose offers to build a community dog park adjacent to his kennel facility—an amenity that selectively benefits dog owners, who make up a politically powerful and cohesive group in the community. These dog owners (who would get all the benefits of the park and who are less bothered by barking from the kennel than other community members in any event) might be able to push the deal through, even though the community's dogless contingent will suffer significant uncompensated losses.

The nexus test could indeed help to flag such opportunistic deal-making. But the real problem with the dog park scenario is that those making the deal are not acting in the interests of those who are impacted. Blocking entire categories of potentially beneficial exchanges does not respond in a tailored manner to that concern. Not only is the response overinclusive, it is also underinclusive. Because those with sufficient political power may be able to push through land use changes that harm the interests of a minority without resorting to any bargaining at all, monitoring bargains will not stop all inefficient and unfair land use changes. The problem of bad bargains would be better addressed through procedural safeguards that involve all impacted parties in land use transactions.

The difficulty in efficiently adjusting land use rights is quite general. Zoning shifts control from landowners to the collective in an effort to enhance a resource held in common, such as neighborhood ambience, but makes scant provision for moving in the other direction when necessary for optimal management of that resource. To be sure, some degree of flexibility is imported through mechanisms like variances and special exceptions. Likewise, the potential to rezone small areas—while presenting additional concerns—offers a means for shifting control back to landowners.[29] But inefficiently tight control of land uses remains a problem that can in some cases rival or eclipse the problem of spillovers resulting from unconstrained land use. The same concerns, although clothed in a different set of legal restrictions, appear in private developments governed by covenants and homeowners associations.

Private Land Use Controls

Private residential communities that employ covenants administered through homeowners associations have proliferated in recent decades, now making up a significant and steadily growing market share of housing.[30] As a result, private land use controls are becoming increasingly important mechanisms for controlling neighborhood externalities. One source of controversy surrounding private neighborhoods—their interaction with the larger community—relates to topics I take up in Part III.[31] But land use controls in private communities may also fall short for the households subject to them.

An Overview of Private Communities

There are many reasons why people might choose to purchase a home within a private residential community. Perhaps they want access to premium amenities like a golf course or a swimming pool, are seeking associational or social advantages, or simply desire a neighborhood environment with tighter controls (and more localized control) than zoning provides.[32] In some cases, the choice may be made almost by default—homebuyers in some parts of the country will have difficulty finding a new home that is *not* located in a private covenant-bound community.[33] One reason for this phenomenon is that local governments are increasingly refusing to approve new residential developments unless they are structured as private communities.[34] Whatever the motivation, purchase of a home in a private development automatically subjects the household to a reciprocal, community-wide set of covenants, conditions, and restrictions (here referred to simply as "covenants") that control each homeowner's use of his own property, the use and maintenance of common property and amenities, and other details of community life and governance. In addition, the household becomes a member of a mandatory homeowners association that will administer the covenants.[35]

Covenants typically operate in a more restrictive manner than traditional zoning by controlling matters like exterior paint colors and the height and type of fencing. The details vary significantly from community to community, but the overarching goal of these land use controls is to produce a local public good that we might call "premium ambience." By controlling negative externalities and requiring households to undertake certain actions that produce positive externalities (such as lawn maintenance), covenants are designed to effect an upgrade of the neighborhood's feel or ambience from that which would prevail in the covenants' absence. In addition, the existence and content of the covenants may serve as signals that help households sort themselves into particular communities.

This premium ambience comes at a literal premium, however. Whether or not residents pay more out of pocket for a home in a private development, they pay "in kind" by ceding property rights that they would otherwise hold. A simple example illustrates this point. Imagine a group of ten households on a residential block. Each landowner attaches some value to the ability to place items of his own choosing in his own front yard but believes that, in general, objects placed in front yards detract from the neighborhood's ambience. If each piece of yard art brings $100 worth of benefits to its displayer but imposes $200 worth of costs on the group— that is, it inflicts $20 worth of aesthetic dismay or reduced property value on each resident, including the displayer himself—then people would be expected to put out too much yard art. Like Hardin's overgrazing ranchers, displayers internalize the full benefit while bearing only a fraction of the cost—a standard tragedy of the commons scenario.[36] Accordingly, there is a possible gain from trade. It is worth $80 (net) to a displayer to place the art in his yard, but his neighbors are $180 better off if he refrains from doing so. Likewise, the would-be displayer stands to suffer losses of $180 if each of his neighbors displays a piece of yard art.

Thus, it would be worth it to each neighbor to refrain from displaying his own art if he could obtain similar surrenders from the other nine residents. Land use covenants reciprocally binding all residents to forbear from yard art would provide significant gains to all of the residents under these assumptions. By agreeing to such a reciprocal covenant, a household grants some control over its own parcel to each of its neighbors; at the same time, the household receives some control over each of the neighbor's parcels by virtue of the covenant.[37] Figure 4-2 presents a stylized representation of such an exchange from the point of view of one homeowner within the community, Ada.

Ada's initial (precovenant) entitlements in her land are represented by the square in Figure 4-2 (a). Figure 4-2 (b) shows the impact of the covenants. The white, gridded triangular area broken away from the left-hand side of that square represents portions of control over her land that Ada is giving up by agreeing to a covenant. The tiny squares indicated by the grid pattern represent the fact that this control is not granted to a single person or entity but rather is broken up and dispersed among all other members of the community. For example, if the covenant that Ada is agreeing to prohibits yard art, she effectively grants a veto over her yard art choices to each other household in the community. In exchange, every other household in the community grants Ada veto rights over its yard art; this grant is represented by the grid-patterned black triangle to the right of Ada's initial square. Once the set of reciprocal covenants is fully executed, Ada's new holdings are represented by the parallelogram shown in Figure 4-2 (c).

In theory, everyone making such a trade views it as a worthwhile one; the expanded control over the property of others more than compensates for the diminished control over one's own property. Someone who netted more in benefits from displaying yard art than he stood to gain from being shielded from the yard art of others would not be expected to enter into such a covenant arrangement. The "no yard art" covenant provides a convenient way of drawing together those for whom such a covenant would represent a gain and delivering that gain to them, while screening out those for whom such a covenant would represent a loss.

Of course, if Ada and all of her neighbors attempted to construct a community-wide web of reciprocal covenants from scratch, the transaction costs would be prohibitive. Because the developer of a private community is able to act as a central locus for forming these reciprocally binding covenants, however, transaction costs for bargains of the sort depicted in Figure 4-2 are quite low, even in relatively large communities.[38] Ada is able to alienate property rights to dozens, hundreds, or even thousands of other

(a)

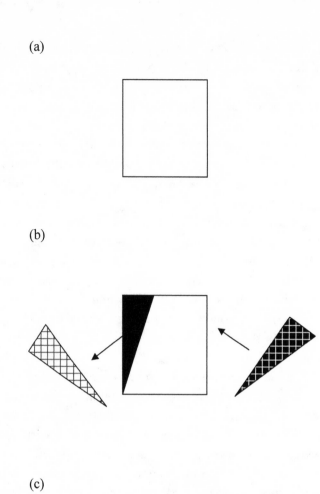

(b)

(c)

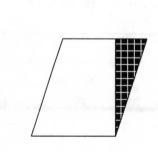

Figure 4-2. Covenants in a community

individuals, while simultaneously receiving property rights from the same number in exchange, simply by purchasing a lot in a private development that is subject to a particular set of covenants. But this advantage also generates a concern: undoing a covenant turns out to be much harder than putting it into place. From one perspective, this is a positive and functional feature of covenant regimes generally. It would be impossible to provide residents with an assured level of ambience in the community if covenants could be costlessly shed at will by various households. But it also means that households may be forced to abide by land use constraints even when they would be willing and able to fully compensate their neighbors for any loss in value associated with the forbidden land use.

To return to Figure 4-2, the entitlement that Ada surrendered through the covenant has now been fragmented among her many neighbors, each of whom holds the right to enforce the prohibition on yard art against Ada. If Ada wished to reclaim her entitlement to display yard art, she would have to cobble together the entire lost entitlement triangle by repurchasing display rights from each of the many community members to whom it was alienated. In a community of any significant size, the transaction costs, including holdout problems, are likely to make obtaining releases from a given servitude from all other community members a logistical impossibility. Every member of the community faces the same difficulty in assembling the rights necessary to engage in activities prohibited by covenant. The resulting situation has the structure of an anticommons.[39] Because of the difficulty each household faces in assembling fragmented entitlements, efficient incursions into the ambience created by the covenants may not occur. The covenants may, therefore, generate a level of premium ambience that is inefficiently high.

The covenant scheme does not just fragment control, however; it also consolidates it. When Ada disperses land use rights to her neighbors, she also collects rights over neighborhood aesthetics from each of them, as represented by the right-hand triangle in Figure 4-2 (b). That process of collection brings together in Ada's hands something that was previously fragmented among the neighbors—power to control certain aspects of neighborhood aesthetics. The private development form of ownership thus solves one problem of fragmentation, even as it creates a new one.[40] The challenge, then, is to find a way to obtain gains from reciprocal covenants without locking inefficient restrictions into place.

Governance and Flexibility

A private development's reliance on an internal governance structure—the homeowners association—represents a partial response to the challenge just raised. Homeowners entering a private development agree not only to be bound by a set of initial substantive constraints but also to submit to the governance structure established by the development's declaration. The homeowners association generally has the power to change the original covenants, add new rules, remove old rules, interpret the prevailing rules, and make enforcement decisions—all on less than unanimous consent.[41] Because one or a few holdouts cannot block a change desired by the great majority of residents, this governance structure adds flexibility that enables the community to respond to changing conditions and preferences. That flexibility comes at a price: the risk that decisions adverse to the individual homeowner will be made.[42] By ceding control to a collective decision-making body capable of acting on less than unanimous consent, the landowner risks losing entitlements in his own property that were reserved to him after the initial reciprocal exchange of covenants (represented by the white area shown in Figure 4-2 (c)) as well as entitlements to control other people's land that were granted to her in that initial exchange (the black triangle area on the right in Figure 4-2 (c)).

More fundamentally, the flexibility delivered by the governance structure will not respond to the plight of an individual household for whom a particular covenant is inefficient. Legal restrictions often keep homeowners associations from making changes in the applicable covenants on a parcel by parcel basis.[43] Homeowners associations may attempt to import discretion into the enforcement process, but doing so invites charges of favoritism and could have unwanted legal consequences.[44] For example, an association's decision to ignore a violation in one instance could compromise its ability to enforce similar violations in the future.[45] Thus, the fact that individual households cannot freely bargain over the rules in private communities presents difficulties akin to those already explored in the zoning context. Yet it is no simple matter to design an alternative.

Sorting and Its Limits

At this point in the argument, the reader may well ask whether the problems I have described are really such a big deal. Can't people simply sort into like-minded communities, Tiebout-style, and avoid all of these controversies? Chapter 2 introduced some reasons why sorting, even when augmented by a set of internal rules, may not adequately address localized spillovers in neighborhoods. Revisiting those issues in the present context will sharpen the dilemmas to which land use controls both respond and contribute.

Consider a controversy over localized spillovers that has recently received media attention—the choice whether to treat one's lawn with herbicides or whether to rely instead on organic treatments.[46] Some fear that the chemicals used to kill weeds will make their way into local water sources, into neighbors' yards, and ultimately into the bodies of people and pets in the neighborhood. But organic treatments have shortcomings as well. They tend to be more expensive than herbicides and are reputed to be less effective at weed control, at least in the short run.[47] Thus, organically maintained lawns may be less visually attractive, or may permit the spread of weeds to neighboring yards (via, for example, wind-blown dandelion seeds). Not surprisingly, some households prefer applying herbicides, while others prefer to use organic treatments. Meanwhile, residents are bothered in varying degrees by weeds and lawn chemicals in the yards of others.

It might seem at first that sorting is an obvious and complete solution to this dilemma: one neighborhood (Organic Oaks) goes fully organic, while another (Herbicide Hills) happily drenches its lawns in chemicals. An initial problem is that households do not decide where to live based on lawn care rules alone. Instead, they must make a home purchase decision that bundles together many land use rules at once, as well as all of the other attributes of the home. Because sorting on every attribute is impossible, homeowners may not respond in a highly sensitive manner to individual covenants. They may buy a home in spite of the content of a covenant, or without giving it much thought.[48] But even if we assume that lawn care rules are of paramount importance to homebuyers and feature prominently in their purchase decisions, sorting falls short.

Suppose everyone in Herbicide Hills is bound together by a shared appreciation for chemically enhanced lawns. Individual households may still
put too much or too little herbicide on their own lawns for their neighbors' aggregate tastes, while suiting their own preferences perfectly. Likewise, even if all households in Organic Oaks are united in their distaste
for lawn chemicals, they may put less money and effort into producing attractive results through organic care than they would if they could internalize all of the benefits of doing so. Recall that in the standard tragedy of
the commons situation, all of the ranchers were assumed to have identical
preferences, yet each was tempted to overgraze in the absence of constraints. The problem was not heterogeneity but rather a divergence between each rancher's private calculus and an overall social calculus that
would take account of all costs and benefits.

Beyond disagreements about the degree of lawn care of a specified type,
some households may actually prefer that their neighbors engage in a kind
of lawn care different from that in which they themselves engage. For example, we can easily envision a heavy herbicide user, Hank, who would
prefer that all of his neighbors engaged in organic lawn care so that he
could enjoy the most beautiful lawn on the block without being exposed
to the cumulative effects of chemical runoff from his neighbors' lawns. Or
consider Olga, an organic lawn care maven who nonetheless would prefer
that her neighbors engaged in herbicide use instead of allowing weeds to
proliferate and potentially spread to her own lawn.

Even setting aside these complications, people can only sort into communities that actually exist—and there is no guarantee that communities
will offer all the alternatives that residents might want. John Miller and
Scott Page make this point using a stylized example of two cities made up
of three citizens each.[49] Each city must decide whether to serve red or
green chili peppers at an annual event. If two of the three residents in each
city prefer green peppers, and if a simple majoritarian decision process is
used in both cities, both cities will opt for green peppers. The fact that a
substantial minority of the citizens of the two cities would prefer red peppers does not ensure that this choice will be made available—the re-sorting necessary to create a local red pepper majority seems unlikely without
a red pepper rule already in place in one of the communities.[50] Put in terms
of our lawn care example, those who prefer organic lawns may not be able

to command a majority in any given jurisdiction, and hence there may be no "organic-only" jurisdiction into which they can sort.

Path dependence, coupled with concerns about adverse selection, may also limit the alternatives that become available. Consider a metropolitan area in which nearly all of the new housing is in private residential communities featuring rules that many homebuyers regard as too restrictive. Perhaps these restrictions were actually preferred by the first private communities that formed in the area but were thereafter copied without much reflection in community after community by developers using standard boilerplate forms. We might think that a new community entering this milieu could profitably offer more lenient rules. But such a community would have to contend with a problem of adverse selection. Those who are most inclined to enter a lenient community that is an outlier in a restrictive field are those who are most likely to press that leniency to its utmost limit. Even households that desire a bit of leniency themselves do not necessarily want to surround themselves with those who are at the most unconventional end of the spectrum.[51]

For example, a development might wish to permit homeowners a free choice of exterior paint colors, and many homeowners might find this idea attractive in theory. But if all of the other developments in the area restrict paint colors to very boring palettes, the "free-painting" development would risk attracting a disproportionate number of people who will choose truly garish combinations, and thus drive away those with only minor preferences for moderately brighter trims. Relatedly, some homeowners might be leery of living with high concentrations of people who really, really care about being able to paint their houses the color of their choosing. Importantly, neighbors do not simply choose an exogenous neighborhood; they also choose each other. Thus, we would expect sorting to be based in part on preferences for people who will prefer or disprefer particular rules, rather than strictly on the content of the rules themselves. To the extent that covenants constitute signals about community member characteristics, developers and residents will be concerned about the content of the signals that they send.[52] In a world where most communities strictly regulate aesthetics, permissiveness about an aesthetic element sends a stronger signal than it would in a world where permissiveness of that sort is widespread.

Even if a full set of options were to somehow become available, sorting offers only a temporary solution, given the many ways in which the costs and benefits of particular policies can evolve in response to new information or changes in technologies, preferences, or household composition. For example, the best lawn care rule for a given community might change if the cost of organic treatments drops, if more effective organic treatments are developed, if safer herbicides are developed, or if new information (whether positive or negative) is obtained about the long-term effects of herbicides on human beings and animals. Similarly, the cumulative effects of chemicals or weeds may make the lawn care choices of neighborhood households nonlinear. Perhaps the fifth chemically enhanced lawn on the block creates marginal costs that are many times worse than those generated by the fourth chemically treated lawn on the same block. Alternatively, a cluster of organic lawns might make no appreciable dent in chemical runoff levels while producing a robust supply of dandelions that induce heightened chemical countermeasures by neighbors.

Moreover, the composition of the neighborhood will change over time, as will the composition of individual households within the community, with likely effects on both household-level and community-level preferences. Additional rounds of rule changes and re-sorting could respond to these changes, but at a price. Because the number of communities is necessarily limited, a move that improves matters for a household along one dimension may require it to make new compromises on other dimensions. In addition, the household's costs of moving to a new location are far from trivial. There are social costs associated with relocations as well—social networks are disrupted, as are the local public goods that the residents themselves participate in producing.[53] People who expect to continue interacting with each other over time will be more likely to adopt cooperative strategies than those who view themselves as transient participants in strategic interactions.[54] Frequent re-sorting thus renders impossible one community attribute that generates important social benefits and that may be greatly preferred by many households—neighborhood stability.

To the extent that sorting is imperfect, rules made by the community will inevitably be applied to a heterogeneous group with varying and shifting preferences. But unless people with sufficiently strong preferences about a given rule are able to bargain with the other members of the community for an exemption or otherwise translate the strength of their preferences into political outcomes, the rule is likely to operate inefficiently with regard to at least some of the population. This basic difficulty has been well noted in the context of majoritarian rule-making.[55] Although private communities typically allocate voting rights based on property ownership rather than allocating one vote to each person in the community, property ownership may also fail to serve as an adequate proxy for preference strength.[56]

Suppose Lane wishes to use a clothesline in his backyard, a use forbidden by his community. His near neighbors are only slightly bothered by the sight of laundry hanging out to dry (aggregate costs of $100), while Lane derives enormous pleasure from drying his clothes in the open air, without the use of a dryer (internalized benefits of $500). Although Lane's clothesline use is efficient, he cannot just go ahead with it and pay the neighbors afterward for the costs that this activity inflicts on them. Land use covenants are typically enforced through injunctive relief (in contract terms, specific performance), or through escalating, supercompensatory fines.[57] Zoning proscriptions are likewise enforced coercively. Yet because Lane's vote does not incorporate the strength of his preferences relative to those of his neighbors, he is unlikely to have enough clout in the political process to push through a rule change.

Of course, it is not possible to make all property owners perfectly happy with their community's rules in every particular. And it would be senseless to condemn as inefficient an arrangement that, while admittedly imperfect, cannot be cost-effectively improved upon. But it is interesting that many of the innovations that have gained prominence in contexts such as pollution control have received so little attention in addressing matters of neighborhood ambience. In essence, communities have responded to the threat of negative externalities almost exclusively through command-and-control approaches, rather than by considering whether "draws" against ambience might be the subject of mutually beneficial trades. Mechanisms designed to facilitate such exchanges could offer significant advantages.

This observation raises another question. If innovations of the sort that I am alluding to are such a good idea, why don't we see them? Why don't different communities compete on their procedures for altering rules, just as they might compete with each other on the content of the rules them-selves?[58] Inertia and path dependence may provide at least partial explana-tions. Local governments tend to follow what has been done before, and private developers tend to employ tried-and-true boilerplate forms in setting up new communities.[59] If we view innovative land use control systems as public goods that will benefit every community that eventually makes use of the idea, we may see here a manifestation of a commons dilemma in which every player has insufficient incentive to invest in improvements.[60] Another possibility, of course, is that these problems of blocked bargains are simply not that pressing or costly. Given the amount of attention that deal-making with local governments and dissatisfaction in private communities has re-ceived, however, the possibility that new forms of property might offer meaningful improvements deserves a fair hearing.

Property Rules, Liability Rules, and Politics

Under current law, both public and private land use controls can be modified, but the dominant mechanisms for carrying out such changes are political in nature. Thus politics, not property rules or liability rules, determine whether land use entitlements stay in the hands of those who currently hold them or shift to another party's control. It is worth exam-ining how these political protections work, and how they compare with other ways of protecting entitlements.

In private communities, the political apparatus of the homeowners as-sociation softens the rigidity that would otherwise result from a web of property-rule-protected covenants. Provisions in the governing docu-ments that permit change on less than unanimous consent circumvent holdout problems that would result from widely dispersed veto powers.[61] The price of this flexibility, of course, is that those who are outvoted can lose valuable entitlements, without compensation.[62] The private com-munity's political mechanism thus operates like a toggle that can move property-rule-protected entitlements from the community as a whole to its members severally, or vice versa. For legal and practical reasons, the po-litical apparatus typically changes the restrictions (or not) for the entire community at once, rather than selectively for particular households—the switch is thrown for all at the same time, or for none.

Zoning changes are also mediated by a political mechanism. As land use restrictions are added, entitlements formerly held by individual landowners are transferred to the community as a whole. While these restrictions are in force, they are generally inalienable in the sense of not being freely marketable. Some such restrictions are truly "not for sale," such as those designed to safeguard health and safety, but most land use restrictions are negotiable in a broad sense. The limits on bargains discussed above place some constraints on the governing body's capacity to negotiate the transfer of entitlements to developers, but deal-making manages to proceed. Thus, piecemeal changes in zoning are often possible.[63] The political mechanism determines both *whether* a particular restriction is alienable at all, and, if it is, the price (whether in cash or in kind) at which it can be alienated. The political apparatus may also realign entitlements without any money changing hands at all.

Politics therefore imports flexibility into land use controls, but it is not the only possible vehicle for doing so, and it has some drawbacks. Suppose Beasley lives in a community that, through either private covenants or public regulations, has banned the display of various forms of yard art, including concrete gnomes like the ones Beasley favors. Suppose further that gnome privileges will win Beasley $600 in intangible psychic benefits, an amount in excess of the $500 aggregate cost the gnomes will impose on the community as a whole. Because Beasley has unusual tastes for his community, resort to politics is unavailing. He cannot convince the local land use authorities to roll back the gnome ban, make an exception in his case, or allow him to pay for display privileges. With no easy way to strike a bargain with his neighbors, he is stuck in an inefficient gnomeless state. (Lest readers think Beasley's gnome-related travails too trivial to repay their attention, it is worth emphasizing that the same analysis could be applied to any other land use that a community prohibits, from parking certain kinds of vehicles in driveways, to building fences over a certain height, to drying clothes on clotheslines, to putting chemicals on lawns, to painting homes in particular colors, to keeping pets of certain types or sizes; yard art conflicts serve merely as convenient illustrations.)

A liability rule solution comes immediately to mind: rather than ban Beasley's gnomes outright, the community could permit them and merely require Beasley to remit a gnome fee to the community that is calibrated to compensate it for the costs suffered as a result.[64] But there are some problems with this solution. First, it may be quite challenging to quantify the damage caused to the community in the aggregate—much less the way in which those costs are distributed among the community's members. The difficulties mount if the activity in question (here, gnome placement) does not deliver a steady marginal increase in harm for each increment of activity, but rather operates in a nonlinear manner to produce cumulative or synergistic impacts. Imperfectly calibrated damages would not only keep the community's members from receiving adequate compensation for each marginal gnome but would also send the wrong price signals to would-be gnome displayers like Beasley, leading to an inefficient number of gnomes. Moreover, even if we could know for certain just how much to compensate the affected community members, involuntarily taking away their right to veto gnome use might still seem problematic.

These concerns—undercompensation and the loss of control over property entitlements—resurface whenever liability rules are used in place of property rules to govern changes in an entitlement regime. Much of the uneasiness surrounding liability rules stems from concerns that compensation will be too low.[65] When entitlements change hands through voluntary transactions, we have some assurance that any completed exchange was, in fact, value enhancing for both parties. Reliance on consensual exchange also saves the state the trouble of trying to make the necessary valuation calculations.[66] But requiring parties to resort to market exchange does more than insulate owners against too-low valuations of their interests; it also protects the autonomy that is typically associated with ownership.[67] Perhaps due to these advantages, interests in real property are predominantly protected with property rules.[68]

For example, owners of real estate usually have the right to prohibit others from entering their property, even when the trespass would cause no damage. This right is backed by the coercive power of the state; interlopers can be ejected by force, kept off through injunctive relief, and punished through supercompensatory civil penalties or even criminal sanctions.[69] In one Wisconsin case, punitive damages of $100,000 were upheld when a mobile home delivery company defied a property owner's instruction to stay off the land, even though the company's traversal of the land did no damage to the property and was undertaken to avoid having to take a more dangerous and circuitous route along a curving, snow-covered road.[70]

Similarly strong protection has also been extended to the entitlements contained in covenants. In a New York case, Judge Cardozo refused to overturn a restrictive covenant in order to permit a church to be built, even though all but one homeowner had signed consents releasing the church from the covenant. As Cardozo observed, that homeowner "took the position that he had bought his lots for the purpose of a home, and that his peace and comfort would be disturbed by a meeting house across the way with the parking of cars, the tooting of horns, and the invasions of privacy attendant upon crowds."[71] Given that there was no evidence of bad faith on the part of the covenant-holder or undue hardship on the part of the church, Cardozo concluded that the homeowner was entitled to stand on his rights and refuse to allow the church to be built, explaining that "[h]e will be protected in his refusal by all the power of the law."[72]

Of course, the stirring image of a property holder insisting on absolute veto rights over his entitlements has never been the law, nor could it be. Exclusion rights and covenants alike are softened or suspended under some circumstances, and even the ultimate sanctuary of the home can be the subject of a forced transfer if the standard for "public use" is met.[73] In the context of land use controls, we have just observed how politics makes entitlement transfers more readily available than they would be in a purely property-rule-protected world. Comparing property rules with liability rules thus presents something of a false dichotomy. The better question is whether the brand of flexibility imported through political mechanisms is better or worse than that achievable through liability rules. Of course, we might wish to dial back both forms of flexibility in order to gain the advantages associated with property rules in contexts where the lack of flexibility presents few risks. But in contexts where granting strong veto rights to a large number of parties introduces an unworkable level of rigidity that must be softened somehow, we should compare different means for doing so.

Property rules, liability rules, and politics thus represent alternative protocols for transferring entitlements. Under a strong version of the property rule approach, consent would be required from all affected parties before any transfer could occur. The best example of this approach is a covenant regime without a political apparatus in place that is empowered to make changes on less than unanimous consent. For example, if we start out in a regime that allows herbicides and a herbicide hater wishes to impose a ban, he must somehow induce all members of the relevant community to give up their herbicide rights. Conversely, if a prohibition were already in place, a would-be herbicide sprayer could attempt to buy back his previously alienated rights from each of his neighbors. In both cases, an anticommons dynamic would likely preclude success.

If liability rules were instead in place, transfers could occur on the initiative of one party and over the objections of other affected parties. A traditional liability rule regime would set a predetermined price for making a shift from prohibition to permission, or vice versa. The party desiring the shift initiates the change and accomplishes it by making the specified payment; nobody else needs to agree. The herbicide applier, for example, simply pays and sprays. If the price is set too low, these shifts may occur too easily. Alternatively, prohibitions may be lifted or imposed through political processes. Where this is the case, political power, whether wielded through votes or through special interest pressures, is the relevant currency. Money cannot be overtly translated into political outcomes, but within applicable legal limits, cash and in-kind payments may be part of bargains mediated by the political process. Though political shifts can sometimes be inefficiently difficult to accomplish, at other times these shifts are inefficiently easy. Rule changes can override the interests of those who are powerless or in a political minority in cases where the benefits thereby gained do not outweigh the costs inflicted on those who lose out.

Unlike liability rules, political adjustments to property entitlements often proceed without providing the losers any compensation (except that which comes from being part of a reciprocal system in which such adjustments are possible). Liability rules and politics might also be combined. For example, eminent domain uses a political toggle (a legislative body's choice to condemn property) to switch from a property rule to a liability rule. Under such an approach, resort to a liability rule is mediated by politics, while the compensation requirement arguably offers some protection against majoritarian overreaching.[74]

Too Hard or Too Easy?

It is no simple matter to design an entitlement transfer protocol that consistently permits efficient shifts while blocking inefficient ones. Property rules may make change too difficult, but liability rules may make change too easy. Political rules, which seem to offer a middle way, too often produce errors running in both directions. Presenting property rules, liability rules, and politics in terms of the difficulty or ease of shifting from one legal rule to its opposite presents an interesting question: If we aren't sure whether a given rule is optimal, should we err on the side of making it too hard to change or too easy to change? Here, it is helpful to think more broadly about the way in which different arrangements generate surpluses or losses. Under what circumstances is it especially important to make certain that all efficient transactions occur (even at the risk of allowing through some inefficient ones), and under what circumstances are the costs of a missed transaction lower? To hint at the intuition, compare a jigsaw puzzle, which might be enjoyed (albeit suboptimally) by a group of children even if one piece is missing, with a machine that will absolutely not run without all of its parts. In both cases, complementarities are present, but the surplus associated with assembly does not follow the same curve in both cases.[75]

Likewise, we might compare two different land assembly projects—one to construct a railroad or highway, and another to construct a shopping mall.[76] In the case of the railroad, the risk of a holdout is greater, and the costs of the holdout blocking the assembly are greater as well. This is because the social surplus from the railroad route assembly occurs all in one big jump when the full route has been acquired—at least if we assume that there is just one viable route.[77] A noncontiguous railroad track is not useful, just as a partial bridge is not. These are examples of "step goods" that deliver their benefits in a great lump rather than a bit at a time.[78] Because of the step characteristic, each fragment is indispensible to the overall project. As a result, the owners of the land occupy monopoly positions vis-à-vis the land assembler, and they are likely to react to that market power by attempting to extract as much surplus as possible in selling their parcels. If everyone attempts this, there is a good chance that the assembly will not be successful. In situations like these, the economic case for exercising eminent domain (that is, substituting a liability rule, which makes the transactions much easier to complete, for a property rule) is perhaps at its apex.[79]

Now consider land assembly for a shopping mall. Unlike a railroad, for which a particular route may be necessary, shopping malls can be and are located in many different sorts of locations. Also unlike a railroad, which requires a particular linear configuration, a shopping mall can be designed in many different ways to take advantage of the available space. As a result, it is not necessary for an assembler to have "all the pieces" in order to gain any benefit from the assembly project. Vivid examples of development around holdouts suggest that it is often possible to obtain a significant part of the available surplus associated with land assembly in such cases without acquiring every last fragment that might be efficiently transferred.[80] Where the assembler does not need to obtain all the parcels, bluffing on the part of a fragment holder becomes riskier. A true holdout—that is, someone who is simply bluffing in an effort to get a higher price—will recognize the chance that his plan will backfire, leaving him with his property fragment rather than with an outsized share of the surplus. Keeping in place the relatively more difficult shifting mechanism of property rules presents less risk that an efficient assembly will be blocked through strategic behavior under these circumstances. At the same time, it avoids the possibility of an inefficient involuntary transfer from a fragment holder who actually values the fragment at a price higher than that which the assembler can profitably offer.

The difference between these two prototypical assembly problems—the railroad and the shopping mall—can easily be seen if we consider the shape of the production function for the surplus that each assembly generates. Figure 4-3 depicts the assembly problem presented where ten parcels are needed to construct a railroad connector that will link up two other portions of a major rail system. Each of the ten parcels is essential to the whole operation, and the owner of any one parcel can block the realization of the entire surplus, absent eminent domain (or some other mechanism for overriding the holdout's veto).[81]

We might imagine that the shape of the production function for a shopping mall project would be significantly different. Even if the land assembler has his eye on a specific set of ten parcels ideally suited for the mall, he will probably be able to obtain most of the surplus associated with the

Surplus

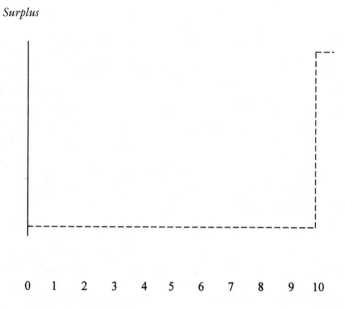

0   1   2   3   4   5   6   7   8   9   10

No. of Fragments Assembled

Figure 4-3. The railroad track

project by assembling less than all ten parcels—whether by choosing a different site, building around troublesome holdouts, building a smaller mall, or changing the physical design. While the production function for the surplus will vary as an empirical matter from situation to situation, one possibility is shown in Figure 4-4.

Of course, it may not always be empirically true that a shopping mall assembly will be less prone to holdouts. Some sites may be so unique and so well located—say, in the heart of a particular urban neighborhood—that there is simply no good substitute elsewhere. But the basic intuition presented by this example is helpful in returning to the question of neighborhood ambience. In that context too, we find difficult problems of entitlement assembly.

Consider again Beasley's situation as a would-be gnome displayer. If a large set of reciprocal covenants ban Beasley's gnome and the political process does not come to his aid, he cannot display his gnome until he buys back rights from everyone in the community. (I assume here that a

Surplus

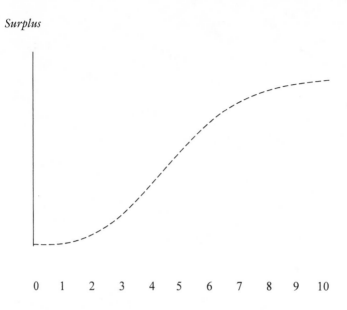

0   1   2   3   4   5   6   7   8   9   10

No. of Fragments Assembled

Figure 4-4. The shopping plaza

homeowners association stands ready to enforce the no-gnome rule, should Beasley try to skirt it.) His plight is like that of the railroad assembler, in that he can enjoy none of the surplus from the display until he has consent from everyone. The likelihood that one or more holdouts will keep the deal from going through is great; this will produce an inefficiency if we assume that Beasley's benefits are so large relative to the costs to the community that his gnome placement would be efficient.

Consider now the case of Cora, who despises gnomes. Suppose we start in a legal regime in which gnomes are permitted, and Cora has no chance of pushing a ban through the community's political process. Under ordinary property rule protection, Cora would only be able to secure for herself a completely gnome-free community by buying up display rights from everyone in the community. As suggested already, this will be difficult—it seems to present an anticommons situation much like the one faced by Beasley. However, Cora's situation is probably more akin to that of the shopping mall assembler than that of the railroad assembler. Cora may greatly value a gnomeless neighborhood, but it is still likely that she de-rives some benefit from gnome reduction, even if she cannot completely eradicate the cheerful statuary from her viewshed. In other words, the pro-duction function for the surplus she will glean from buying up gnome en-titlements probably does not look like the one in Figure 4-3; it more likely resembles that shown in Figure 4-4, or some other curve in which signif-icant surplus is available short of assembling all of the entitlements. In contrast, a person who wants to put a gnome in the yard but is forbidden to do so until she obtains permission from every neighbor faces a situation more like the one shown in Figure 4-3, in which the surplus is a step good that requires assembly of all the entitlements.

The shape of a production function does not decide matters on its own. We still must consider the relative magnitude of the harms threatened, as well as a variety of other factors, including administrative costs. But the production function tells us something about the likelihood of producing an anticommons tragedy as we strive to solve tragedies of the neighbor-hood commons.

To bring the discussion back to its starting point, both public and pri-vate land use controls grapple with important commons problems. Without such controls, communities would be exposed to serious neg-ative externalities. Yet enforcing prohibitions without allowing any op-portunity for individualized customization can lock inefficiencies into place. As we have seen, both public and private land use controls man-ifest this tension.

Making entitlements alienable offers some ways out of this dilemma, but difficulties remain. Property rules, by giving entitlement holders a veto power, can block the efficient assembly of entitlements. Liability rules, which remove the veto power, can permit entitlements to change hands at a price that is too low. They can also raise autonomy concerns. Political so-lutions offer an alternative means for overcoming holdout problems, but at the risk of generating inefficient decisions that will visit uncompensated harm on minority interests. The next chapter explores some alternatives to these standard solutions.

5

ADAPTIVE OPTIONS

A merchant ship pitches wildly as a raging storm intensifies. Cargo must be jettisoned immediately or the ship will be lost. But whose cargo should be tossed, and how should the owner of the goods be compensated? The law of general average contribution provided elegant answers.[1] Every merchant was required to place a value on her goods. That valuation carried two implications: first, it established the amount that the merchant would be compensated if those goods were lost en route; and second, it determined how the cost of that compensation would be divided among the other merchants whose goods arrived intact. Goods could then be stowed in accordance with these valuations to facilitate quick and efficient action in the event of a storm. Value one's goods too low, and they are more likely to be tossed overboard, in which case one will get too little compensation. Value one's goods too high, and they are less likely to be cast into the sea, but one will have to pay proportionately too much to compensate the owners of the goods that are jettisoned.

This example, drawn from a fascinating literature on self-assessed valuation, points to an innovative way around the difficulties posed in the previous chapter.[2] It suggests how entitlements to engage in acts with off-site impacts might be made adaptive and autonomy preserving without sacrificing the key advantage associated with liability rules—their capacity to avoid holdout problems. Such tools may enable us to solve tragedies of the commons without creating tragedies of the anticommons. To see where they fit in and how they work, however, it is necessary to revisit the problems introduced in the previous chapter and the shortcomings of standard solutions to them.

Pursuing Efficient Adjustments

Chapter 4 explained how responses to potential tragedies of the commons can themselves carry the potential for inefficiencies. Homeowners are understandably concerned about the impact of off-site factors, such as their neighbors' aesthetic choices, on their stream of consumption and likely investment return from the home. Animated by the impulse to reach out and control factors lying beyond the corners of their own parcels, homeowners reflexively resort to familiar institutional arrangements that make such control possible—covenants and zoning. But these are, at least typically, blunt command-and-control techniques that rely on blanket prohibitions. Each time the law decides to forbid an activity with extra-boundary impacts, it drains away property owners' privileges to engage in the activity in question. The collective exercise of control therefore ends up stripping homeowners of part of what gives their property value—the freedom to make use of it in desired ways. What is needed is an escape hatch for undoing these restrictions when, but only when, it is efficient to do so.

Ideally, we would want to make neighborhood ambience rules self-adjusting, so that efficient moves are encouraged and inefficient moves are deterred without any need for potentially costly or ineffective bargaining between the parties. Traditional liability rules are self-adjusting in one sense: they induce an actor to compare the established price for engaging in the conduct in question with the internalized benefit that she will receive. As that internalized benefit changes in size, so too does the actor's assessment of whether engaging in a particular act, such as putting a plastic flamingo in the front yard, is worthwhile. If an individual who was previously indifferent to flamingos develops a special affinity for them after a trip to Peru, for example, a fee for placing a flamingo figure in her yard may suddenly seem well worth it to her. A traditional liability rule thus constitutes a call option that gives an actor the right, but not the obligation, to purchase an entitlement (here, display privileges) at a price set by a third party.[3] The benefits accruing to the actor determine whether or not the particular aesthetic act is "in the money" at a given time, and hence whether the option is worth exercising.

The "call option" characterization of traditional liability rules has led scholars to consider "put option" variations as well.[4] For example, a community might allow flamingo placement as an initial matter but permit individual flamingo displayers to give up their entitlement to display flamingos in exchange for a preset payment from the community. In effect, displayers could force the community to buy back their flamingo privileges. Like a call option, a put option would induce the would-be displayer to compare the internalized benefit from flamingo display with the price placed on that display. With a put option, however, the displayer would be deciding whether to engage in a forced sale rather than a forced purchase of the display privileges.

We might worry, of course, that people would engage in gratuitous flamingo display just to receive a subsidy upon ceasing display.[5] Because of such concerns, put options more commonly take the form of subsidies for socially valuable conduct in which relatively few people are already engaging. The introduction of tax subsidies for hybrid cars illustrates this point, as does the subsequent phase-out of subsidies for the more popular models.[6] Even where subsidizing desirable conduct does not involve making payments to an unmanageably large group, concerns persist about perverse incentives (perhaps people switch not only from SUVs to hybrids but also from bicycles to hybrids), as well as the possibility that monetary payments might "crowd out" intrinsic motivations to engage in certain desirable behaviors.[7] Thus, liability rule discussions usually focus on the call option (actor pays) variety, rather than the put option (actor collects) version, although both design choices might play a role under appropriate circumstances.

Because of the capacity of liability rules to self-adjust to changes in the actor's valuations, their introduction could bring more flexibility and efficiency to the neighborhood commons. However, as we will see, they do not adapt well to changes in the valuations of others in the community. In the discussion that follows, I consider two ways of packaging traditional liability rules—fee schedules and tradable permits—both to illustrate the advantages of such systems and to provide a clearer picture of their shortcomings. I then turn to a more innovative twist on entitlement structuring that is based on self-assessed valuation.

Fee Schedules

Some of the concerns typically associated with liability rules—loss of autonomy and valuation difficulties—might be ameliorated if community members consented in advance to a damages-only scheme for addressing rule violations.[8] This approach would be feasible in a newly formed private neighborhood, where homebuyers could indicate their consent simply by purchasing a home in the community. The need to determine damages on a case by case basis could be avoided by establishing a schedule of fees for violations at the outset. The fee schedule would allow homeowners to consent not only to the *type* of relief that will be available in the case of rule violations but also to the *amount* of relief.

Such a fee schedule would serve two purposes. First, price lists could help prospective buyers sort themselves in a more meaningful way than is possible when every community the homebuyer encounters features a fairly similar laundry list of prohibitions. For example, a homebuyer could meaningfully distinguish between two different neighborhoods that disfavor herbicides if one charges a tax of $100 per application and the other charges a tax of $10 per year for unlimited use of herbicides. People also might be inclined to pay more attention to lists of prices than to lists of prohibitions, especially if the background expectations that they bring with them to the home-purchasing context make them disbelieve that absolute prohibitions would really be enforced.[9] And because households could choose whether to enter a prohibitory or fee-based regime, self-sorting could occur along remedial as well as substantive lines.

Second, the fee schedule reduces the risk that a given community member will be prevented from engaging in an activity that is efficient, or that later becomes efficient. The price list quite literally gives homeowners options. The initial sorting based on prices will be imperfect, both because people are making bounded decisions about bundled goods and because preferences will change over time. But if preference swings are drastic enough, residents will find it worthwhile to pay the price and engage in the activity in question. Thus, homeowners in such a regime hold an option that is not available to people living under prohibitions backed by injunctive relief. Where the fees for engaging in desired behaviors are lower than the cost of exiting the community altogether for a given individual, that person is better off in a neighborhood with a fee schedule than in a neighborhood with flat prohibitions. Given the spillover effects associated with long-term residency, the neighborhood is better off too.

There are, however, at least three problems with the fee schedule approach. First, getting the fees right will be difficult. The developer would need to set the fees in advance of selling homes, and she would only know whether she had made an error if she encountered sales resistance. Even if we assume that some homebuyers might pay a bit more attention to fee lists than to lists of prohibitions, many homebuyers ignore covenants and other governing documents altogether, choosing a home based on other attributes, like price and location. Thus, the market might not provide useful signals to developers about consumers' preferred fee levels for violations of land use restrictions. Even if consumers do provide market feedback to developers, it may come too late to be of much use, given that changing the fees midstream would require difficult renegotiation with those to whom sales had already been completed. Because of these risks, developers may be reluctant to experiment with this approach.

Second, and closely related, it may be difficult to specify exactly what a particular fee does and does not entitle one to do. For example, if herbicides are allowed for a particular "per application" fee, what counts as an application? What, for that matter, counts as a permitted herbicide? Likewise, if a fee is charged for yard art, the schedule would need to specify how much art can be displayed, and of what type. Does a family grouping of plastic deer (a doe, buck, and fawn combo-pack) qualify as one piece of art, or three? Does paying the fee to display a plastic flamingo entitle one to erect a forty-foot mechanized flamingo that dances all night to show tunes?

Third, a fee schedule deals well with fluctuations in homeowners' valuations of the right to engage in specified conduct, but it does not address fluctuations in the amount of damage that such conduct causes. Fees that are fixed in advance cannot respond dynamically over time to changes in information, neighbors' preferences, or cumulative or other sorts of nonlinear effects. The fees could be indexed to keep pace with inflation and updated annually within some designated bounds, but these adjustments would not deal with problems like changes in the social meanings or documented effects of particular activities, or unwanted spatial or temporal concentrations of those activities. It is one thing to allow herbicide use for a low fee when few people choose this option, but might be quite another to allow it at the same low fee if many begin to do so, or if a new study is released showing previously unknown adverse health effects. Similarly, the twenty-eighth flamingo may cause more (or less) marginal damage to the neighborhood's ambience than the second flamingo. By extending a unilateral option to the homeowner, the fee leaves the community exposed to the risk that its own valuation will change.[10]

To be sure, political responses would typically be possible. For example, if the perceived tackiness quotient of flamingos were to rise unexpectedly (perhaps due to negative treatment in popular culture), the community could simply reset the price of flamingo display in an effort to convince some displayers to desist. But this action undermines the supposed autonomy and consent advantages of having a fee schedule in the first place—what is the point of moving into an apparently flamingo-friendly environment if the rules can suddenly change? At the same time, even a politically adjustable fee schedule may not fully ameliorate the overlay of compromised autonomy for the rest of the community that goes with a "pay and spray" or "pay and display" regime. Those who are subject to the effects of the aesthetic act have no choice in the matter, aside from the (typically minor) input that they may have as participants in the political community that establishes the price. Hence, a homeowner who despises flamingos must simply grit her teeth and bear the visual assault once her neighbor pays the applicable flamingo fee.

Nonetheless, fee schedules could work reasonably well for activities that are highly salient to homebuyers, easy to define, and already well understood—such as keeping a dog. We have a sense of what it means to "keep a dog" because we have in the back of our minds a large set of legal restrictions—leash laws, waste removal rules, prohibitions on dogfighting and other forms of cruel treatment, laws requiring proper maintenance of the dog, nuisance laws that would forbid excessive barking or odors, and laws addressing aggression by dogs against people and animals. Thus, a well-developed body of background law with respect to a given activity may be important to making a fee schedule work.

Tradable Permits

Another set of alternatives would take a page from environmental law—tradable permits to engage in activities that are otherwise prohibited by a covenant or zoning ordinance. This approach will be promising if it is easier to determine the optimal overall level of violations in a given community than it is to determine the appropriate price for each violation.[11] For example, if the community knew how many lapses in lawn mowing or how many concrete gnomes it could tolerate before the overall ambience begins to deteriorate, it could issue exactly that many permits for the activity in question, either assigning them by lottery or through an initial auction. If the permits were made freely alienable, they would presumably find their way to the highest valuers. A neighborhood could facilitate such trades through a physical or virtual bulletin board.

Some important design challenges would remain, however. For one thing, the community would have to decide whether to set a single limit for aesthetic violations of all types and allow the permits to be used for any of those purposes, or whether instead to create a separate limit for each violation type. For example, should the neighborhood issue a specified number of gnome permits and a specified number of flamingo permits, or should it issue permits that can be used for any kind of yard art? Moving to an even higher level of generality, the tradable scheme could group together entirely different categories of violations, issuing an all-purpose "tradable eccentricity permit" that allows the bearer to disregard any one of a wide range of prohibitions—whether it be adding an extra pet beyond the specified number, painting her front door a nonapproved color, changing her car's oil in her driveway, or letting her grass grow beyond the specified length.

As these examples suggest, there would be difficult definitional problems involved in specifying what counts as a "single" violation. But even more fundamentally, we would need to know whether the tragedy of the commons that the community hopes to avert involves generalized tackiness or more specific forms of "overgrazing" of the commons. A similar issue involves the spatial and temporal distribution of incursions into the neighborhood commons. In the environmental realm, there are concerns that tradable emissions regimes will lead to "hot spots"—spatially and temporally concentrated emissions that generate greater aggregate harm than they would if they were more dispersed. Similarly, habitat acreage that is part of a contiguous preservation area cannot be equated with the same number of acres of habitat in scattered sites.[12] If the location and timing of particular draws against neighborhood ambience make those draws nonfungible, we would need to design the trading program accordingly.

Scholars have developed a variety of interesting proposals to deal with such issues in the environmental realm.[13] Yet a fundamental tension persists between making trading systems workable (both in terms of administrative costs and in terms of creating "thick enough" markets) and making them precise in generating the desired set of results. James Salzman and J. B. Ruhl have helpfully explained this essential difficulty as a trade-off between making tradable currencies "fat and sloppy" and "thin and bland."[14] The more things that a given tradable currency can be spent on, the more robust will be the trading opportunities. On the other hand, if the items that are lumped together through the currency are not truly fungible, then the trades may operate to reduce value overall. The trade-off becomes more complicated if unfolding events and new information bear on the question of fungibility itself.

Introducing Entitlements Subject to Self-Made Options

Scholars have explored how liability rules might be reformulated or combined to address some of the problems raised above. For example, "second-order" and other "higher-order" liability rules specify a series of permitted moves in which the parties essentially take turns choosing whether or not to initiate a shift from the (then) current rule.[15] Other mechanisms replicate the results of this process by inducing the parties to submit truthful information about their valuations.[16] Such procedures represent a significant change in how transfer prices are determined. Liability rules have traditionally been understood to involve a predetermined price, usually established by a third party such as a court or administrative agency. But it is also possible to involve the parties themselves in setting the prices, while still giving one of the parties a unilateral right to force a shift in the legal regime.

Consider a simple example in which a seller owns a parcel of land, and a buyer wishes to purchase it. Because this piece of land is part of a larger whole that the buyer wishes to assemble, the seller may be tempted to behave strategically by holding out. If the seller's entitlement is protected by a property rule, she has an absolute veto power and hence complete control over whether an exchange occurs. The risk, of course, is that a transfer that would leave both parties better off will fail to occur. If we downgrade the seller's entitlement to ordinary liability rule protection, as eminent domain does, this risk is removed. But it is replaced with another risk—that an inefficient transfer will occur.

With the shift from property rule protection to ordinary liability rule protection, the seller's control over the bargain plunges from absolute to nonexistent. Not only can the land be taken over her objections, she also has no control over the price at which it can be taken. Instead, a third party such as a court or an administrative agency will determine the compensation—perhaps aided, in the land example, by a professional appraisal. Between these two poles of the seller's absolute control and the seller's complete lack of control lie additional possibilities. The buyer might be given control over *whether* the transaction occurs, just as with an ordinary liability rule, but the seller might nonetheless retain control over *the price* at which the transaction occurs. Alternatively, the seller might be granted unilateral control over whether the transaction occurs (that is, a put option that enables her to force a sale), while the buyer sets the applicable price.[17]

What is fundamentally valuable about liability rules—their ability to sidestep holdout behavior and other sources of high transaction costs—can be obtained without requiring one party to surrender all control over the terms of the transaction. The key to splitting up control over the transaction between the buyer and the seller lies in the use of self-assessed valuations to set transfer prices. To return to the land assembly example, the seller could set the price at which the buyer, acting unilaterally, could obtain the property for a given window of time (the option period). Of course, we cannot simply depend on the seller to provide an honest valuation. But a large and interesting literature on self-assessed valuation suggests that mechanisms capable of eliciting reasonably truthful statements of value can be devised.[18] While I will save the details of these mechanisms for the discussion below, the essential idea is to formulate self-executing penalties for both understatements and overstatements, as illustrated by the law of general average contribution discussed at the start of this chapter.

With such an information-forcing device in place, the seller in our example would have an incentive to name a value for her property that is close to its actual value to her. By doing so, she would effectively write an option for her property that the buyer could choose to exercise, or not. The seller's entitlement in this story would be protected neither by a traditional property rule nor by a traditional liability rule. Instead, it would be an "entitlement subject to a self-made option," or ESSMO.[19] The ESSMO requires one party to package her subjective valuation in the form of an option, while allowing the other party to act unilaterally on that option. In this way, the ESSMO dodges the primary sources of inefficiency associated with property rules and ordinary liability rules—holdout problems and undercompensated transfers, respectively.[20] It also avoids the need for governmental or community valuation.[21]

The law of general average contribution, introduced above, offers an excellent illustration of the ESSMO in action. In placing goods on a vessel, each merchant enters an ESSMO system in which the captain (acting for the merchants as a group) may choose to exercise a call option on the goods at a price set by the merchant herself. Thus, the merchant is entitled either to the safe delivery of the goods or the stated valuation amount. The captain also holds what amounts to a put option; he can force the owners of the nonjettisoned goods to buy back their intact shipments at a premium that covers any loss experienced during the shipment. Significantly, the amount of that premium is keyed to the merchants' own valuation statements.

Perhaps most important for our purposes, ESSMOs work well in dynamic, multiparty settings marked by radical uncertainty about future conditions. In these settings, the costs associated with an actor's entitlement to do a particular thing—whether to refuse a land sale, emit a pollutant, keep her goods on the ship, or select a bold color for her front door—do not stay constant. ESSMOs offer fresh traction on these dynamic problems by doing two things. First, they provide a vehicle for eliciting (relatively) truthful valuations from parties. Second, they offer a way to distribute decisions among the parties over time, without the need for the parties to come to agreement each time an entitlement shift would be efficient. Because of these two features, explored in the sections below, ESSMOs can be used to construct land use controls that can adapt to changing circumstances and valuations.

Eliciting Valuations

In general, people cannot be counted on to volunteer honest and accurate valuations of entitlements that they own or might wish to own. Because it is usually evident whether a higher or lower valuation will better serve the self-interest of the person asked to do the valuation, there is a temptation to lie or unconsciously shade one's answer in a self-serving direction.[22] For example, if awards following the exercise of eminent domain were simply based on the self-reported valuations of those whose homes had been condemned, we would expect upward deviations from the truth. Likewise, if a voluntary neighborhood organization asked each household within its service area to state the amount it would be willing to contribute toward an amenity that the organization is considering purchasing, such as a set of tennis courts, we would expect undervaluations from those hoping to free-ride on the contributions of others.

The same pattern holds true in ordinary bargaining between buyers and sellers. Suppose one party, Aurora, owns a house and another party, Borealis, is interested in purchasing it. As a seller, Aurora will try to represent that her true valuation or reservation price is very high, perhaps equal to her original asking price, even if she would actually be happy to sell for much less. Borealis, in contrast, may make an offer much lower than the price he would be willing to pay, while attempting to convince Aurora that this represents his true valuation. As the parties work through rounds of offers and counteroffers, each can add verbiage to the proposed numbers (such as "This is my last and final offer!" or "That's my rock bottom price, take it or leave it!"), but these statements may or may not be truthful. There is some cost to lying about one's valuation when bargaining—the chance that a mutually beneficial deal will fail to occur, or (less dramatically) that money will be wasted in the course of wrangling.[23] But because neither Aurora nor Borealis will fully internalize these losses, whereas each of them will garner the full benefit of squeezing a little more surplus out of the deal, there will be a tendency to misstate valuations in a self-serving direction.

A mechanism capable of eliciting reasonably honest valuations requires built-in sanctions for both overstatements and understatements. As scholars have noted, one way of building in these sanctions is to keep the valuer in the dark about whether she will be a buyer or a seller at her stated price—that is, whether she will be subject to a call option or a put option based on her valuation.[24] The "Texas Shootout" approach to dissolving partnerships illustrates this point.[25] In a simple two-partner situation, the mechanism first requires one partner, Paula, to name a price for half of the partnership venture. The other partner, Peter, can then choose to pay that amount to acquire Paula's half of the venture, or he can instead require Paula to buy out his own half-interest at that same price.[26]

Paula's valuation statement thus grants Peter two options that he must choose between. First, he receives a call option on Paula's half of the enterprise and can acquire it at her price. Second, he receives a put option on his own half; he can force Paula to buy it at her own stated price. Peter will exercise one option or the other after learning Paula's valuation, and Paula must live with the result; she cannot backpedal on the valuation once she learns which alternative Peter has in mind. This approach leverages Paula's uncertainty about whether she will emerge as a buyer or seller of partnership shares into a more accurate valuation statement.[27] If she values her partnership share too high, she may get stuck buying out Peter at a price that is higher than the buyout is worth to her. If she values her share too low, she may lose it at a price that is less than it is worth to her.

In this example, sanctions against overstatements and understatements are self-enforcing; one's potential roles as a buyer and as a seller, respectively, provide the necessary deterrents. While it is not always literally possible to keep parties providing valuations in the dark about whether they will be buying or selling, it is possible to devise other mechanisms that contain self-executing sanctions for understatements and overstatements. A simple example can be found in the well-known formula for fair cake division between two people: one party cuts the cake into two pieces, and the other party gets to choose between the pieces. The cutter will endeavor to divide the cake equally, knowing that any inequality in the slicing will work against her. Important for our purposes, when the cutter slices the cake, she is revealing that she values the two pieces equally; in other words, she expresses the value of one piece of cake in the currency of the other piece of cake. If she announces (through her slicing behavior) that a tiny sliver is of equal value to the remaining 95 percent of the cake, this misstatement will come back to bite her—she will end up with the less valuable of the two things she has pronounced equivalent.[28]

The law of general average contribution works similarly. By putting a value on the goods, the merchant states indifference between getting that value and getting the goods back at the end of the voyage after paying a premium that is keyed to that same valuation. Like the cake cutter, the merchant will endeavor to make these two packages as equal as possible; the captain then controls which of the outcomes the merchant will receive. What is crucial in all of these examples is that the valuation plays a dual role, effectively appearing on both the debit and credit sides of the valuer's ledger. By making the valuation higher, the valuer potentially gains something, but also potentially owes more to the other party; by making it lower, the valuer potentially loses something, but also concedes less to the other party.

The same ideas can be translated into the land use arena. For decades, scholars have discussed the use of a self-assessment mechanism to overcome valuation problems in property tax assessments or in eminent domain proceedings.[29] For example, it is possible to link the valuations used in these two contexts, so that the value the landowner announces for purposes of property taxes will also determine her compensation in the event her land is condemned. Indeed, Taiwan and several other countries have adopted self-assessment approaches to land valuation at various times.[30] It is not difficult to imagine how the same basic approach could be applied to land use entitlements in the neighborhood commons. For example, a resident who wished to display a plastic flamingo in a neighborhood that otherwise bans such ornaments might be asked to place a value on the privilege. This valuation would have two implications: it would be the basis of a "flamingo tax" that she would remit to the community, and it would also represent the amount that the community could pay to take away her flamingo display privileges at some later date.

Distributing Decisions over Time

ESSMOs do not merely elicit information; they also allocate decision-making authority over time. Like all options, ESSMOs give one party (the option holder) increased flexibility during the option's exercise period, while giving the other party (the option writer) diminished flexibility during that same period. Consider an option to purchase a house. During the time that the buyer holds the option, she can buy the house at the specified exercise or strike price. She is not obligated to complete the transaction, but she has the right to do so on the agreed-upon terms if she so chooses.[31] The added flexibility that the buyer enjoys constrains the flexibility of the seller—he must sell if the buyer decides to exercise the option, but he has no guarantee of being able to make the sale. The option thus fundamentally changes the way in which risk is allocated, enabling the option holder, but not the option writer, to respond to new information or price changes during the option period.[32] For example, the buyer in our story will benefit if home prices rise, but she will not suffer if home prices fall; conversely, the seller bears the risk that home prices will fall, but he will get none of the benefit if home prices increase.

ESSMOs operate similarly in that they extend control to one party (for a time) while withdrawing it from another party, but they incorporate two important refinements. First, ESSMOs may be part of a regulatory regime that requires particular parties to write options for other parties. With property-rule-protected entitlements, parties are under no obligation to offer options to others. But in a community that is faced with trying to solve a difficult collective action problem, requiring everyone to provide valuations in the form of options may be an essential move in overcoming holdout problems and reaching efficient solutions. For example, all households in a neighborhood might be required to indicate their valuations of their own flamingo placement privileges by writing options that would extend to the community (acting collectively) the right to buy up those privileges at each household's stated price. Under this approach, the individual households would be option writers who, after writing the option, hold ESSMOs—that is, entitlements that are vulnerable to the household's own "self-made" option. The community as a whole would hold a call option on each household's flamingo display privilege.

An option writer can use all of the information available to her about the likely course of future events and its impact on her personal valuation to select an appropriate, customized exercise price for the option period. In turn, the option holder can monitor events over the option period and ex-

ercise the option if it becomes valuable to do so. Of course, the writer of
the option may experience changes in valuation too, after the option has
already been written. For example, imagine a merchant learns, after her
shipment is halfway across the Atlantic, that one of her crates contains a
rare artifact that she had previously believed was merely a replica. Ideally,
we might want to allow the merchant to update the valuation information up until the time that the option is exercised. This will be infeasible,
however, if communication is impossible or if the cargo would be prohibitively costly to rearrange en route. Thinking about options in this light focuses attention on important design choices, such as the length of the
option period, the opportunities that the option maker will have to update
her valuation, and the crucial question of which party should write the option and which should hold the option.

In my simple example involving flamingo options, I made the individual households the option writers and the community as a whole the option holder. This arrangement makes sense if we believe that the
preferences of households are either more stable or more predictable (by
the households themselves) than are those of the community as a whole.[33]
As the community's preferences change, or as it learns about the interaction effects of phenomena like large flamingo clusters (the aesthetic equivalent of environmental hot spots), it can act to buy back flamingo
privileges. In contrast, if we believed that the preferences of the community were completely fixed and that it knew in advance the costs of each
marginal aesthetic act, then the community could simply write options for
households—that is, the community could be governed with ordinary liability rules that allow the households to pay and display.

More likely, however, both the households and the community will experience valuation changes over time. To respond to this possibility, an
enduring system for managing spillovers may require an iterated series of
options that effectively allow the parties to take turns in acquiring and
reacquiring entitlements.[34] Put differently, entitlement transfer protocols
can be designed with reversibility in mind. The initial exercise of an option
need not be the end of the matter for all time, nor need the situation re-
vert to a property-rule-protected baseline in which any further changes
require consent by all affected parties. Instead, an entitlement regime can
be devised in a way that consciously distributes decision-making over time

by alternately giving one party and then the other unilateral control over whether a transfer occurs. That choice is exercised, or not, in response to valuations provided by the other party, who lacks current control over whether the transfer occurs. These ideas can be more clearly conveyed by examining how such a system would work in a neighborhood setting.

ESSMOs in the Neighborhood

ESSMOs might be developed as either public or private land use control mechanisms. It is perhaps easiest to imagine how they might operate in a private neighborhood, however, given the relative freedom of such neighborhoods to engage in creative entitlement restructuring. As self-contained land use control regimes formed ab initio and by contract, these communities could offer excellent small-scale testing grounds for different land use alternatives.[35]

Above, I discussed the possibility of a fee schedule that residents might accept upon entering a community. Under that approach, the community can be viewed as holding a type of ESSMO, in that it would provide a valuation (by setting a fee) while extending a call option based on that valuation to households. But the valuations could not really be viewed as "the community's" except insofar as community members endorsed it by moving in—the fees would have to be set by the developer before the homes in the community were sold. The fee schedule leaves the community with no tools for responding to preference changes, nonlinearities (such as hot spots), or even unexpected manifestations of the items on the schedule (such as a forty-foot dancing flamingo). As a result, a great deal would turn on the developer's ability to accurately foresee the sorts of impacts that would matter over time and to craft well-tailored rules and associated fees to manage those impacts. If we are skeptical about the ability of any mortal to excel at such a complex forecasting and drafting task, we might want to consider a more adaptive way of bringing the ESSMO idea to the neighborhood.

The Customized Callable Call

Instead of making the community (through the developer) responsible for writing options that can be exercised by households, we might instead ask households to write options for the community. This approach would require homeowners in the first instance to undertake the work of specifying what they plan to do and placing a value on their right to do it. The community would then be given a choice between two alternatives: (1) allow the practice and collect a tax based on the valuation; and (2) stop the practice by paying the valuation. For example, suppose Hank wishes to spray herbicides on his front lawn every week. He could reveal the details of this lawn care regimen and state how much he valued the privilege of continuing with that preferred lawn care program for a particular temporal period, such as a season or a year. By doing so, he would effectively write an option that would permit a collective decision maker, such as a homeowners association, to buy back his lawn care privileges by paying the price set by Hank himself. In the meantime, he would be assessed a tax based on his own valuation.

Hank would receive a customizable callable call—a type of ESSMO—once he had entered the community and made his valuation. The ESSMO would be made up of two components. First, Hank would hold a call option to go forward with lawn care upon payment of a tax based on his valuation. Second, the call option would itself be reversible or "callable." The callable feature would be customized by Hank himself; his own valuation would determine the strike price. Thus, the community would receive an option to "call back" Hank's lawn privileges upon payment of that sum.

Since the amount of harm caused by particular actions depends on multiple factors that change and interact over time, the ability of the decision-making body to monitor the situation and respond appropriately to unfolding events is very valuable.[36] While collective entities can always engage in a regulatory response as circumstances change, ESSMOs structure that later decision-making authority in ways that are more likely to produce efficient outcomes. If each householder selects an exercise price based on the expected trajectory of her individual valuation over the relevant time period, the public body can readily survey the territory to select which options to exercise.

The customized callable call could also be combined with a fee schedule, as the following example illustrates. Suppose the developer of a new private community in Middletown wants to experiment with allowing some aesthetic diversity in the community but also wants to reassure buyers that things will not become too tacky overall. While there are many real-world land uses that might contribute to perceived tackiness, for purposes of simplicity I will let the much-maligned lawn flamingo serve as a representative (readers should feel free to mentally substitute another land use that they find more troublesome or compelling). Suppose, then, that the developer establishes a fee schedule that gives homeowners a call option to, say, display a lawn flamingo for $50 annually. This fee schedule would facilitate sorting into the community by signaling that lawn flamingos are not banned, but also not completely welcome. Within the community, the fee would divide the population into those who valued flamingo display at $50 or more and those who valued it at less than $50. The former would display a flamingo and pay the fee, and the latter would go flamingoless and avoid the fee.

For the reasons suggested above, however, the developer cannot stop there. Homebuyers will want to protect themselves against prospects like an unexpected overabundance of flamingos, costly concentrations of flamingos, or especially egregious flamingo specimens. They will also want to preserve flexibility to crack down on flamingos if such lawn ornaments should become increasingly unfashionable over time or are found to pose some as yet unknown danger to the ecosystem.[37] To leave greater control with the community (and hence provide greater protection to homebuyers), the developer could make the call option extended to households callable by the community. This callable feature would enable the community to reacquire any individual's flamingo permit upon payment of an exercise price. The exercise price for the community's call option would be made up of two elements: a default component and a customizable component. The default component would simply be the community's standard flamingo fee (here, $50). If the homeowner did nothing to "customize" her option to display a flamingo, the community could call back her flamingo entitlement at any time by simply refunding her standard fee.

The individual could, however, choose to customize the exercise price at which the community could buy back her flamingo entitlement. She could raise the community's price of recalling her flamingo permit by paying, in addition to the $50 minimum fee, an extra premium based on her valuation of flamingo privileges (which she could adjust from year to year, or at other preannounced intervals). This customized valuation would raise the exercise price for the community's recall of the flamingo. The flamingo fees and premiums would go into the central coffers of the homeowners association to be used for administering the system; any excess would go toward providing benefits to the community at large.

If the community decides that it has become too flamingo heavy, it can begin to "call in" outstanding homeowner call options. If the problem is the overall level of flamingos, then it could simply look for the flamingos that could be recalled at the lowest exercise price. If there are troublesome spatial concentrations, the community could scan the concentrated area for the cheapest recall options. Individuals who highly valued flamingo display could try to immunize their call options against being called by raising the exercise price to a high level and paying a correspondingly high fee, but the community would remain free to apply whatever criteria it found relevant in deciding which, if any, flamingos to recall. A system like the one just described holds promise, but operationalizing it would require confronting a number of complications and concerns.

Strategic Valuations

The flamingo displayer's valuation choice in the context of the customized callable call is constrained by two conflicting design features. First, because her payment into the community's tax system is linked to her valuation, she has an incentive to make her valuation as low as possible. Second, because her neighbors' recall rights are based on her valuation, she will want to set the valuation high enough to keep them from recalling the entitlement too easily. But these conflicting incentives will not necessarily induce the displayer to disclose her actual valuation.

Consider first the potential for strategic undervaluation. A homeowner who truly values flamingo display would prefer to offer a valuation that is lower than her actual valuation, but still high enough to stave off retakings. She might look around at the values placed on other similarly situated pieces of lawn art and value hers just a bit higher, so that the others will be better targets for reacquisition. This is a risky strategy insofar as lawn art is nonfungible, and it will always be at least somewhat nonfungible spatially. Alternatively, the homeowner might try to predict the reservation prices of the community and its members, and attempt to price her entitlement just a touch higher than that. Again, she runs the risk that someone will call her bluff. In general, the more idiosyncratically elevated her true valuation is relative to the impact of her actions on the community, the greater will be her ability to succeed in making a strategic understatement. Other design features, such as the time period for which one's valuation is binding and the protocols and timing features for regaining lost entitlements, will help to determine the extent to which undervaluation strategies may be employed.

It is worth pinpointing precisely why we should worry about strategic understatements. From an efficiency perspective, there are at least two concerns. First, parties may waste time and effort—their own, and that of others—in trying to game the system. Second, people may misgauge how low they can get away with pricing their entitlements and end up losing them to those who actually value the entitlements less. Recall that from an efficiency perspective our goal is to facilitate transfers that "should" occur—those to higher-valuing users—while filtering out transfers that "should not" occur—those to lower-valuing users. If a party strategically states a low valuation to avoid paying premiums that correspond to her true valuation, she could lose her entitlement to another party whose valuation is lower than the strategic party's true valuation. This is an inefficient result. Because all of the costs of the inefficiency fall on the undervaluing party, however, a strategizer has a strong incentive to obtain reasonably good information or to protect her interests with a reasonably accurate valuation, whichever is cheaper for her.

Strategic understatements also have distributive implications. For example, suppose the community's valuation of the entitlement exceeds that of the displayer's dishonestly low valuation—but also exceeds the displayer's true valuation. In this case, the community would have exercised its call option even if the valuation had been honest; the resulting transfer is efficient and generates a surplus. But because the displayer must be paid only the stated valuation, the community enjoys any difference between that amount and its own valuation. Not only does the community reap the full surplus of the transfer, it also receives an additional transfer from the displayer in the amount of the displayer's undervaluation. But this sort of result is not unique to the ESSMO. Even when transfer prices are set perfectly, liability rules assign all of the surplus to the party exercising the call option.[38]

Indeed, the distributive effects of ESSMOs generally seem normatively palatable. A party holding an ESSMO does not stand to lose an entitlement at a price set by the government; rather, she will only lose it if she is compensated at the level she herself selected. Likewise, autonomy concerns associated with involuntary transfers of entitlements may be alleviated if people have the opportunity to opt into ESSMO regimes. Again, the law of general average contribution is illustrative. No merchant can justifiably complain that her compensation is too low or that she is required to pay too large a share toward covering the losses of others; she herself chose the valuation on which these outcomes were based. Of course, there may be settings where our intuitions about the fairness of ESSMOs would be less clear. For example, a scheme in which self-stated home values determine both property taxes and compensation in the event of eminent domain might be criticized for unfairly burdening a community's most vulnerable constituents or unfairly taxing subjective value.[39]

Another concern is strategic overvaluation among those who lack any genuine interest in retaining the entitlement. Consider Caralessa, who couldn't care less about flamingos one way or the other but knows that her neighbors despise them. She blithely selects a flamingo (the tackier the better), sticks it in her yard, and places a high value (say, $3,000) on her right to do so, in the hopes of extorting that amount from her sensitive neighbors. Note that the only check on her behavior is the display tax she must pay, which is based on her valuation. If strategic overstatements are a real concern, it may be necessary to set taxes that are not merely a fraction of the valuations claimed by actors but represent instead the full valuation amount for a given time period. In this case, the community's exercise of its call option would amount only to a refund of taxes previously paid, dulling any incentive to engage in gratuitous statuary display.[40] This move would of course sharpen the pressures toward strategic understatement—a displayer made to pay her full valuation would reap no surplus from the entitlement.

Additional Considerations

The customized callable call raises a number of additional issues that merit consideration.

DEFINING THE COMMUNITY, AND THE ROLE OF SPITE Thus far, I have been referring to "the community" as if it were a composite person with well-defined preferences. This is clearly not the case. Consider a back-yard flamingo display that is very obnoxious to the five neighbors whose backyards border that of the flamingo displayer. This display is inoffensive to everyone else in the neighborhood; it cannot be seen from the street or from anyone else's property. On a majority-rule vote, the people bothered by the flamingo will lose out to people who would prefer to keep the flamingo fees rather than exercise the option. How can the preferences of individuals be translated into decisions about things like flamingo recalls?

One alternative would be to bypass voting mechanisms altogether and simply allow any community member to contribute private funds to a "flamingo buyback," based on the strength of her preferences; when the buyback fund reached the option amount, the original call option held by the displayer would be recalled. However, spite could generate perverse results under this regime. I have been assuming in this discussion that the display fees would be paid into a centralized fund that would inure to the general benefit of the community. Attempts to allocate the fees to specific neighbors based on the amount of damage that a particular display caused each of them would open up new valuation problems and could lead to strategic interactions among neighbors. But we must also consider the implications of a system that routes flamingo fees into a central coffer while making harmed individuals personally responsible for funding buybacks.

Specially harmed neighbors are made worse off by a display that they must pay to stop. So long as the buyback money only serves to refund amounts that the flamingo displayer previously chose to pay in taxes, it does not create any perverse incentives for a purely self-interested home-owner to gratuitously display flamingos. It would, however, offer a dia-bolical opportunity to the homeowner who wished to raise costs for his neighbor by effectively forcing her to fund a buyback. Even though the displayer would be no better off than at the outset (he would only get his fees refunded), he would hold the power to make his neighbor worse off. Conversely, a spiteful individual who is not bothered at all by a neighbor's flamingo display could threaten to fund a buyback in order to bluff the neighbor into paying a higher flamingo fee. Once again, this effect would probably not be produced by self-interest. Because flamingo fees go into the community's central coffer, the neighbor does not benefit (much) when the flamingo displayer pays a higher fee. But the neighbor might relish the opportunity to inflict costs on her neighbor.

Although it would be foolhardy to underestimate the role of spite, this problem does not seem insurmountable. For one thing, the "spited" party in each situation can call the bluff of the other party. The gratuitous flamingo displayer could simply be ignored, for example. If he does not actually value display more than the display fees he is paying, the financial burden should eventually prompt him to desist. Likewise, the flamingo displayer who is bullied by a neighbor's buyback threats might call the neighbor's bluff by refusing to pay higher fees.

WHEN IS A CALL FINAL? Another design issue raised by this example is the question of what should happen once flamingo buyback occurs. Should it be "final," so that the individual can never again display a flamingo? Should the recalled entitlement be protected (in the hands of the community) with a property rule? Should the community's entitlement "run with the land" so that nobody on that site can display a flamingo ever again without gaining clearance from every neighbor? Making the buyback permanent seems unnecessary and potentially inefficient. Adding features like a waiting period or a hefty "reissue" fee, however, would deter people from lightly forfeiting and reobtaining display permits. Certainly, any amounts the erstwhile displayer collected in abandoning her display would have to be surrendered in a lump sum in order to obtain a new permit, along with the tax for the new year.

COMPLEXITY AND IRREVERSIBILITY We might also worry about the complexity of the ESSMO device and question whether the efficiency gains that it produces are really worth the trouble. In addition, some community impacts are less amenable to this mechanism than is a decision to place objects in the yard. Sometimes the problem relates to the difficulty of reversing an impact. Structures and certain sorts of pollution cannot readily be "undone," for example.

In other cases, it is technologically possible but socially costly to reverse an impact. Consider, for example, applying this customized callable call to pet keeping. The prospect that one's right to keep a dog could be "called" seems plainly unacceptable, especially in a society already characterized by high levels of pet abandonment. Additional fine-tuning (for example, safe harbor periods during which an exercised option would not be callable) could offer an alternative, but again, this fine-tuning comes at the cost of increased complexity. It may instead be better to use a simple fixed fee schedule or tradable permit scheme for entitlements of this nature.

Experimentation with different entitlement forms in private neighborhoods has lagged far behind the proliferation of this ownership form. Yet there is perhaps no setting in which experimentation with entitlement forms is more feasible and appropriate. Communities might address spillovers through creative entitlement restructuring of the sort discussed here, rather than rely only on community homogeneity or command-and-control approaches to solve commons (and anticommons) problems. Of course, readers may protest that if people wanted options of this sort in private communities, they would already have them; it is, after all, the job of developers to give people what they want.[41] But innovation in entitlement design is costly and risky, and a developer who innovates must bear all of the costs and risks alone.[42] Moreover, consumers are not the only audience that developers must please—to move forward with their projects, developers must present plans that meet with the approval of lenders and local government regulators.[43] All of these factors create pressure to stick with tested formulas. As a result, we cannot tell whether prevailing arrangements reflect the marketplace's considered judgment on the merits or merely the influence of path dependence, inertia, and institutional influences.

Adding new alternatives to the mix could help test this question. To be sure, the ESSMO is not a perfect solution. It presents opportunities for strategic or spiteful behavior that may produce inefficiencies or unwanted distributive consequences. However, these problems are not unique to this entitlement form. Property rules feature a higher-octane set of strategic risks—the equivalent of a Chicken Game. The ESSMO effectively replaces the open-ended Chicken Game with a set of iterated moves that sidestep mutual bluffing behaviors and leave strategizers with most of the risk associated with their machinations. Traditional liability rules (the usual response to high bargaining costs) threaten inefficient transfers and undercompensation, while also encroaching on autonomy. ESSMOs restore a measure of autonomy and make inroads against inefficiency and unfairness by letting the party vulnerable to the transfer set its price.

COMMUNITY COMPOSITION

6

ASSOCIATION AND EXCLUSION

Part II considered the interhousehold difficulties that can arise *within* a given jurisdiction or neighborhood and explored how entitlements might be designed to address those problems. If we zoom out from this highly localized view to examine an entire metropolitan area, we see similarly structured strategic dilemmas playing out *between* communities. Although interjurisdictional conflicts can arise over a variety of issues, the most challenging and controversial of these involve the inclusion and exclusion of residents. In this part, I suggest that associational patterns can amount to resource dilemmas that might be usefully addressed with the theoretical tools of property.

Compliance Effects and Membership Effects

Homeowners view their neighbors as extremely important inputs into their property values and residential consumption experiences. Accordingly, land use restrictions targeting the characteristics and behaviors of residents are ubiquitous. Although land use controls with associational purposes or effects are often discussed under the rubric of "exclusionary zoning," that label can be confusing; it means different things to different people, often carries an emotional charge, and applies by its terms only to public land use controls. Instead, I want to distinguish between two fundamental ways that land use controls impact communities. First, land use controls can directly alter the actions of those people who would live in the community whether or not the controls existed ("compliance effects"). Obviously, compliance with behavioral rules falls within this category, but so too does a household's choice to purchase and pay property taxes on a house that meets local zoning standards (rather than some other home that it might have purchased in the absence of those standards). Second, land use controls can impact the community's membership by actually changing who lives there, in terms of numbers, characteristics, or both ("membership effects").[1] The same land use control can produce both sorts of impacts, and both effects are likely to be well represented within any overall scheme of public or private land regulation.

Part II focused primarily on the compliance effects of land use controls. As explored there, rules that limit choices within a community can avoid localized tragedies, but can also produce new inefficiencies. While sorting (a membership effect) was discussed as a potential response to these inefficiencies, its limitations required us to consider other ways to reduce the costs of compliance effects, such as through entitlement design. In this part, I shift my focus to the membership effects of land use controls. As we will see, controls can have membership effects even if no conscious intent to exclude is present. Moreover, these effects can involve not only keeping people out of the community but also attracting people to the community. Overt efforts by governments or private neighborhood associations to fence out unwanted residents thus account for only a subset of the membership effects of land use controls.

In Chapter 2, I surveyed some of the motivations for land use controls: apportioning property tax burdens among residents ("collecting"); controlling the behavior of people who choose to live in the neighborhood ("controlling"); facilitating the sorting of people into like-minded communities by providing information about local rules ("sorting"); and keeping people with particular characteristics, such as low incomes or wealth levels, from moving in ("screening"). While screening consciously involves membership effects, such effects can also be a by-product of measures that are primarily concerned with collecting or controlling. For example, a zoning restriction that is entirely premised on fiscal considerations will keep out families who cannot afford the "cover charge" of purchasing a particular sort of home just as surely as would a zoning restriction animated by outright snobbery. In addition, land use controls that appear to encourage self-sorting along one dimension may also shape community membership along other dimensions, as Lior Strahilevitz has explored. For example, a community centered around a golf course may encourage the entrance not only of people who love to golf but also of those who like to associate with people who golf—including those who have taken notice of the demographics of golfers relative to the population at large.[2] Significantly, land use controls that keep out some households (whether intentionally or unintentionally) do more than simply make it expensive or impossible for some residents to enter; those controls also provide a framework within which other households exercise residential choice. Recognizing this point allows us to refine our understanding of membership effects. The most direct impacts are on what I will call "constrained households"—those that find it impossible to enter the residential subgroup as a result of the land use control. But the existence of land use controls, including the controls' anticipated effects on constrained households, will also influence the locational decisions of many "unconstrained households"—those who could enter the jurisdiction despite the land use control. For some of these unconstrained households, the land use control makes entering the subgroup more costly or less beneficial; if they enter the jurisdiction, they must bear the associated compliance costs, such as buying a larger house than they would otherwise prefer. For other unconstrained households, however, the land use control makes entering the subgroup more attractive; these households expect to internalize net benefits from the restriction's combined compliance and membership effects.

Although membership effects on constrained households clearly contribute to the changes in grouping wrought by land use controls, much of the action takes place in the decision-making of unconstrained households. This should not be surprising, if we recall that land use controls are often consciously sought by homeowners in order to preserve the value of their investments in their homes. Such controls will therefore be one of the dimensions along which homebuyers assess housing bundles. Because the "product stabilizing" nature of land use controls may cause households to enter a community they would not otherwise select, membership effects can stem from land use controls that do not operate to zone out anyone. Membership effects also interact with compliance effects in complex ways. Sorting, one type of membership effect, can forestall what might otherwise be inefficient compliance effects of land use controls. For example, a gnome-forbidding rule adopted by a given jurisdiction may never operate inefficiently if no gnome-appreciating household ever enters that jurisdiction. On the other hand, conscious efforts to produce membership effects may generate inefficient compliance effects. For example, jurisdictions that zone for costly housing types in an effort to keep out lower-income people will produce not just membership effects but also compliance effects: some households that enter the jurisdiction will consume more housing than they would otherwise prefer.[3]

Finally, the anticipated membership effects of a given land use control can induce other changes in membership. For example, a community's exclusion of one group can be attractive to—and induce entry by—another group. Each wave of moves that households make in response to land use controls will have impacts on the subsequent decisions of homebuyers and residents. The pathbreaking work of Thomas Schelling has shown the powerful effects of interdependent locational choices on spatial patterns.[4] Because residential choices are strongly interdependent, land use controls can set in motion chain reactions that will dramatically alter the composition of multiple subgroups. Changes in membership caused by land use controls can in turn trigger behavioral changes within the group, such as heightened or diminished levels of cooperation in the production of local public goods. These indirect behavioral changes arising from membership changes can be usefully distinguished from compliance effects, which are directly induced by the land use controls themselves.

A System-Level View

Sorting by tastes—a type of membership effect—underpins the Tiebout Hypothesis and is credited with enhancing efficiency. We can see the theoretical advantages of sorting when we imagine populations that split cleanly into two camps on a particular issue, such as yard art or lawn care. But many real-world conflicts do not take this form. Often, sorting is invoked to defend a rule adopted by one subgroup (such as a private neighborhood or local government) that has very high compliance costs for some would-be group members. It is often true that if those who cannot cheaply comply with that rule go elsewhere, the subgroup under examination will become more homogeneous, and intragroup inefficiencies arising from compliance effects will be reduced. But membership effects in one spatial or political subgrouping within a larger system such as a metropolitan area cannot occur in isolation; they necessarily produce membership changes in one or more other subgroups as well.

To assess the efficiency or inefficiency of a land use control's membership effects, then, we must look beyond the subgroup adopting the control. In other words, we must conduct our analysis at the "system level" rather than at the subgroup level.[5] The reason why the efficiency assessment at the system level may differ from that produced by a narrow focus on a single subgroup becomes obvious if we consider the possibility of a collective action dilemma among the subgroups. Like the ranchers in Hardin's classic tale, each subgroup may act in ways that maximize the joint utility of its own members while imposing higher aggregate costs on the system as a whole. To illustrate this, let us consider a group of local jurisdictions that share a physical resource such as a lake.

Figure 6-1 depicts a lake that extends across the jurisdictional boundaries of towns A, B, C, and D, which together make up the entire system (metropolitan area) under review. Absent legal restrictions emanating from a higher level of government or coordination through formal or informal agreements or norms, each jurisdiction will be motivated to adopt policies with respect to the lake that maximize the returns for the individual jurisdiction, even when doing so generates higher aggregate costs for all of the jurisdictions sharing the lake.

The same sort of dilemma might be produced by land use controls that generate membership effects. Suppose that the irregular shape in Figure 6-1 contains not a lake but rather newcomers from the hinterlands who plan to locate in one of the four towns. Suppose the agglomeration benefits of living within the metropolitan area are so great that each household will make the move, and therefore must end up in one of the four jurisdictions. The households' choices are unlikely to resemble pure Tieboutian shopping. Rather, land use controls that individual jurisdictions put in place can keep some households out (whether by design or as a side effect of some other function), and, in so doing, attract other households. Significantly, every time a household is pushed out of or pulled into a given jurisdiction, there is a resulting impact on a neighboring jurisdiction. If

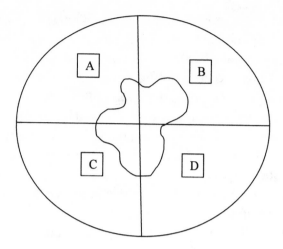

Figure 6-1. A shared lake

we make the simplifying assumption that every household must end up somewhere within the four-jurisdiction system, there is a principle of conservation at work: exclusion from one place requires inclusion in another.

None of this would matter from an efficiency perspective if we believed that the distribution of households among jurisdictions was a zero-sum game. Depending on how quickly and aggressively the various jurisdictions acted to attract and repel households, each might end up with lower or higher concentrations of residents possessing certain traits, such as community-spiritedness, law-abidingness, or wealth. These membership effects, although potentially unfair, would be purely distributive in nature—the interjurisdictional equivalent of children grabbing slices of a fixed pie. However, if the game is not zero sum—that is, the entire system can suffer gains or losses depending on how households are distributed among the jurisdictions—then the membership effects of land use controls can produce inefficiencies as well as inequities.

One reason the distribution of households among jurisdictions might not be zero sum has been considered already. Populations that are homogeneous in their tastes for public goods and services and that have preferences for similar rules can be more efficiently served in a single jurisdiction. As we have seen, heterogeneity within a given jurisdiction requires some residents to accept rules that are suboptimal. Entitlement design can ameliorate some of these problems, but those solutions are costly as well. Other things being equal, it would be better for the gnome friendly and the gnome averse to enter different communities. But because households have more than gnome policies (or policies on any other single dimension) on their minds when they choose a home, other things are rarely equal.

Moreover, there is no guarantee that a land use control that increases homogeneity of tastes in one jurisdiction through membership effects will also increase homogeneity of tastes in other affected jurisdictions. To see this, suppose that we have just two jurisdictions in a metropolitan area. The first, known as Bluetown, has traditionally favored exterior paint colors that fall along the cool part of the color spectrum (blues, greens, and purples), while the second, known as Redlands, has historically favored a palette of warmer tones (reds, yellows, and oranges). This arrangement is preserved informally through voluntary sorting until the day that Bluetown passes an ordinance outlawing certain colors that, although indisputably falling on the cooler side of the spectrum, are deemed by majoritarian interests to be "too bright."[6] If some of the Bluetonians (and would-be Bluetonians) who wish to paint their homes in one of the now-forbidden colors enter the (still unregulated) Redlands as a result, Bluetown will indeed become more homogeneous in its paint color tastes. Redlands, however, will become more heterogeneous.

We can of course imagine new land use controls enacted by Redlands, additional moves, and an eventual equilibrium in which each household ends up in a jurisdiction in which the costs of complying with the prevailing paint regime are lowest. I will not revisit here the reasons that sorting does not always proceed smoothly to produce efficiency. My point is simply that the composition of a given jurisdiction matters not only for that jurisdiction but for surrounding jurisdictions as well. To determine whether a given land use control enhances or diminishes efficiency through its membership effects, we must look at those effects on a systemwide basis. In the sections that follow, I explore another mechanism through which membership effects can produce efficiency gains or losses systemwide: the impact of subgroup members on the quality of local public goods.

Membership Effects and Local Public Goods

Membership effects directly bear on two of the goods that are most essential to quality of life—education and public safety. Although these local public goods are nominally provided by local governments (or, in some cases, by the private governments operating within common interest communities) the households that consume them are also important co-producers of them.[7] The cost and quality of education and safety crucially depend on factors like the school-readiness of the students and the community-mindedness of the residents.[8] When land use controls influence the composition of different residential subgroups within the metropolitan area, the impacts reverberate through the schools, sidewalks, and streets. This is an issue of obvious importance from the perspective of distributive justice, but it can also have efficiency implications. There can be net gains or losses to the metropolitan area as a whole, depending on how the households are divided into subgroups within that system.

The reason why grouping patterns might matter in this way is intuitive: residents and students often interact with each other or with service providers in ways that produce negative or positive synergies. The significance of peer effects for student achievement has been well established.[9] As Caroline Hoxby has explained, peer-effect spillovers might occur through any of a number of mechanisms, from direct student-to-student "knowledge spillovers," to impacts on resources in the classroom, to influences on "classroom standards" or on teachers' reactions.[10] Recent work by Thomas Nechyba modeling school choice takes into account these effects by including the students themselves among the resources that institutional arrangements must distribute in some manner.[11]

Neighborhood effects also appear to play an important role in public safety, although again the mechanisms producing these results are difficult to pin down.[12] It is not just a question of whether individuals within the community obey or break the law—although there is evidence that peer effects can influence young people's involvement in crime and use of drugs and alcohol.[13] As Jane Jacobs convincingly argued decades ago, neighborhood safety also depends on "eyes upon the street"—law-abiding people out and about, engaged in casual observation and enforcement.[14] If people do not believe an area is safe, they will stay off the streets; their withdrawal then makes the area even less secure.[15] Sociological work in Chicago likewise supports the relevance of "indigenous informal social control."[16] Manifestations of such control include, for example, "the willingness of residents to intervene to prevent acts such as truancy, drinking, vandalism, and street-corner disturbances (e.g., harassment, loitering, fighting)" in maintaining public order.[17] Tenant groups in housing projects have made similar use of informal social controls to reduce crime and maintain order.[18]

Clearly, residents differ in the way they consume, and hence produce, local public goods like education and neighborhood security. In the analysis that follows, I employ as abstractions two polar types of individuals to capture the heterogeneity among potential group members—the quality-enhancing group member (designated "E"), and the quality-detracting group member (designated "D"). Examples of Es would include the well-behaved, attentive student who participates in class and the neighborhood resident who keeps eyes and ears open for trouble and makes frequent, purposeful use of the local sidewalks and streets. Examples of Ds would include students who bring drugs and violence into the school and people who use their local streets and public parks as venues for drug sales and gang activity.

These labels are simplifications, but they broadly denote individuals with the current capacity and propensity to engage in behaviors that enhance or detract from the local public goods generated by a residential subgroup within a metropolitan area. Three factors are important to keep in mind when encountering Es and Ds in the analysis. First, the factors that make one an E or a D are not immutable characteristics but rather behavioral ones; hence, the number of Es and Ds is not fixed in advance but subject to change over time.[19] Second, to the extent that certain resources are necessary to foster the development of E-like capacities, the distribution of those resources may be relevant. Third, real-world individuals typically fall somewhere in between these archetypes, exhibiting E- or D-like characteristics to a greater or lesser degree. Thus, the binary distinction used here only scratches the surface in accounting for heterogeneity.

If land use controls have membership effects that influence the relative numbers of Es and Ds in a jurisdiction or private community, those controls will also influence the proportions of Es and Ds in other jurisdictions or communities within the same metropolitan system. Enacting such land use controls can, therefore, be understood as draws against a common resource, which we might call an "associational commons."[20] Like other common resources, the associational commons is vulnerable to tragedy.

Associational Tragedies

Neither governments nor individuals take into account the full, systemwide effects of their grouping decisions. This is an unexceptional fact, and one that will generate tragedy only when certain conditions hold. To understand those conditions, it is helpful to have in mind the idea of "associational surplus," or gains from grouping. These gains, which go by a variety of names in the literature, may be produced through economies of scale, complementarities of various sorts, or political or institutional advantages.[21] Tragedies of the associational commons, as defined here, cannot occur unless the total quantum of associational surplus is capable of expanding or shrinking based on the way in which households are configured into subgroups within an overall metropolitan system. We must worry about these outcomes when conditions are such that households or groups are both tempted to make and able to make grouping decisions that will diminish the total amount of associational surplus available systemwide.[22]

Whether the total amount of associational surplus can change in this way depends on how people within variously constituted groups produce negative or positive synergies, such as neighborhood or peer effects. Put in terms of our stylized analysis, we need to know how different ratios of Es to Ds within a given subgroup influence the production of local public goods. In other words, we need to know something about the production function for associational surplus. Consider first a situation where the production function for associational surplus is perfectly linear. Here, the movement of a quality-enhancing E from one group to another produces perfectly offsetting gains and losses for the gaining and losing groups.[23] Assuming that the process of group formation and reconfiguration over time is costless, grouping becomes a matter of pure distribution that does not implicate efficiency. That is, the same total associational surplus is produced, and is merely allocated in various ways among the groups depending on their respective compositions.

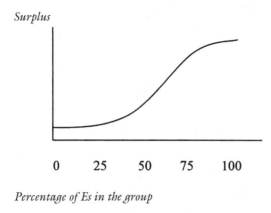

Percentage of Es in the group

Figure 6-2. S-shaped production function

Where production functions take a different shape, however, net gains or losses can result from different grouping configurations.[24] In these cases, one pattern of groupings is not just as good as another. Consider, for example, the production function shown in Figure 6-2, which tracks one possible relationship between the percentage of Es and the total associational surplus produced in a grouping.

In the Figure 6-2 case, a movement of Es from groupings where they constitute a large majority or a small minority into groupings where E membership falls in the 50 to 75 percent range can produce net gains. This shape fits with the intuition that a small number of quality enhancers may do little good, but once a "critical mass" is reached, gains will increase at an increasing rate. Eventually, however, surplus will plateau; further additions will produce increasingly smaller marginal improvements.[25]

Of course, the production function might instead take a very different shape, as an empirical matter. Consider, for sake of comparison, the curve in Figure 6-3. Here, Es do the most good in marginal terms when loaded into groups already containing a large majority of Es. In this case, a systemwide shift from mixed groups of Ds and Es to groups containing all Ds or all Es would generate net gains. It is, of course, an empirical question whether the production function in a given setting is linear, or, if nonlinear, whether it takes the shape shown in Figure 6-2 or Figure 6-3, or some other shape entirely.[26] But it is at least plausible that many grouping situ-

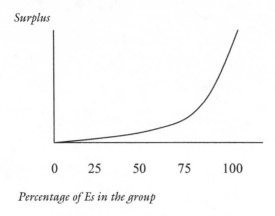

Surplus

0   25   50   75   100

Percentage of Es in the group

Figure 6-3. Increasing returns

ations involve nonlinearities that generate the possibility of tragedy in the associational commons.

A nonlinearity in the production function for translating inputs into outcomes is not enough on its own to produce tragedy, however. Recall that for a tragedy to occur, actors with access to the resource in question must have incentives to make suboptimal decisions with respect to it. Such incentives often exist when the costs and benefits of individual decisions about harvesting, cultivating, or degrading a common resource are not fully internalized. Even then, tragedy is not inevitable; actors may still internalize enough of the costs and benefits to make efficient decisions, especially if norm-based nonpecuniary sanctions and rewards are present. But inefficient outcomes become more likely.

For reasons that have already been explored, residential subgroups may engage in exclusion precisely because it offloads costs onto other subgroups. But even if land use controls with membership effects are adopted for other reasons, any resulting drop in systemwide associational surplus will not be fully internalized by the subgroup adopting the control. Moreover, when unconstrained households choose a residence, they do not fully internalize the effects of their choices on the membership pools in the various subgroups that they join or fail to join. Thus, land use controls, when coupled with the individual locational decisions of unconstrained households, can create tragic results that will leave the system as a whole worse off. These tragic effects may be concentrated on one or a few subgroups or spread among all of them. Regardless of how the losses are distributed, if the total amount of associational surplus could be increased by changing the composition of subgroups within the system, there is a potential for value-enhancing trades.

Behavioral Effects of Grouping Rules

At this point, the reader may complain that the foregoing line of argument proves too much. There are many settings outside of neighborhoods where the reconfiguration of subgroups within a system might be said to produce net gains, and in which people likewise pay no attention to the external effects of their grouping choices. Consider, for example, how employees within a particular industry are grouped into firms, or how the total pool of law students is split up among law schools. Perhaps an excellent worker would add more productivity to a mediocre firm than to an elite firm that is already filled with exemplary workers, or perhaps a top-notch law student would add more to the intellectual climate of a lower-ranking school than to that of a top-tier institution. The same argument might even be made about the allocation of individuals among households. Reshuffling such groupings in the name of avoiding tragedy would be absurd, but it is worth exploring why.

A layer of analysis that has remained in the background thus far offers some traction on the question. Systemwide associational surplus depends not only on groupings but also on a series of past and ongoing decisions by group members about whether to cultivate associational surplus and the capacity to produce it. For example, suppose Es within a given system produce diminishing marginal returns as they are added to any of the four subgroups that make up that system. Viewed as a problem of how best to allocate a fixed number of Es systemwide, we would do best by dividing up the Es among the subgroups. But the number of Es may not be fixed. Instead, it may depend on the payoffs to being an E, and these payoffs may depend, at least in part, on society's grouping arrangements.

We have already seen how the quality of goods like education and security can depend on those who are consuming—and hence also co-producing—those goods. Thus pooled-together Es are likely to receive better-quality local public goods than Es that are split up into groups containing significant proportions of Ds. If it is costly to become an E and to act like an E over time, changes in the rules governing group formation could reduce the willingness of households to invest in developing and practicing E behaviors. The result could be a change over time in the total number of Es.

The ground rules for group configuration could affect incentives at two decision points: at the "investment" stage in deciding whether or not to develop the characteristics that make one an E, and at the "cooperation" stage, in deciding whether to manifest E-like characteristics within the group in which one finds oneself. In some settings, such as employment and higher education, individuals invest heavily in human capital development in hopes of securing a place in a desired grouping that practices strong exclusion. In such cases, the long-run incentive effects associated with selective grouping likely outweigh any short-run gains from reallocating group members. Grouping protocols can also influence the behavioral choices of group members once they are assembled into groups. An individual who joins a group freely might be more cooperative (other things being equal) than a group member who has been forced into a group.[27] Conversely, someone who is trapped in a group she hopes to escape from soon may do relatively little to pursue the group's goals. Rules for removing members from a group can matter as well. For example, if a group has the power to expel noncontributors, members may be more likely to cooperate or otherwise contribute to group goals.[28]

These caveats might make us question whether common-pool resource analogies are tenable when it comes to assessing how human beings choose to live and work together. But consider again the analogy of a replenishing common-pool resource, such as fish in a pond. Optimizing involves limiting extraction enough to foster a thriving population capable of renewing itself over time. In associational settings, the number of Es that develop will depend in part on how suitable the associational conditions are for fostering E-like behaviors and investments. Following the logic of replenishing resource games, if Es move too quickly from the background population into exclusive groupings, the overall number of Es may drop over time. A slower rate of migration of Es from the background population could foster the development of more Es—at least up to a point. Too little movement of Es into more-selective groups could discourage the development and exercise of E-traits, if part of the incentive to become an E is the chance to participate in selective groupings.

A related point involves interactions among various groupings throughout the life cycle. Perhaps certain groupings, such as those encountered in early childhood, are especially formative in developing the E-like or D-like behaviors that will carry over to later groupings. If so, then group configuration choices at these early stages could produce costs or benefits for a given cohort long after the specific groupings in question (such as assignment to particular primary or secondary schools) have ended. Some recent research supports the idea that social interactions early in life are correlated with social capital, trust, and community engagement later in life.[29] Although the mechanism responsible for this connection is unclear, one potential implication is that early interactions—and hence early groupings—matter a great deal. Nonetheless, such results should be interpreted with caution. As Nancy Rosenblum has observed, we cannot simply assume that particular forms of associational participation will spill over into new and different realms; it is even possible that some associations compensate for or act as counterweights to others.[30]

There is yet another wrinkle that deserves attention. The simple example just given assumes that everyone can tell who is an E and who is a D, so that Es could easily self-segregate (and exclude the Ds) if only they were permitted to do so. We rarely find this level of discernment in real-world settings. If it is difficult to tell Es from Ds, some rough proxy might be used instead that, on average, screens out more Ds than Es and lets in more Es than Ds, but that generates both false negatives and false positives. Such a screening system has real risks: it might be expected to reduce the investments of would-be Es who know they are very likely to be mislabeled as Ds, given the proxies in use. Suppose, for example, that the standard screening proxy is wealth or income. If we assume that prospects for group membership represent a primary motivation for cultivating E-traits, then less well-off individuals would have diminished incentives to make such investments. Interestingly, wealthy people (that is, those who possess the proxy characteristic) might also see less need to invest in developing the underlying characteristics deemed valuable to the group.[31]

Games Neighbors Play

In all, unconstrained households participate in three sets of decisions with implications for local public goods throughout a metropolitan area. First, they must decide where to live—that is, choose a subgroup within the overall system. Second, they must decide how to act in the place that they choose to live—that is, whether or not to exhibit E-like behaviors within the subgroup. Third, as part of the local governmental or private association's political process, they must decide whether to adopt, revise, or maintain land use controls that will have effects, whether intended or incidental, on membership. Decisions by current residents about land use controls with membership effects will not only limit the choices of constrained households but may also serve to attract or repel unconstrained households.

This third set of decisions directly implicates law, and it provides the usual analytic point of entry for scholars concerned about the impacts of grouping and exclusion on society. Adding new property tools to these centralized political decisions is the primary focus of the next chapter. But the other two sets of household decisions—where to live and how to act— must be examined first. Land use controls with membership effects shape those decisions, often in complex ways. Because each household's payoffs from its own choices will be strongly influenced by the actual and anticipated choices made by other households, interactions among households can take the form of strategic games.

In the balance of the chapter, I consider in simplified form how the choice about where to live might constitute a strategic dilemma among unconstrained households. I close by considering some of the standard and not-so-standard responses to this dilemma, as well as shortcomings associated with those responses. One important limitation is the prospect of behavioral changes, including altered cooperation levels within the subgroup, that might occur in conjunction with some of the possible responses.

Choosing a Subgroup

In choosing a residential subgroup, a household is opting not only for an exogenous set of goods and services provided by the local governmental entity, but also for a set of neighbors who will be both co-consumers and co-producers of local public goods like education and security. Under certain plausible assumptions, this choice can look like a Prisoner's Dilemma (or its structural equivalent, a tragedy of the commons) among unconstrained households.

One caveat must be stated at the outset. For purposes of the stylized example presented here, I will assume that key local public goods are geographically determined. For example, I ignore possibilities like private schools and personal security forces that would allow households to consume services different from those enjoyed by their immediate geographic neighbors. Where such goods are in fact decoupled from geography, the strategic game of choosing the subgroup with which to co-consume may still take the form presented here; however, households must play it on an à la carte basis for each service, rather than all at once by choosing where to buy a home. Given this book's focus on the home, I will assume a tight nexus between location and services, while recognizing that decoupling could matter in at least two very different ways. First, selective decoupling, as where parents send children to private school, could erode the effects of residence-based reforms in associational choice. Second, broad-based decoupling of, say, schooling and residence might be part of a strategy to achieve selective associational reform by lowering the stakes within a given associational realm.[32]

It might seem at first that unconstrained households choosing where to live face no strategic dilemma at all. We might simply expect them to maximize their consumption value by selecting, Tiebout-style, the subgroup that suits them best. But the residents of metropolitan areas do not consume only the safety provided in their own neighborhood, or the education provided in the school that the household's children attend. As the diagrams presented in Chapter 2 suggested, residents are likely to cross local jurisdictional boundaries frequently in the course of daily life, and hence will be influenced to some extent by the quality of local public goods in neighboring jurisdictions within the overall system. For example, if Homeria lives in a perfectly safe suburban or private community but her commute to work takes her through streets regularly punctuated with automatic weapon fire, she will be worse off than if a higher quality of security prevailed along her commuting route. Similarly, if Homeria regularly frequents shops, banks, and other service providers throughout the metropolitan area, she will suffer if people working at the establishments she patronizes lack basic reading, writing, and computing skills. Moreover, as a citizen of the metropolitan area, she may have preferences about the well-being of others who share that larger system with her; she may wish for them to enjoy at least some decent minimum of education and security. Thus, she may occupy a dual role as a consumer and as a citizen.[33]

If these intuitions are correct, many residents of metropolitan areas receive a two-part payoff associated with the local public goods under discussion. One part corresponds to the direct consumption value the household receives from consuming the good in question, and the other part corresponds to the value that is generated by the overall pattern of consumption of this type of good throughout the larger system ("composite value").[34] Of course, residents are likely to be quite heterogeneous in the relative weight placed on direct consumption and composite value, depending on (among other things) the degree to which they are other-regarding, and the extent of their interactions beyond their own residential enclave. But among unconstrained households for whom a concern about composite value is sufficiently strong, a strategic dilemma may emerge with the structure of a Prisoner's Dilemma. I illustrate this dilemma here through the use of a stylized two-person game, but the same principles could be extended to a multiplayer game with many participants.[35]

Consider two individual heads of household, Rudy and Carrie, who are moving into the metropolitan area of Metropolis. Both have young children, and each is quite concerned about the public schools and about the level of neighborhood safety. Each must decide whether to locate in Optoutia, a quiet suburban community zoned for single-family homes on large lots, or in Coopersville, a dense sector of the central city.[36] Both choices are open to both Rudy and Carrie—each is an unconstrained homebuyer who is not precluded from either choice by land use controls. For each household, local public goods will be the deciding factor; the locations perfectly balance out on all other attributes. For example, suppose each is comparing a Coopersville condo that features a short walk to work, lavish finishes like granite countertops, limited living space, and no yard, with an Optoutia colonial-style house that has more than twice the square footage, a generous yard, outdated finishes, and a seventy-minute commute.

For present purposes, I will assume that both Rudy's and Carrie's households will be Es in whichever subgroup they decide upon, enhancing both the quality of public safety and of public education. In other words, I assume that their propensity to cooperate will not be affected by their choice of residences. This may not be a realistic assumption. For example, perhaps Rudy will be so exhausted by his daily commute to and from Optoutia that he will be suboptimally lenient with his children about homework completion, or Carrie will feel less comfortable in Coopersville and, accordingly, will spend less time interacting with her neighbors.[37] Nonetheless, we can begin with this simplifying assumption.

In this game, local public goods are rated "rotten," "decent," or "premium"—labels that denote absolute quality levels. The game's structure assumes that both Optoutia and Coopersville have S-shaped production functions like the one shown in Figure 6-2. In Optoutia, however, more than 75 percent of the population is already made up of Es, so that Rudy and Carrie would be entering in the relatively level plateau range on the right side of the Figure 6-2. Thus, local public goods in Optoutia will be provided at the premium level regardless of what Rudy and Carrie do. Their contributions as Es will be made in an environment that has already been enhanced to a very high level by other Es, and will therefore add little in marginal terms.

In Coopersville, however, the quality of the local public goods depends to a much greater degree on the locational choices that Rudy and Carrie make. The current percentage of Es in Coopersville stands close to the 50 percent mark in Figure 6-2, so that each additional E household will produce significant gains. If both Rudy and Carrie choose Coopersville, their (and their children's) participation will produce local public goods at the premium level in Coopersville. If only one or the other opts for Optoutia, the remaining player will still be able to keep the local public goods quality at the decent level in Coopersville. If, however, both head for Optoutia, the local public goods in Coopersville will fall to rotten. In other words, I am assuming that some critical mass of quality enhancers will make the local public goods premium in quality and that some smaller number of quality enhancers is necessary to make those goods decent. While it is clearly unrealistic that one or two individual house-holds would make such a large difference, setting up the game in this way is a necessary stylization in the two-player context. The interaction between Carrie and Rudy thus models the strategic interaction that would more plausibly occur between dozens or even hundreds of un-constrained households like Rudy's and Carrie's.

People care not only about the absolute quality of their children's edu-cation but also about how that education stacks up against the education received by relevant others. In part because elementary and secondary ed-ucation is used to obtain other valuable goods in a competitive economy, such as admittance into better colleges and eventual employment at bet-ter jobs, it is a "positional good"—a good for which the surrounding con-text of consumption matters greatly.[38] Thus, in our two-person game, local public goods that are premium in absolute terms can be "premium and su-perior" (if only one player receives that quality level) or "premium and equal" (if both players receive that quality level).

Finally, because Rudy and Carrie will travel daily into Coopersville for work, shopping, and recreation, they care about the quality of its local public goods, even if they do not end up living there (although, of course, they will care much more if they do live there). Thus, their payoffs will be made up in part by their own consumption experience in the subgroup in which they choose to reside, and in part by the overall "composite" local public goods experience in Metropolis as a whole. Given the setup of this simple game, the composite element can be directly measured by consid-ering the quality of local public goods in Coopersville, since any degrada-tion of overall composite quality will be felt there. The pieces of the resulting two-part payoffs for the players are as follows:

> *Direct Consumption Component*
> Rotten public goods where I live = -2
> Decent public goods where I live = 2
> Premium (and equal) public goods where I live = 5
> Premium (and superior) public goods where I live = 7
>
> *Composite Component*
> Rotten public goods exist in Metropolis = 0

All public goods in Metropolis are decent = 2

All public goods in Metropolis are premium = 3

As this schedule indicates, I have also made the possible payoff range for the direct consumption component larger than that for the composite component, which reflects the intuition that people have a much larger stake in the former. Those valuations yield the payoff grid shown in Table 6-1.

To see how this game amounts to a Prisoner's Dilemma, first look at things from Rudy's point of view. No matter what Carrie does, Rudy is better off selecting Optoutia. If Carrie chooses Coopersville, Rudy can do better in Optoutia—he can reap the benefits of a metro area in which all public goods are decent, while at the same time enjoying good and superior public goods where he lives (total payoff of 9). Choosing Coopersville would reduce his payoff to 8. Even though it would make the public goods in Coopersville premium rather than merely decent, his household would receive only premium and equal public goods rather than the premium and superior education available in Optoutia. Of course, if Carrie is going to choose Optoutia, Rudy has an even greater incentive to do so as well. Otherwise, he will be bearing the burden of keeping the public goods across the metropolitan area decent, while subjecting his own household to those merely decent public goods. Meanwhile, Carrie gets the benefit of decent public goods throughout the metro area while securing premium and superior local public goods for her family's consumption.

Things look identical from Carrie's point of view, of course. The result is that choosing Optoutia is the dominant strategy for both, making the lower right-hand cell the equilibrium solution. In that cell, some local public goods in the metro area (that is, those in Coopersville) fall to rotten, but Rudy's and Carrie's households directly consume premium and equal local public goods in Optoutia. The total combined payoff associated with the lower right-hand cell is the lowest of the bunch. Rudy and Carrie could collectively do much better if they could agree to choose Coopersville, but the temptation to defect presents an obstacle.

This game structure and the resulting dominant strategy depend on the specific payoffs I have built into the example, which depend in turn on a number of assumptions about the players that would not hold true for everyone. One could easily imagine different orderings of valuations that

Table 6-1 The homebuyer's dilemma

	Payoffs for (Rudy, Carrie)	
	Carrie chooses Coopersville	*Carrie chooses Optoutia*
Rudy chooses Coopersville	I. (8, 8) (5+3, 5+3)	II. (4, 9) (2+2, 7+2)
Rudy chooses Optoutia	III. (9, 4) (7+2, 2+2)	IV. (5, 5) (5+0, 5+0)

would present no dilemma at all, because no weight would be given to local public goods other than those in one's own subgroup. Similarly, different valuations might turn the game into Chicken, an Assurance Game, or some other game structure.[39] Nevertheless, the scenario set forth above demonstrates that under at least some imaginable circumstances, unconstrained households that would collectively be better off choosing one community will nonetheless choose another.

Responses and Shortcomings

Many different mechanisms might alter the payoff structures faced by unconstrained households like Rudy's and Carrie's and thereby change the dominant strategy. In shorthand form, we can refer to these as locks, bribes, norms, and pacts. Locks, which would force both parties into Coopersville and make them stay there, are problematic for obvious reasons, even if it would make the unconstrained households in our story better off. Not only would the coercive action required to accomplish the lock intrude into autonomy in ways that seem objectionable, it is likely that parties forced to associate with each other in residential settings will act significantly less E-like than those who make their subgroup choice freely.[40] Unfortunately, analysis of the impacts of associational choice often comes to a dead end after considering and rejecting coercive alternatives. Just as there are alternatives to "command and control" in the intragroup context explored in Part II, there are also alternatives that might influence choices between groups.

Pacts, for example, would accomplish the same result as a lock, but through a voluntary agreement among unconstrained households rather than through coercive external action. Because individual consent would be involved, the autonomy concerns are alleviated. Coordinating the pact, however, could quickly become unwieldy as we move from our stylized two-party game to an interaction involving hundreds or thousands of households. Even if these difficulties could be overcome, a conceptual objection remains: Once the pact is in place, can it be lifted for individual households when it is efficient to do so? Suppose, for example, that after Rudy signs a pact to stay in Coopersville, his child is diagnosed with a medical condition that requires thrice-weekly treatment in an Optoutia hospital, dramatically shifting his locational cost-benefit calculation in the direction of Optoutia. In theory, Rudy could negotiate a release from the pact, but Part II's analysis of covenants and their capacity to lock in inefficient results might give us pause, especially if we move to the many-player context. By creating a response to what amounts to tragedy of the commons, we might end up with an anticommons in which even efficient moves from Coopersville to Optoutia would be impossible to accomplish.

A further problem with pacts stems from heterogeneity. In the two-person game just presented, both Rudy and Carrie would have been better off if they could have reached an agreement whereby both would go to Coopersville. However, there may be many unconstrained households whose preferences are such that a "go to Coopersville" agreement would not make them better off—they would unambiguously prefer Optoutia. Such households' decisions may still be inefficient, but the losses are heaped on others; the household itself shares none of the pain. Put differently, these unconstrained households do not have a sufficient "composite" local public goods element in their payoff structure to make a pact advantageous for them.

Norms and bribes (or, less pejoratively, incentives) both operate to alter the relative payoffs of competing courses of action. Game theorists have long recognized that intangible factors, such as social norms, can change the effective payoffs that the players experience. For example, notions of honor and disgrace powerfully alter the payoffs that soldiers experience when confronted with a collective action problem, such as whether to stay and fight or flee to safety.[41] Yet, even though such norms exert considerable influence in some settings, it is fair to say that they are not robust checks on residential decisions. Competing norms in favor of consumer choice seem to dominate, and concerns about the side effects of individual decisions are often only vaguely apprehended. Of course, the possibility remains that norms could be shifted in favor of collective action in this context. This is only likely to happen if those within the relevant reference group (probably, other unconstrained households) widely share a consensus about the choices that would lead to higher payoffs. Like pacts, norms are unlikely to take hold unless unconstrained households would, in fact, reap a benefit from cooperation.

Finally, financial inducements, whether framed as bribes, incentives, subsidies, or rewards, hold the power to alter payoffs and hence change strategies that produce suboptimal results. Decades ago, James Buchanan discussed the possibility of paying well-off residents to remain in central cities.[42] The notion of paying higher-income people for their continued presence seems offensive, in part because money flows to those who already have plenty of it—in our schema, the unconstrained households. Yet, there are many other ways that arrangements might be structured to influence locational choices.[43] For example, money might flow in the other direction; choices to move to Optoutia could require the payment of a fee.

Innovative property mechanisms have already been devised to address problems of pollution and resource conservation. Similarly, the rich literature surrounding the allocation and protection of entitlements[44] could illuminate certain problems of association. In order to even consider these ideas, much less give them the detailed design attention necessary to sidestep objectionable features, we must have a way of thinking and talking about what is at stake. In short, we need the concept of an associational entitlement.[45] The next chapter introduces this idea and explores how it can shed new light on the most difficult and controversial of metropolitan problems.

7

PROPERTY IN ASSOCIATION

When people buy a home, they also buy proximity to a current and prospective set of neighbors.[1] These associational purchases usually attract little attention. Yet, the resulting pattern of subgroups within a metropolitan area can be inefficient, even tragic.[2] Two responses to this state of affairs have dominated the public discourse. First is the assertion that the individual decisions of municipalities, private communities, and homebuyers make up a free-market system that produces results that are not only efficient but also essential to personal autonomy. A second, and diametrically opposed, response takes the existence of concentrated poverty, especially when it involves the residential isolation of racial minorities, as prima facie evidence of discriminatory exclusion that must be addressed through absolute prohibitions. Significantly, neither approach views residential patterns as a species of resource dilemma that might be addressed through property theory. Each side in the debate instead assumes that residential spatial association is an all or nothing matter—either a particular choice must be allowed absolutely or it must be banned categorically.

To be sure, both complete prohibitions and zones of free choice are essential when it comes to associational decision-making. Some forms of exclusion, such as discrimination based on racial identity, are so reprehensible and destructive that they must be banned categorically in all but the most intimate spheres. Likewise, certain kinds of associational choices, such as one's religion or one's life partner, should receive broad protection from state interference. But these realms of prohibited and permitted decision-making represent only two ends of a spectrum of associational decisions relevant to housing patterns. At other, carefully delineated points along that spectrum, entitlement designs analogous to those we have already explored in the neighborhood context could help to avert tragedy.

It is worth emphasizing that such alternatives would not interpose a novel form of social engineering into an otherwise pristine field of free-market activity. Land use controls, whether public or private, already aggressively shape the associational landscape using regulation and politics, not free-market transactions.[3] It would be equally mistaken to view a system of associational entitlements as introducing unseemly market-based loopholes into a system that currently offers categorical protection against residential exclusion. Exclusion is, and has long been, a reality. The ideas in this chapter, then, are not about championing regulation or facilitating exclusion but rather about restructuring these already pervasive features of metropolitan life to address the externalities they produce.

Property and Association

Property theory has dealt uneasily and incompletely with matters of association for at least two reasons. First is a concern that property is simply the wrong conceptual tool for the job, and that, instead, "rights-based" notions of constitutional law, civil rights, and political philosophy should govern inquiries about inclusion, exclusion, and association.[4] Second is a conviction that property law and theory already deal with associational conflict to the extent necessary through existing forms of private property, as augmented by land use controls. After all, if property's signature attribute is the right to exclude (and, by extension, to selectively include), then why is it not sufficient to create well-defined rights in property and let association take care of itself?[5]

Taken together, these ideas lead us to view property as an associational envelope of sorts, with hard outer boundaries that protect an invitation-only enclave. What happens inside the envelope is usually understood to involve "privacy" or "freedom of association," while what happens outside the envelope is usually deemed beyond property theory's jurisdiction—work better suited for constitutional law or civil rights scholars. Charles Reich's characterization of property as a mechanism that establishes "a boundary between public and private power" exemplifies this dichotomy. In Reich's words, "Property draws a circle around the activities of each private individual or organization. Within that circle, the owner has a greater degree of freedom than without. Outside, he must justify or explain his actions, and show his authority. Within, he is master, and the state must explain and justify any interference."[6] Unsurprisingly, debates about associational matters tend to center on line-drawing—locating the point at which the baton of associational control properly passes from private owners to public lawmakers.[7]

This way of framing associational issues carries some descriptive force, but it offers no coherent account of where the dividing line should fall between completely free association and association that is properly regulated by public law. Parcel boundaries are an unsatisfactory answer for many homeowners, for reasons that have been emphasized throughout this book. Households' predictable attempts to expand control outward collide with public law concerns, however, leading to showdowns between the two absolute positions of banning exclusion or permitting it. Entitlements that allow some associational questions to be determined through prices or bargains offer a middle way.

Using property tools to order at least some subset of associational choices offers important advantages. First, an entitlement structure can harness information about the costs and benefits of various arrangements by putting individuals in the position of revealing valuations or acting on valuations revealed by others. A command-and-control approach, in contrast, depends on a central planner's possession of all of the relevant information about the costs and benefits of different grouping arrangements. Such an approach cannot elicit or capitalize on information in the possession of the parties who are actually affected by grouping arrangements.

Second, and similarly, entitlements might be structured in ways that facilitate discovery of the best way of addressing a particular grouping-related problem. It is intuitive to think about addressing inefficient grouping patterns directly, by changing group formation incentives. But it is also possible that actions taken earlier—either by society or by would-be group members—could eliminate the features of the situation that later make exclusion rational for the excluding groups. Just as conditions prompting the impulse to quarantine might be greatly reduced by earlier actions to vaccinate, so too might motives to exclude be dampened by earlier actions that affect the distribution of resources or the accumulation of human capital throughout society.[8] Alternatively, or in addition, community development efforts, monetary inputs, training programs, and the like could transform the population from within and foster the formation of internal social capital networks. Ideally, we would structure entitlements in a way that induces the parties themselves to find the most efficient solution. An analogy can be drawn here to Calabresi's notion of locating the "cheapest cost avoider" of an accident.[9]

Significantly, "propertizing" association does not require the single-minded pursuit of efficiency to the exclusion of other normative goals. The manner in which a society chooses to assign and protect entitlements will inevitably have distributive implications, and these implications might properly become the primary focus of attention in entitlement design. However, the capacity of transferable entitlements to harness private information and thereby produce efficient results is one of their most attractive features, making them especially well suited to settings where distributive and efficiency goals can be advanced simultaneously. Residential association seems to be just such a context, at least if we suspect that certain grouping patterns tend to be inefficient as well as unfair.

Associational Entitlements

In designing entitlements to govern residential patterns, the insights from Part II can be transplanted—with some important limitations—to a larger scale. Just as households may make individually rational decisions that degrade the neighborhood environment in ways that are socially costly on balance, public and private governmental entities may enact land use controls with membership effects that are beneficial to a subgroup but suboptimal for the system. And just as communities have reflexively resorted to prohibitions on particular uses to control intensely local tragedies, policymakers have assumed that larger associational tragedies can only be addressed by forbidding exclusion or mandating particular residential patterns. At both scales, gains could be realized through mechanisms that price behavior rather than allowing it unconditionally or forbidding it categorically.

Expanding the Menu

Adding price-based alternatives is more complicated and controversial in the associational realm than it is in the aesthetic or environmental realm. Indeed, some exercises of associational decision-making are not normatively comprehensible as alienable entitlements at all. Thus, it is crucial to begin by marking out areas of inalienable associational rights. Doing so reveals a middle ground in which alienable associational entitlements can play a role. Table 7-1 breaks out categories of inalienable associational decision-making authority by collectives and households, as well as alternatives that fit in between those inalienable categories. The two rows in Table 7-1 reflect the fact that residential patterns of association are shaped by both collective and household decision-making. Local jurisdictions and private neighborhoods enact land use controls, and constrained and unconstrained households make residential decisions within the resulting choice structure. The three columns in Table 7-1 reflect three different levels of decision-making control that an actor might hold with respect to an associational choice.

In the leftmost column, the decision maker holds an entitlement to make the decision in question, and that entitlement cannot be sold. In Calabresi and Melamed's terms, the entitlements are protected by inalienability rules. Cell A includes land use controls that are genuinely designed to protect health, safety, and morals. Local governments and private collectives can enact such controls, but selling violation rights would be inconsistent with important normative goals. For example, a jurisdiction is entitled to keep a household from adding more members than the structure can safely contain, but it cannot sell the rights to violate that rule. Indeed, we would take a dim view of a local official who offered to turn a blind eye toward unsafe overcrowding in exchange for a cash payment, even if the payment were dutifully deposited into the jurisdiction's coffers.

Cell B similarly contains decisions that households are entitled to make but that they cannot alienate. Here, we find decisions to live within a particular grouping in order to further certain constitutionally protected ends, such as those relating to religious exercise or expression. While this area of constitutional law is complex and conflicted, such an entitlement could potentially exist in some residential settings. To the extent it does, it cannot be infringed by collective decision makers, nor can it be sold. In ad-

Table 7-1 Inalienable and negotiable decisions impacting residential patterns

	Permissible choice; cannot sell rights	*Potentially negotiable*	*Impermissible choice; cannot buy rights*
Collective decisions	A. Land use controls for the protection of health, safety, and morals	C. Most land use controls addressing externalities and aesthetics	E. Discrimination based on protected characteristics; interference with residential choices for constitutionally protected reasons
Household decisions	B. Residential choices for constitutionally protected reasons; choices free of discrimination based on protected characteristics	D. Most residential choices	F. Residential choices prohibited for protection of health, safety, or morals

dition, households have an inalienable right to be free of discrimination based on protected characteristics when they make their locational choices. This right is grounded in both statutory and constitutional law, and is enforceable against both public and private governmental entities, as well as private sellers, landlords, realtors, and others who control access to housing.[10] Individuals cannot be excluded from a residential subgroup because of their race, for example, and cannot accept a payment in exchange for tolerating this exclusion.

In the rightmost column in Table 7-1, we find a converse set of limitations to those displayed in the leftmost column. Here, the decision maker has absolutely no right to make the decision in question, and is further disabled from purchasing that right from the party holding it. Cell E is the flip side of Cell B. It tells us that collectives, whether public or private, cannot discriminate against those who are in protected classes, nor can they purchase the right to do so. Similarly, collectives cannot interfere with (or buy the right to interfere with) any association that is constitutionally protected because of its connection to religious or expressive ends. In Cell F, we see the flip side of Cell A. When a household encounters a land use control enacted for the protection of health, safety, or morals, it has no right to override that control, nor can it buy the right to do so.

Given the existence of inalienable health and safety regulations on the one hand and inalienable protections against discrimination or interference with constitutional rights to associate on the other, it is perhaps not so difficult to understand why a dichotomous view of property's interaction with association has been so tenacious. Yet, these two categories do not begin to cover all real-world associational decisions. The middle column in Table 7-1 recognizes the possibility that a decision maker might be given conditional or negotiable rights over a particular associational choice.

As Cell C suggests, local governments and private communities routinely adopt land use controls that address matters such as aesthetics, which by no reasonable stretch of the imagination could be said to preserve health, safety, or morals. That is not to say that these controls are necessarily illegitimate or valueless—as we have seen, they may solve important collective action problems. But there is no good reason to make them inalienable. Likewise, as Cell D indicates, the vast majority of households choosing a residence are not pursuing expressive or religious ends that would require special constitutional privileging of their choices. Again, this does not mean that households should be precluded from choosing the location they prefer, only that their entitlements to do so need not be inalienable.

So far, I have concentrated on making the general case for a middle category of alienable associational entitlements—the middle column in Table 7-1. But a series of further decisions would have to be made as well: How should those entitlements be assigned in the first instance? Will they be protected by property rules (and hence be alienable only by mutual consent) or by liability rules (so that transfers in entitlements can occur on the unilateral initiative of one party)? How will the transfer price be determined? And so on. The next section explains.

Making Association Alienable

We can begin to flesh out some details about alienable associational entitlements by translating Calabresi and Melamed's basic approach, which helpfully breaks down society's choices about entitlements, into the setting of residential association.[11] Society must make two decisions when addressing a struggle between two parties over a given entitlement—which party will be initially assigned the entitlement, and how the entitlement will be protected.[12] In the associational context, however, defining the parties is tricky—after all, groups are simply more or less fluid collections of individuals. Therefore, some preliminary work must be done to frame the problem in a way that is amenable to entitlement analysis.

To give the analysis traction, I will make two simplifying moves. First, I will focus on the land use controls imposed by collectives rather than on the locational choices made by individual unconstrained households. While both play important roles in generating residential patterns, the latter occur in the shadow of, and are strongly shaped by, the former. Second, I will assume that constrained households are empowered by an entity such as a state agency acting on their behalf, so that their associational preferences can be successfully aggregated and translated into dollars as needed. In the simple example highlighted here, the immediate point of conflict is between a subgroup (a local government or homeowners association) that wishes to enact a land use control with membership effects and a constrained household that wishes to be included. The entitlement in question might be framed as the right to exclude, which if held by the household would entail the right to keep the household from being excluded. From these premises, we can generate a menu of alternative entitlement forms, as shown in Table 7-2.[13]

Rules 1 through 6 in Table 7-2 represent transferable associational entitlements. Rules 1 through 4 were part of the original Calabresi and Melamed framework, while Rules 5 and 6 were added by other authors elaborating on that framework.[14] To put those alienable rules into context, I have also included Rules 0a and 0b, which correspond to the two categories of inalienable entitlements shown in Table 7-1. Rule 0a represents inclusion rights held by individual households that the subgroup may not purchase (such as the right to be free of racial discrimination), while

Table 7-2 Alienable associational entitlements

Rule	Household holds	Subgroup holds	What does it mean?
0a	Entitlement protected by an inalienability rule	Nothing	Exclusion is forbidden; subgroup cannot purchase exclusion rights
0b	Nothing	Entitlement protected by an inalienability rule	Inclusion is forbidden; household cannot purchase inclusion rights
1	Entitlement protected by a property rule	Nothing (except the opportunity to negotiate)	Exclusion is forbidden, except as otherwise negotiated
2	Entitlement subject to a call option	Call option	Exclusion is taxed
3	Nothing (except the opportunity to negotiate)	Entitlement protected by a property rule	Exclusion is permitted, except as otherwise negotiated
4	Call option	Entitlement subject to a call option	The household's admission into the subgroup requires payment of a fee
5	Nothing-minus	Entitlement plus a put option	The subgroup can exclude the household or include it and collect a fee
6	Entitlement plus a put option	Nothing-minus	The household can demand inclusion or collect an exclusion fee

Rule ob represents exclusion rights held by the subgroup (such as the right to enforce maximum occupancy restrictions for safety reasons) that individual households may not buy out.

Transferable entitlements differ along two dimensions: who holds the entitlement initially, and who controls whether or not the entitlement will be transferred to the other party. Entitlements that are protected by property rules (Rules 1 and 3) cannot be transferred unless both parties agree to the transfer. Under Rule 1, the household cannot be excluded unless the subgroup pays a price that the household deems acceptable. Conversely, under Rule 3, the household can only gain entry if it offers a price acceptable to the exclusive group. Entitlements protected by liability rules can be subdivided into "call options" (Rules 2 and 4) that permit a unilateral transfer on the initiative of the party who is not initially assigned the entitlement, and "put options" (Rules 5 and 6) that allocate the power to initiate a unilateral transfer to the same party who is initially assigned the entitlement.[15] Under Rule 2, then, the subgroup can exclude by paying a fee, while under Rule 4 the household can gain admission to the subgroup by paying a fee. Under Rule 5, the subgroup starts off with the right to exclude but can collect a fee if it includes the household. Under Rule 6, the household has the converse option—it can demand inclusion, or it can collect a fee for staying out.

I am setting aside for the moment the manner in which the transfer price is determined. Standard discussions of liability rules assume that the transfer price will be set by a third-party governmental entity, such as a court or an administrative agency. But the literature of self-assessment raises the possibility of allowing the party against whom the option may be exercised to set its price in advance, as discussed in Chapter 5.

From Rules to Policies

Although the preceding list of entitlement forms might seem rather abstract and alien, counterparts to many of these variations exist either on the ground or in the literature. To start with the most pervasive example, local jurisdictions typically have broad latitude to adopt land use controls that have membership effects, such as those zoning out multifamily dwellings.[16] Zoning restrictions are not freely salable and hence might seem at first glance to be inalienable. But developers and local governments routinely engage in deal-making in which zoning designations are changed or zoning restrictions are relaxed. The predominant regime thus corresponds more closely to Rule 3, in which exclusion is permitted except as otherwise negotiated. Of course, households can enter any jurisdiction by purchasing housing of a type permitted in the jurisdiction. This might seem to give them a Rule 4 call option to get into the group by a paying a fee—the price of the permissible home. Such a characterization seems strained, however. It is a bit like saying that a ban on bicyclists along a particular stretch of road actually extends a call option to bicyclists, who can win inclusion by purchasing and driving a car instead. In any event, the payment is not made to the excluding jurisdiction and is not keyed to the costs that the community would incur by including the household.

In contrast, a "head tax" set by a jurisdiction to cover the cost of local services and amenities—coupled with a repeal of all zoning restrictions distinguishing among kinds of residential uses—would constitute a clear example of Rule 4. Edwin Mills suggested just such an approach thirty years ago.[17] A variety of other scholarly proposals for introducing transferable entitlements in association have appeared in the literature over the years. Robert Ellickson discussed an approach that would allow municipalities to enact exclusionary policies if they paid damages to affected landowners or housing consumers—a Rule 2 solution.[18] Michelle White suggested that a Pigovian tax on exclusion (another Rule 2 alternative) might be a superior instrument for achieving efficiency.[19] Both proposals were designed to make actors internalize the costs of their exclusionary policies.

James Buchanan's recommendation, mentioned earlier, takes a different tack.[20] Buchanan suggested that the differential fiscal impacts of low-income and high-income residents within a central city would justify policies that effectively "bribe" the wealthier households to stay put.[21] Such an approach corresponds loosely to Rule 5, if we understand the act of exit by the well-off (who are likely to be more mobile than their less well off counterparts)[22] as a form of exclusion. Other scholars have proposed a different variation on Rule 5—that of subsidizing inclusive communities. Here, the municipality has the right to exclude but can collect a fee by being more inclusive. The subsidy is not collected directly from an included individual but instead comes from a higher level of government, where it is financed by a broader demographic group than those at risk of exclusion.[23]

Similar ideas have gained policy attention in the education context. Title I funds directed to schools with high percentages of students from low-income families could be characterized as a form of subsidized inclusion, and scholars have discussed various ways of expanding the subsidization idea.[24] Given the currently tight connection between residential housing and schooling, such innovations could have important implications for residential patterns as well as educational groupings.[25] A recent proposal by Mechele Dickerson attacks the problem of residential segregation from a different angle. Dickerson suggests that school assignments be delinked from residence, and that parents who locate in integrated neighborhoods be given priority in an auction for school placements.[26] Here, inclusive residential choices are subsidized as in Rule 5—but not in cash. Instead, the subsidy takes the form of associational priority in the educational domain.

Perhaps the most interesting (albeit flawed) real-world associational entitlement framework was developed by the New Jersey legislature in the wake of the controversial *Mount Laurel* decisions. In the first *Mount Laurel* decision, the New Jersey Supreme Court struck down Mount Laurel's exclusionary zoning regime and held that such municipalities must take on their "fair share" of low-income housing as a matter of state constitutional law.[27] After eight years of foot-dragging by Mount Laurel and other municipalities, a second decision followed up with clarifications and potent judicial remedies.[28] The litigation sparked controversy and, ultimately, a legislative response in the form of the New Jersey Fair Housing Act. The Act, upheld in *Hills Development Company v. Township of Bernards,* authorized the use of Regional Contribution Agreements (RCAs) as an alternative way for municipalities to meet up to 50 percent of their fair share obligations. Recent legislation has eliminated RCAs, but the devices remain worthy of study.[29]

RCAs work like this: a sending jurisdiction purchases the right to be free of its obligation to house some number of low-income households, while a receiving jurisdiction assumes that obligation at a price. For example, Mark Hughes and Theresa McGuire note that under one such RCA, taxpayers in Tewksbury, New Jersey, "agreed to pay an additional $800 a year in taxes for six years to send 45 [low-income] units to Perth Amboy."[30] Low-income households are not involved in the negotiations, but developers are intimately involved, usually serving as the catalysts for formulating and consummating deals.[31] The associational nature of the entitlement in play has not gone unnoticed. Hughes and McGuire observe that even though "[t]he conventional point of view is that lower-income housing units are being traded," it is really "the right to exclude lower-income households that is being traded."[32]

Put into the framework outlined in Table 7-2, the RCA approach replaces the background Rule 3 regime (in which exclusion is permissible unless otherwise negotiated) with a three-stage regime. In the first stage, which lasts until the municipality has met the first half of its fair share obligation, Rule oa (exclusion forbidden) applies. In the second stage, as the municipality meets the remaining half of the fair share obligation, Rule 1 applies. Exclusion is prohibited unless otherwise negotiated—here, by finding another jurisdiction willing to take on the obligation. The jurisdictions negotiate the transfer price themselves (often with intercession by an interested developer), and if they fail to strike a mutually acceptable bargain, no transfer occurs.[33] Once the entire fair share obligation has been met through some combination of negotiation and inclusion, a third and final stage is reached in which Rule 3 applies—exclusion is permitted unless otherwise negotiated. Notice here that the parties who might seek to "buy up" the jurisdiction's exclusionary prerogatives include not only individuals or developers but also other jurisdictions that are looking to transfer the second half of their fair share obligations.

RCAs are innovative devices, but they present several concerns. First is the concern that unequal bargaining power between "sending" and "receiving" communities produces unfair results.[34] Second, RCAs have been criticized for improperly commodifying governmental obligations.[35] While commodification concerns might arise with any entitlement regime that permits exchanges of associational interests for cash, some of the concerns in the RCA context may be attributed to an entitlement design that leaves low-income households out of the conversation. Bargains can be struck without their participation or approval, presenting the possibility that they may be harmed by the resulting arrangements.[36] Third, because the RCA system is not sensitive to the spatial distribution of poverty, it could facilitate troubling concentrations of poverty within certain receiving jurisdictions. This shortcoming is not surprising, given that the *Mount Laurel* court did not focus on associational patterns as such.

Notwithstanding the well-deserved criticisms RCAs have received, these mechanisms underscore two central points. First, the value that home-owners derive from their property is importantly connected to their pref-erences for residential association. Second, pricing those preferences represents one way to respond to the social harm that those preferences can inflict. What is most surprising about RCAs is not that they have been roundly condemned—they do have quite serious flaws—but rather that so few scholars and policymakers have thought creatively about how the basic idea of transferable association rights might be redesigned to better serve social purposes. It is to that task that I now turn.

An Alternative: Options in Space

Could a redesigned RCA-like instrument address the distributive and spatial concerns raised above, without losing the informational and other efficiency advantages of an alienable entitlement? The self-assessed valuation approach discussed in Chapter 5 offers a starting point. Rather than striking pairwise bargains on a piecemeal basis, each community might be required to state, at annual or other regular intervals, the value it placed on a given exclusion increment (corresponding to a standard number of low-income housing units). Two consequences would attach to that valuation statement. First, the community would be required to pay a tax into a state coffer based on its valuation. Second, the valuation would create a call option that could be exercised by the state agency; the agency could acquire the community's right to exclude the housing units by pay-ing the community's stated valuation. These dual consequences would help to induce honest valuations: a too-high valuation would result in un-necessary tax payments, and a too-low valuation would create the risk that low-income housing might be placed within the jurisdiction at a price that the jurisdiction deems insufficient.[37]

This approach corresponds to Rule 4 in Table 7-2, if we posit a state agency able to exercise the call option on behalf of the individual house-holds. Note that the predetermined price at which transfer may occur (that is, the exercise price of the call option) is set by the community itself rather than by a third party. The array of valuations provided by communities throughout a metropolitan area would permit a state agency to easily iden-tify the lowest-cost sites for the low-income units. The agency could then build in spatial criteria (or any other criteria) in deciding when and where to exercise its options. For example, concentrations of low-income housing above a critical threshold could be avoided altogether, or each potential site could be evaluated based on a combination of price and spatial attributes.[38] As the holder of a set of call options, the state agency could use valuation information along with any other informational inputs to respond flexibly to changing conditions over time.

Because a community that places a lower true valuation on exclusion saves tax dollars under this scheme, communities should be willing to undertake efficient steps to make exclusion less central to their visions of the good life. Such efforts might take the form of innovations like better crime control, after-school enrichment programs, or neighborhood design that would reduce the impacts of poverty within the community and thereby reduce the costs of including low-income housing. Of course, some efficient cost-reduction efforts might not be undertaken, if the benefits will be shared broadly throughout the metropolitan area.

A remaining problem is that the state agency responsible for siting low-income housing may not do a good job of choosing the criteria that will best advance the interests of the low-income households themselves. A possible solution would be to delegate siting decisions to nonprofit organizations or private developers who might do a better job of aggregating the interests of low-income households. Coalitions of low-income households might be given either an advisory role or a veto power. More direct preference aggregation systems might also be devised, although not without introducing additional complexities.

Another concern relates to the risk of inappropriate commodification of associational interests. Explicitly attaching monetary valuates to associational preferences might be viewed as an especially harmful kind of discourse. Rather than being told subtly through land use controls (or the simple absence of affordable housing) that they are not welcome, low-income people would be confronted with a dollar figure that tells them just how unwelcome they are. This criticism assumes that subtle means of communicating associational distaste are less harmful than overt ones. Some traces of this view can be seen in antidiscrimination law. The so-called Mrs. Murphy exception in the federal Fair Housing Act exempts landlords who own buildings made up of four or fewer units and who actually occupy one of those units as a residence from liability for certain discriminatory acts. Yet the Act does not exempt those landlords from liability for discriminatory advertisements and statements. The result is a regime in which these landlords can legally discriminate (except as prohibited by other laws, such as Section 1982 of the Civil Rights Act of 1866) as long as they keep quiet about doing so.[39] Among the justifications for this apparent anomaly is the concern that certain kinds of statements and advertisements are particularly harmful to members of protected groups and may make them feel unwelcome even in places where the law does protect them from discrimination.[40]

Nonetheless, transparency is often beneficial precisely because it provides opponents with a clear target and exposes the actor to the risk of public disapproval. It is an empirical question, but social norms could produce a shaming control that limits the willingness of municipalities to present themselves as having an extraordinarily high willingness to pay for exclusion. Whether a high price would be deemed shameful depends not only on the existence and strength of anti-exclusion norms but also on whether payment was deemed an inadequate or inappropriate alternative to inclusion.[41] In this connection, the fact that land use controls with membership effects are at issue cuts in two directions. Characterizing the payment as one designed to keep out particular uses or structures rather than groups of people arguably softens the exclusionary message. On the other hand, it may make shaming either ineffective (because people believe that pricing decisions are based on structures and not on people) or inappropriate (if it truly is the case that pricing decisions are based on structures and not on people).

The idea sketched above is only one of many possible ways that entitlements in association might be approached. It is presented not as a finished proposal but rather as an example of the kinds of ideas that property scholars should be exploring. In the balance of the chapter, I turn to some more general questions about this family of approaches.

Objections and Implications

Explicitly recognizing associational entitlements in the neighborhood context would be a major theoretical move, and one to which a number of objections might be raised. Interestingly, analogues to some of these concerns can be found in the intellectual history of incentive-based approaches to environmental law. As Wallace Oates explains, arguments against using economic ideas to control pollution emanated both from polluting industries who resisted any new taxes on their activities and from environmentalists who saw the system as "basically immoral."[42] Likewise, criticisms of the notion of associational entitlements include both skepticism about any new limits on associational freedom and alarm about putting prices on associational interests.

I will begin by explaining why making the theoretical move suggested in this chapter need not undermine existing notions of associational freedom. I will then discuss my approach as a new tool for countering exclusion, and address concerns about its interaction with antidiscrimination law.

Rethinking Freedom of Association

Talk of curtailing the exclusionary prerogatives of local jurisdictions or private communities usually elicits strong protestations based on the asserted right to freely choose one's neighbors. This objection is almost entirely a red herring. It suffers from a rarely acknowledged logical defect: where people in a bounded metropolitan area form geographic subgroups, is not possible to extend rights of exclusion to each of those subgroups simultaneously, unless people happen to have perfectly congruent grouping preferences. Because every household must end up somewhere, and because adjacency to other households is an inevitable spatial fact in a metropolitan area, each household's associational choice affects the associational outcomes of others.

When people invoke freedom of association, they typically have in mind association that is based purely on mutual consent: entry into a group is by invitation only, but nobody is compelled to enter. Mutual consent logically requires granting veto or exclusion rights to every party to a would-be association: each individual can exclude himself from an unwanted association with a group, and an already formed group can exclude unwanted would-be members. This system of mutual consent works uncontroversially and well in a wide range of contexts—consider the choice of friends, spouses, partners, and housemates. In other broad classes of situations, the principle of mutual consent remains foundational, even though it is modified somewhat by public law—here, consider the matching of employees to workplaces, and students to institutions of higher education. In still others, such as membership in religious communities and social groupings, mutual consent remains important, even though practical, institutional, and familial considerations may cabin it to varying degrees.[43]

Mutual consent remains a workable organizing principle as long as any individual can opt out of all available groupings of a given type. As a matter of logical possibility (not normative desirability) one can remain completely outside all of the grouping types just mentioned—single, friendless, and unaffiliated with any religious group, workplace, or college. If an individual, Igor, is excluded from all of his preferred groupings in these realms, he is not summarily grouped together with a set of unchosen others with whom he must live, worship, or work. It is true that he might view himself as forced to be a member of an amorphous group known as "the friendless" or "the unemployed," and that outsiders might place a label such as "atheist" on him that lumps him into a category with others not of his own choosing.[44] But Igor is not required by virtue of these labels to engage in any interactions with the others sharing the group label, nor is he placed in spatial proximity with them.

Residential groupings within metropolitan areas present a different dynamic. To simplify a little, the background population must be, in the language of set theory, partitioned into subsets; every member of that population must occupy a place in exactly one subset.[45] In such a case, it is impossible for anyone to stand outside all subsets. This observation is of no consequence if each individual can make up a subset of his own if he so chooses. But if we further posit subsets of fixed (or even relatively inflexible) capacity, then the logic of set partitioning begins to have interesting consequences. Most notably, unless everyone happens to have perfectly nonconflicting preferences about grouping, basing group formation purely on the principle of mutual consent is no longer possible. Some people will end up in groupings that they did not choose and do not wish to be in.[46]

Exclusion in spatially bounded settings thus involves elements of forced inclusion. A dramatic example of the logical connection between exclusion and forced inclusion can be seen in the facts of *Korematsu v. United States*, the 1944 Supreme Court case that addressed the constitutionality of internment camps for U.S. citizens of Japanese ancestry during World War

II.[47] Korematsu was convicted of violating an exclusion order that made it a crime for him to remain in any part of the zone in which his home was located *except* a designated "assembly center," where he would have been detained for relocation to an internment camp. Another military order precluded Korematsu's exit from his home zone.[48] This second order effectively set a hard boundary around two possible locations: the assembly center, and the rest of Korematsu's home zone. Exclusion from the latter therefore translated into forced inclusion in the former. While the majority framed the case as involving only the violation of an exclusion order, the dissenters recognized it as directly implicating a question of forced inclusion—that is, whether an American citizen could be forcibly relocated to a concentration camp based on his ancestry.[49]

Turning to the residential context, if we suppose that everyone must live in exactly one of two available jurisdictions within a metropolitan area with fixed boundaries, exclusion from one jurisdiction operates as forced inclusion in the other. Of course, the lines between residential groupings are usually less stark and consequence-laden than this two-jurisdiction hypothetical would suggest. The boundaries between different residential areas may be fuzzy, people may engage with each other in more than one geographic area, and group membership lines may be drawn differently for various residence-linked groupings (for example, the school attendance zone may be different from the neighborhood watch zone).[50] But even where exclusion does not push households into a specific unchosen grouping, it reduces the available choice set.[51]

It will also often be inaccurate to describe group membership as truly "forced." It is usually possible to drop out of the background set completely by shunning the entire domain. For example, instead of locating within an undesirable residential grouping in a metropolitan area, a household might strike out on its own into rural or wilderness areas and avoid at least the spatial elements of forced grouping. Even so, the household would still be a member of some local political subdivision, which would entail some consequences of group membership based on residence. Grouping situations occupy various points on a spectrum as to the practical and normative viability of opting out of all groupings of that type (in other words, forming one's own "group of one"). On one end might be various forms of intimate association, and at the other end might be school districts, residential areas, or other spatially configured groupings that actors have limited ability to avoid.[52] At the latter end of the spectrum, opting out may be so unsustainable a choice that it seems descriptively accurate to treat the choice to remain in a residual group as involuntary.[53]

The structure of such set-partitioning situations makes it impossible to honor all associational preferences simultaneously, unless those preferences turn out to be perfectly congruent throughout a given system—an unlikely result. Those excluded from one subgroup (or set of subgroups) must end up somewhere else. Because of the set-partitioning feature and the relative inability to opt out of all subgroups within the system, being kept out of particular subgroups not only denies association but also compels it. Thus it is impossible to grant one residential grouping associational autonomy (the ability to choose its members) without interfering with the associational autonomy of other residential groupings in the same metropolitan area. The choice, then, is not how much associational autonomy we wish to allow but rather whose associational autonomy shall be given priority.[54]

In short, residential associational choice within metropolitan areas is an inherently scarce resource that must be rationed in some fashion among competing claimants. Currently, however, it is neither priced appropriately nor even properly acknowledged as a potential subject of resource dilemmas. Instead, the status quo grants associational priority in de facto ways that are not sensitive to the external effects produced by aggregation choices. It does no violence to overall levels of freedom of association to rethink systems for assigning associational priority in a system that cannot, as a matter of logic, accommodate everyone's associational preferences. Two points require further elaboration, however. First is the relationship between associational entitlements and the Tiebout Hypothesis. Second is the appropriate interface between associational entitlements and residential groupings that are formed for constitutionally protected expressive or religious reasons.

The Tiebout Hypothesis emphasizes the benefits of interjurisdictional competition, which might seem to require a certain degree of associational selectivity. But competition only works to deliver the advertised benefits when the inputs to that competition are priced to reflect their true social cost. Here, one input to interjurisdictional competition, exclusion, is currently consumed on an unpriced basis from a common pool. The resulting overconsumption by some jurisdictions visits externalities on others and leaves the system as a whole worse off. Nothing is lost by requiring competitors to refrain from appropriating entitlements from (or offloading costs onto) others while carrying out their competition.[55]

Another challenge to a new system of transferable associational entitlements is found in grouping choices that serve ends that are tightly linked to constitutionally protected expression or religious exercise.[56] How would the analysis presented here apply to voluntary assemblies formed to pursue such constitutionally protected ends? First, it is possible that these groupings would meet the condition of congruence, so that anyone who wishes to join is included in the group; if so, exclusion does not even enter the picture. But the question of congruence is complicated by the fact that exclusion can take many forms, including what Lior Strahilevitz has termed "exclusionary vibes" that convey unwelcomeness to certain would-be members.[57] Where exclusion does occur, however, such groups may be so small relative to the overall population in a metropolitan area as to have only de minimis effects on associational patterns. Still, suppose a grouping practice initiated for constitutionally protected reasons were carried out on a broad enough scale to generate or exacerbate problems like concentrated poverty. To the extent that the constitution would prohibit interference with these assemblies—a question that I do not take a position on here—the constitutional constraint could be accommodated by spreading the resulting costs across society as a whole rather than imposing them upon the excluding group, while still providing compensation to those harmed by the exclusion.

Associational Entitlements and Antidiscrimination Law

One advantage of the approach taken here is that associational externalities would become legally cognizable and subject to control without excluded households having to prove anything about the motives behind a particular land use control's membership effects. Given the multiple motivations that can underlie particular zoning or covenant choices, removing this burden is quite significant.[58] The idea of addressing exclusionary impacts without the need to show an improper exclusionary motive raises another important set of questions, however. How would an approach that focuses on associational externalities interact with antidiscrimination law—both as that body of law exists today and as it might develop in the future?

As an initial matter, it bears emphasis that associational entitlements, as developed here, are not designed to address discrimination based on protected characteristics. Rights vouchsafed by antidiscrimination law are, and should remain, inalienable. Nor do I envision my approach as in any way substituting for the further development or more rigorous enforcement of antidiscrimination law. Nonetheless, it is likely that a good deal of the exclusion that actually takes place today has at its heart some element of discrimination. It is necessary, therefore, to explain how associational entitlements would complement rather than impede efforts to advance antidiscrimination law.

Clearly, there are huge swaths of exclusion that are not actually reached by antidiscrimination law, as currently formulated and enforced.[59] My approach would price exclusion in those contexts, whether or not some discriminatory element is actually present. To do otherwise would be perverse. Because we are speaking of discrimination that is not currently reachable on constitutional or statutory grounds, carving out such an exception would give a free pass for those suspected of discrimination. Significantly, pricing exclusion regardless of its motive would not amount to accepting payment for discrimination privileges. Nothing in my approach alters the categorical normative commitments embodied in antidiscrimination law. Instead, the idea of associational entitlements represents a supplemental, parallel system that prices impacts, however caused. Any associational entitlement that is purchased through such a system would extend only to *nondiscriminatory* exclusion; no entity or person would be able to buy the right to discriminate. An analogy might be drawn to concurrent civil and criminal liability, where the availability of civil liability does not dilute the moral force of the criminal law or suggest that the right to commit a crime can be purchased.

An important concern is whether the notion of associational entitlements would in any way delay or crowd out the further development of antidiscrimination law or dispel the political will that otherwise would gather in support of such reforms. While it is an empirical question, it seems unlikely that an approach like the one outlined here would hinder antidiscrimination reform efforts. On the contrary, by raising the cost of exclusion in general, an associational entitlement approach should reduce the incidence of exclusion, leaving available more resources to direct against remaining instances of discrimination. Even where a community chooses to exclude and pay, the distributive outcome seems preferable to the status quo system of unpriced exclusion. Nevertheless, no strategy designed to alleviate social problems comes without some risk to other possible strategies. Indeed, closely analogous questions have been raised about the optimal strategy within antidiscrimination law.[60] As long as the impacts of exclusion continue unabated, however, it is difficult to defend a policy of doing nothing.

This chapter had two goals. First, I have tried to show that associational choice is a valuable and scarce resource that society cannot avoid allocating in some manner within a metropolitan system. At present, that allocation occurs haphazardly and below the radar as communities employ land use controls with membership effects on an unpriced basis. These actions amount to uncontrolled and unacknowledged draws against a common-pool resource. Second, I have argued that bringing the tools of property theory to bear on the resulting resource dilemma could produce gains in both efficiency and equity. There are many ways in which access to the resource of associational choice could be structured, and I do not claim to have hit upon the single best design. Rather, I hope to spark interest among scholars and policy innovators in thinking about association in a new way. As part of that project, I have highlighted a policy space between permitting and prohibiting associational choices that can coexist with important inalienable interests on the associational spectrum.

Admittedly, any effort to devise a real-world entitlement scheme for responding to associational collective action problems will be controversial and fraught with conceptual and practical difficulties. But when similar difficulties have beset efforts to address other legal and social problems, creative solutions have been devised—because people viewed the problems as important enough to wrestle with. Problems of residential association are also worthy of our best theoretical tools and our most serious scholarly attention.

PART

IV

RECONFIGURING HOMEOWNERSHIP

8

BREAKING UP THE BUNDLE

A few blocks from my home in Chicago stands the Original Rainbow Cone, an ice cream parlor in its eighty-third year that is famous among locals for its quirky namesake treat—five colorful flavors piled atop a single cone. Unsurprisingly, when I go there for ice cream, I am not required to buy an ownership stake in the business. My limited ownership bundle in the cone itself comes with some risks that are primarily under my control—melting mishaps or ice cream headaches—but the larger risks of running the enterprise are wisely left to Rainbow Cone's owners. Much as I hope Rainbow Cone survives for many decades to come, I am not forced to place a monetary bet on that result in order to enjoy its products.

When I bought my house, however, I had to make just such a bet on the continuing viability of charming local businesses like Rainbow Cone, as well as on innumerable other factors—local housing trends, employment markets, regional growth patterns, larger economic forces affecting lending practices and interest rates, government decisions about highways, schools, land use, and public transit, and so on—all of which are likely to influence the resale price of my home. These gambles were unavoidable if I wanted to enjoy the consumption benefits of homeownership—which, as I explain below, differ in degree and kind from those of renting. As Andrew Caplin and his coauthors put it, "The current market does not allow a household to separate its housing investment decision from its housing consumption decision."[1] To be sure, the expected value of the investment will be positive over time, but the variance in outcomes is high. More to the point, it is unclear why I should be forced to gamble on factors lying wholly outside my control in order to consume homeownership, any more than I should be forced to invest in Rainbow Cone in order to consume ice cream. The mandatory investment component of homeownership has real consequences: households that lack the financial wherewithal or risk tolerance to bet on their local housing markets simply cannot become homeowners.

That current legal arrangements require homeowners to gamble on matters far beyond their sphere of influence and expertise is, on reflection, rather remarkable. Homeownership is widely viewed as one of the most important stabilizing forces in society, but it comes packaged with an enormous dose of investment risk that homeowners are almost entirely powerless to insure against or diversify away.[2] Homeowners typically have no other asset, aside from their own human capital, that makes up a larger share of their portfolios.[3] Thus, households routinely plow a hefty chunk of their wealth into what amounts to stock in a single, risky enterprise—the neighborhood housing market.[4] Placing all of the household's eggs in one basket not only runs counter to basic principles of portfolio diversification but also motivates basket-guarding behaviors that can have high social costs.[5] Those behaviors and their costs have been a primary focus of this book.

I have emphasized from the start that many of the factors that give the modern residence its value are located beyond the property's boundaries. We have seen how the tools households and communities employ to control those factors can misfire, creating new tragedies. We can now see how the very manner in which homeownership is configured contributes to the problem that lies at the core of these dilemmas—the mismatch between a homeowner's exposure and her control. Parts II and III worked on this problem from within the traditional paradigm of homeownership. There, I asked how we might design better mechanisms for addressing spillovers at both within-community and between-community scales, operating on the assumption that households would remain exposed to the full measure of positive and negative impacts. In this last part of the book, I rethink that assumption. Even with the best available spillover-management tools in place, households may not be the parties best positioned to bear the residual risks. Accordingly, I consider here the prospects for scaling back the homeowner's exposure to off-site risks that she cannot efficiently bear.

The present unhappy chapter in the U.S. housing experience relates in two important ways to the arguments in this part of the book.[6] First, as we have seen, homeowners whose gambles turn sour may shift some of their losses to other parties. While this might suggest that homeowners are not really forced to take on unwanted risk after all, the mechanism through which the loss-shifting occurs—foreclosure—carries enormous social costs.[7] Managing the risk of home prices is a central problem for all homeowners that should be taken on directly, rather than through a system that haphazardly delivers downside protection to only those borrowers who fail to meet their mortgage repayment obligations. Second, the faulty belief that homeownership must mean shouldering full upside and downside risk has erroneously put homeownership itself in the hot seat. Policy analysts have begun to conclude that homeownership is not an appropriate goal for certain income sectors, without considering the way in which the mandatory risk package makes homeownership's consumption advantages artificially unaffordable.[8] The affordability shortfall that pushed buyers into unsustainable mortgage arrangements (and that will likely shut significant segments of the population out of homeownership in the wake of tightening credit standards) should also be addressed head on, by asking whether homeowners are buying the right product.[9]

Here it becomes important to understand what mortgages can and cannot do for homeowners. Mortgages spread the cost of the home over a hefty chunk of the life cycle—often thirty years. In their usual form (some variations will be discussed below) mortgages do not change the fact that the owner is purchasing the full upside and downside potential of the home. Mortgages only defer payment (at a price); they are not primarily designed to reallocate housing market risk or change what the homeowner is buying. Of course, mortgagees do bear the risk that the borrower will default, and because that risk rises as housing prices fall, lenders bear some of the risk of downward price movements. Indeed, when buyers purchase homes without putting any money down, a default in the face of price declines can leave the entire loss with the lender.[10] Going after the buyer for the difference between the foreclosure sale price and the original loan amount is legally precluded in some states and usually a practical impossibility, given that defaulting homeowners rarely have significant assets apart from their homes.[11] Thus many homeowners receive at least some downside price protection from their lenders as a practical matter. But a household must go through the often traumatic process of foreclosure to take advantage of this implicit protection, which evaporates as soon as the homeowner has enough equity in the home to cover the price drop.

To be sure, homeowners with significant equity built up in their homes may access mortgage products—home equity lines, refinancing, or reverse mortgages—that draw down that equity and place some risk of price declines on lenders. But again, these products are designed and priced to deliver liquidity, not insurance. Reverse mortgages do make downside protection a standard part of the package.[12] But reverse mortgages are available only to older people with equity in their homes who are willing to bear transaction costs to take on debt.[13] While those costs may be worth it for people desiring the reverse mortgage's liquidity benefits, a reverse mortgage is a cumbersome and expensive way to insure against housing market declines if liquidity is not also desired. Moreover, the reverse mortgage does nothing to change what new homebuyers are required to purchase, nor does it help guard against price declines that occur before the reverse mortgage is purchased.

Thus, while mortgages do have some impact on risk-bearing, their primary purpose is to deliver liquidity rather than change the contents of the homeownership package. That package includes a bet on what the local housing market will do. Because this wager has a positive expected value (homes generally appreciate over time), buyers must pay a lot for it—even if that payment is deferred through mortgage arrangements. But the gamble may or may not pay off for the individual household, for reasons outside the household's control. Of course, if we believed that all homeowners were affirmatively choosing to bet most of their household wealth on this single, volatile asset, then the arrangement would be fully satisfactory. Clearly, some investments in the local housing market are quite deliberate. For example, young households that plan to stay in the same area as their housing needs grow may make an early investment in a home as a hedge against future price increases. If home prices rise in the area, appreciation realized from the sale of the first home can help to fund the newly elevated prices of other homes.[14] But it seems likely that many homeowners gamble on the local housing market only by accident, because existing institutional arrangements offer them no alternative.

In this part, I explore the possibility that a reconfiguration of housing bundles can realign a homeowner's exposure to risk with her sphere of effective control. In practical terms, this would mean breaking off some of the upside and downside investment risk associated with homeownership and transferring it to investors who can hold that risk as part of a diversified portfolio. Quite a few proposals, some of which have been implemented in limited ways, have already attempted to do something like this. In the 1970s, Oak Park, Illinois, introduced a homeowner equity assurance program that promised to reimburse homeowners for certain home value changes experienced after a five-year holding period. The program was designed to accomplish a rather specific goal: stemming "white flight" to ensure a stably integrated neighborhood.[15] But the core idea of changing the way that homeownership risk is held can also be seen in recent, broader-gauged innovations. Home equity insurance programs have been implemented in several other areas, and a number of scholars have envisioned a broader role for such products in protecting against price declines.[16] In spring 2006, futures and options based on housing indexes developed by Robert Shiller and Karl E. Case became tradable on the Chicago Mercantile Exchange (now CME Group).[17] These futures and options make it possible for investors to take on risk associated with specific housing markets and could, at least in theory, allow homeowners to shed that risk.

Many other models for reconfiguring homeownership risk exist: shared-appreciation mortgages and other instruments that exchange cash or favorable financing terms for some of the home's appreciation potential; limited equity cooperatives and similar approaches that attempt to deliver affordable housing over time by limiting the amount of equity that each family can draw out of the home on resale; and "housing partnerships" in which an investor shares in the gains and losses experienced by the occupying owner.[18] These and related ideas have enjoyed a recent resurgence, and new products for repackaging homeownership risk continue to appear on the scene.[19] The current housing crisis has helped to fuel this trend, both by raising questions about traditional homeownership and, more immediately and practically, by generating interest in the transfer of homes' appreciation potential as an element in mortgage restructuring. The Housing and Economic Recovery Act of 2008 requires homeowners receiving government-insured refinanced mortgages under the HOPE for Homeowners program to share equity and appreciation with the government when the property is sold or refinanced, and commentators have urged broader application of the idea.[20]

Although innovators and scholars have devoted decades of research to reallocating the investment risk associated with homeownership, the notion has not yet captured the imagination of the general public or that of key institutional players. Recent events have directed new attention to the problem, however, and it is possible that by the time this book appears, new forms of homeownership will have already attracted widespread support. Even if that should happen, however, we might still ask why it took so long. One important reason, I submit, is a failure thus far to ground the idea of risk reconfiguration in a theoretically coherent account of homeownership. In this chapter, I show how looking at the homeowner's entitlement bundle anew through the lens of property theory might point the way to a new, reduced-risk version of homeownership.

Of Buckets and Bundles

Two metaphors made early appearances in this book. Chapter 1 argued that property can be viewed as a bucket of gambles—a repository for collecting risky inputs and their associated outcomes and charging them to the account of a single owner. Chapter 2 examined homeownership as a bundled good that comprises much more than just the house and the plot of land on which it is situated. Considering the relationship between these ideas reveals how changing the content of the bundle might address the mismatch between exposure and control in homeownership.

The bucket metaphor carries an implicit prescriptive message. If the institution of property exists in order to do a job, we can assess how suitable a particular property form is by asking how well it does that job. The best property arrangements, on this view, are those that form the best buckets for collecting inputs and outcomes. To be sure, the best buckets may not be entirely free of leaks and sloshes—the benefits of making them watertight may not justify the added expense.[21] All the same, a bucket with a hole the size of a dinner plate in its bottom is an objectively bad bucket, if it can even be called a bucket at all. Likewise, when property arrangements cannot collect together inputs and outcomes with some regularity, we might view them as failing in a fundamental way. Either we should look for ways to reconfigure property, or we should question whether property is the right doctrinal category with which to address the problem at hand.

Whereas viewing property as a bucket has a prescriptive punch line, the observation that homeownership consists of a bundle is purely descriptive. The fact that certain elements are grouped together does not mean that they must be or should be so grouped. Nonetheless, we can judge whether a bundle is successful or unsuccessful as a property arrangement by assessing how well it groups together inputs under an owner's control with the outcomes suffered or enjoyed by that owner. In other words (and at the risk of mixing metaphors), we can ask: what homeownership bundle makes the best bucket?

Much of the book has focused on the potential for spillovers to occur among properties and, at a larger scale, among subgroups within a larger metropolitan area. Both sets of spillovers can affect quality of life and property values for homeowners. Other factors influence home values as well, such as local, regional, and national housing market trends, which are themselves influenced by factors like employment patterns, lending practices, and interest rates. When all of the off-site factors capable of influencing home values are considered, we see that the outcomes a homeowner experiences may be linked in only a highly attenuated manner to her inputs on the property.[22]

To return to the bucket metaphor, it is as if a Crusoe figure collecting clams in a bucket routinely stored the bucket below the high-tide line. Some of the clams would stay in the bucket, but some would wash out, and other extraneous matter would wash in. When Crusoe takes the bucket home, what it contains bears little relationship to his own clam-digging inputs. In Crusoe's case, the solution is easy: move the bucket to a place where inflows and outflows do not so profoundly interfere with the connection between inputs and outcomes. In the residential context, however, agglomeration benefits make the pursuit of an isolationist strategy unappealing. All our residential buckets, as it were, need to be clustered together where each will inevitably be both the source and the target of spillovers.

At this point it becomes helpful to distinguish between spillovers, which have a local, identifiable source, and larger "tides"—such as regional housing market trends—that cannot be attributed to any proximate actor. Both spillovers and tides influence property values, and both lie beyond the control of any given household. However, only spillovers can be even roughly and imperfectly addressed with the tools discussed in the preceding chapters. Tides, in contrast, defy any form of collective control by homeowners. From the perspective of households, then, tides represent pure risk. There may be gains associated with allowing homeowners to offload both spillover risks and tidal risks to investors. The distinction is useful to keep in mind, however, because of the relatively greater degree of collective control that households typically have over spillovers, and the resultingly broader array of instruments for addressing them.

The Anatomy of Homeownership

Although the bundle that makes up homeownership can be dissected in many different ways, the present analysis focuses on two distinct elements that are purchased by the homebuyer: (1) a consumption stream that lasts as long as she chooses to occupy the home; and (2) an investment in the home itself, the underlying asset that produces the consumption stream.[23] I will discuss each of these components in turn.

Homeownership as Consumption

Households need not buy a home in order to consume housing; they can rent instead. The leasehold neatly separates consumption of housing from investment in housing—the landlord invests, while her tenants consume. We might think, then, that homeowners must be willing investors or they would not be homeowners at all. This logic breaks down, however, if we think that the consumption streams available to tenants tend to be systematically inferior to those available to homeowners. Thus, it is worth considering what the consumption advantages of homeownership might be.

A much-cited advantage of owning a home is the element of price protection it provides. In housing markets without rent control, tenants face significant uncertainty about the price that they must pay to continue consuming housing in their current location.[24] The rental amount is guaranteed to remain fixed only for the lease term, often a year or less, and may rise thereafter without warning. As advocates of rent control have noted, this uncertainty poses a threat to the plans of residents who wish to put down roots in a given area with an expectation of building a life there.[25] In contrast, the purchase price that a household pays for a home is fixed at the time of purchase, and will not rise thereafter.

On closer examination, however, the homeowner's price protection looks less impressive. Most homebuyers finance their purchases, and credit arrangements can introduce price instability. While mortgages have traditionally offered unbeatable price protection (an equal sum due each month for up to thirty years), the widespread use of adjustable rate mortgages and other nontraditional loan products have exposed many households to large increases in their monthly payments.[26] Homeowners experience other threats to stable housing consumption as well. Homeowners' insurance, required by lenders, can spike upward in cost. Property taxes can rise rapidly and unexpectedly. Maintenance and repair costs can be large and unpredictable. Finally, and perhaps most important, the homeowner may want or need to move. When she does, her ability to obtain a comparable stream of housing consumption elsewhere depends on the price at which her current home sells, a price that is subject to great investment risk.[27]

Still, tenants face another form of uncertainty that is different in kind. At least in the absence of limitations imposed by law, a landlord can sell the property, convert the property to some other use, or decide to occupy it herself as a residence—all events that will physically displace the tenant.[28] While property sales and conversions would be subject to existing leases, most residential lease terms are too short to provide meaningful protection. All homeowners thus possess something very valuable—the option to remain in their current home for as long as they wish, provided they make the necessary mortgage and tax payments. This option is not absolute— it can be overridden by the government through eminent domain or nullified by other factors that make continued habitation impossible—but it is very robust. Indeed, the negative popular reaction to the exercise of eminent domain in *Kelo v. City of New London* suggests the degree to which people associate homeownership with the option to stay put.[29]

In addition, renters are often constrained in matters such as pet keeping, decorating, and landscaping. Often, they cannot add occupants (other than their own children) to the household or sublease the property without permission.[30] While the autonomy of homeowners over such matters has also become increasingly limited as common interest communities featuring tight restrictions have gained market share, owners still generally enjoy greater latitude than renters in choosing how to use and modify the residence.[31] Perhaps more important, homebuyers enjoy a wider set of housing choices than do tenants. In many areas, rental housing stock is dominated by multifamily housing units, with relatively few detached single-family homes available for rent. A household that wishes to locate in a particular size and type of single-family home within a specific neighborhood may find the pickings to be slim indeed. Most of the single-family housing stock in the country is owner occupied, and owners tend to sell their homes when they move rather than offer them for rent.[32]

In addition, rental houses are likely to receive less care and attention, on average, from their owners and occupants, making it less likely that pristine homes will appear on the rental market. As Derek Chau and his coauthors have observed, leaseholds present a "double moral hazard problem."[33] The tenant might be expected to neglect the owner's long-term interests in the property (for example, by taking too little care to avoid damaging the floors). Likewise, the owner might be expected to neglect aspects of the tenant's consumption stream that do not affect the property's value over the long run (for example, by stinting on heat during the winter or delaying minor repairs). A "lemons" dynamic may amplify these phenomena.[34] Tenants who cannot tell ex ante whether a given rental package (including landlord-provided services) is high quality or low quality will only be willing to pay for an average-quality rental package. Because tenant price resistance makes it unprofitable for landlords to offer high-quality packages, the average quality of rentals will drop. Likewise, if tenants have unobservable characteristics that determine how much care they will take of the home, landlords will gravitate toward price-amenity combinations that will be profitable when average-care tenants move in. High-care tenants will find these price-amenity combinations less attractive, and will have an incentive to abandon the rental market and become homeowners.[35]

At least in theory, many of the disadvantages of renting could be resolved contractually through different lease provisions. Residential leases could be extended to terms lasting several decades, for example, and could delegate to the tenant free choice on a wide array of matters that customarily have been left to the discretion of homeowners. While contractual provisions alone would not expand the spectrum of available rental housing, if lease-holds became increasingly attractive along the dimensions just suggested, tenants would be expected to bid up rents and eventually trigger an expansion in the supply of housing stock available for lease. But there are two additional advantages that better leases cannot currently provide.

First, homeowners enjoy significant federal income tax benefits that tenants do not receive. Homeowners pay no tax on imputed rent—the amount of rental income that the home would generate if it were rented out. Yet they can deduct their major expenses (mortgage interest and property taxes) if they itemize.[36] Homeowners can also receive hundreds of thousands of dollars in tax-free gains on the sales of their homes.[37] These tax benefits reduce the cost of consuming owner-occupied housing, at least for those positioned on the upper rungs of the income ladder.[38] Of course, tax advantages are a little different from the other consumption advantages of homeownership, because they can be directly addressed through policy changes. Indeed, it is quite possible that the tax advantages tip the tenure-choice balance just enough to keep the sorts of lease reforms discussed above from being worth the expense of developing and marketing. If this is so, many of the consumption differences between owning and renting would disappear if tax advantages were withdrawn.[39] But while it is not implausible that the tax treatment of homeownership could be changed in ways that would make it less regressive and distortive than it is at present, fully erasing the tax advantages of homeownership seems beyond the realm of current political possibility.[40] Even eliminating the mortgage interest deduction would not produce the desired effects on its own given the ability of some households (especially those with high incomes) to finance their home purchases through other means (say, by paying cash) while still enjoying the core tax advantage—nontaxation of imputed rent.[41]

Beyond tax advantages, the notion of "ownership" carries tremendous psychological appeal in the United States, making homeownership a pervasive aspirational goal. Renting, in contrast, is widely viewed as a transitional state.[42] Here, too, we must ask what underlies the impulse toward ownership. The desire for a stable option—a place that is one's home for as long as one chooses to stay there, and that one can pass down to one's descendents—is certainly part of the story. The other advantages noted above also likely play a role. Yet, there may be something essential about claiming a place as one's own that cannot be reduced to these practical benefits. That essential element of ownership may be related in complex ways to the investment facet of homeownership, or at least to some aspects of it.

Homeownership as an Investment

Homebuyers do not just purchase a consumption stream, they also make an investment. This investment is typically the single largest entry in the household's portfolio, and it is often heavily leveraged.[43] Do homeowners seek out this level of investment exposure, or do they merely tolerate it? If homeownership routinely produces a consumption stream superior to renting, the decision to buy rather than rent would seem to tell us little about how much owners value (or dislike) the investment component. Economic analysis suggests, however, that homeowners would invest differently—and more efficiently—if they had full freedom to allocate their investment dollars between housing and non-housing investments.[44]

Nonetheless, the homeownership consumption stream is one that, by definition, allows the owner to view herself as an owner. Presumably some level of investment is necessary to enjoy in an authentic manner the consumption good of homeownership. But how much? Clearly, the personal shouldering of all risks cannot be a prerequisite to our understanding of ownership. Homeowners typically carry insurance to offload risks of casualty losses that they cannot efficiently bear, yet no one would suggest that an insured home is any less fully "owned." Similarly, most homeowners have a mortgage on the property that places some investment risk on the lender, as discussed above. Yet the existence of substantial mortgage debt does not usually call the title of "homeowner" into question.

A better way of understanding the homeowner's relationship to risk is found in the notion of the property holder as the "residual claimant"—the party who bears any property-related risks that have not been placed on others through contracts or legal rules.[45] That formulation, however, does not tell us anything about the kinds of risk (if any) to which a homeowner must remain exposed in order to be regarded as, and to view herself as, the property's owner. To approach the problem from a different angle, consider Henry Smith's explanation of why owners are residual claimants in the first place. Smith observes that a residual claim captures difficult-to-measure contributions. Thus, the party whose inputs are "hardest to measure" will be treated as the residual claimant or owner—the one who gets whatever outcomes remain after all the other, easier-to-measure claims have been sorted out.[46]

To translate these ideas into the homeownership context, it is helpful to distinguish between sources of property value fluctuation that are within the household's control and sources of variance that are beyond the household's control. The former relate to the household's own day-to-day inputs—things like maintenance and decorating choices—which typically will be hard for others to measure accurately. Indeed, this very difficulty in measurement presents moral hazard problems when responsibility for outcomes under the household's control are shifted to third parties.[47] The idea that factors under the household's control produce the residual for which it bears responsibility fits well with the intuition that investment in the gains and losses that accompany the household's own choices lie at the core of homeownership.

In contrast, local, regional, or national movements in housing prices involve the inputs of others, and seem attenuated from the core of ownership. Just as owners need not gamble on fires or natural disasters in order to be true owners, we might also think that they need not gamble on these other factors occurring beyond the edges of the parcel. If, however, there were no cost-effective way to disaggregate the impacts of these factors from a homeowner's own difficult-to-measure inputs, we might nonetheless be required to make these risks part of the owner's residual package. Although such disaggregation is likely to be very challenging, innovations like local housing indexes may soon bring the price within reach.[48]

If separating out risks that lie beyond the household's control becomes technically feasible at reasonable cost, doing so would not seem to present any intrinsic threat to the notion of ownership. To be sure, some homeowners will wish to take on the risk associated with home price movements outside their control, just as they might wish to engage in any other outside investment opportunity. But a household should not be required to purchase what amounts to a specific number of shares in an undiversified index fund—the local housing market—simply because it desires a particular level of housing consumption. Indeed, it would be mere happenstance if a family's optimal investment in home price movements turned out to correspond precisely to the purchase price of the home that best fits that family's consumption needs.

Thus, we can understand the traditional purchase of a home to be made up of three components: the purchase of a consumption stream, the purchase of rights to the gains and losses associated with inputs under the household's control, and the purchase of the rights to gains and losses associated with factors beyond the household's control. The first two components are conceptually linked and together make up the core of what it means to be a homeowner; the third component lies outside this core. If the third element is so tightly entwined with the others that disaggregation cannot be accomplished cost-effectively, it is efficient for the three parts to stay together. But if innovations loosen these binds, removing the third part from the bundle deserves fresh consideration. Of course, keeping this third component in the homeownership bundle is not problematic to the extent that markets exist that allow the household to alienate unwanted risk. Households are already able to buy protection against uncontrollable threats that may materialize on site (fires, storm damage, and so on). But there is no broadly available mechanism addressing risks associated with off-site factors beyond the household's control, such as housing market changes at the local, regional, or national level.

The analysis thus far has emphasized that some households may wish to accept less risk associated with off-site factors than is required by the traditional homeownership package. But other households (including some who do not own their own homes) might wish to invest at a greater level in a given local housing market than would be feasible through the traditional homeownership model. Returning to the Rainbow Cone example with which this chapter began, a mandatory linkage between investment and consumption would have effects beyond discouraging ice cream consumption by those who did not wish to make an investment in the company. If investors in Rainbow Cone were forced to eat an amount of ice cream corresponding to their ownership shares in the business, we would expect consumption considerations to cap the size of the investment that anyone would be willing to make in the product. So too in the case of owner-occupied housing.

Of course, investors can invest in more housing than they wish to consume if they are willing to enter a landlord-tenant relationship, with its attendant moral hazards.[49] But investment in *owner-occupied* housing, which presumes the presence of an owner-occupant who can be trusted to keep up the house to the investor's standards, currently requires the investor to occupy the property herself. A market that would enable some homeowners to consume beyond their investments would also allow other homeowners—or, indeed, nonhomeowners—to invest in more owner-occupied housing than they personally wish to consume. The fact that our current system of homeownership tethers together consumption of housing with full investment in housing thus creates not one but two sources of potential suboptimality in homeownership.

The discussion above, consistent with a good deal of past scholarship, suggests that many homeowners could enjoy gains if the consumption and investment components of homeownership were not yoked together so inflexibly. Questions remain, however, about the interaction between the consumption and investment elements of homeownership, and the degree to which these components can and should be unbundled.

Building a New Version of Homeownership

Suppose we wanted to introduce a new form of homeownership— call it Homeownership 2.0, or "H2.0" for short—that offers homebuyers a greater degree of choice about investment risks.[50] How would we shape this new alternative? Putting aside for a moment the practicalities of implementation, what kind of homeownership bundle would make good theoretical sense if we were writing on a clean slate? The discussion to this point has emphasized a number of binary distinctions that may be relevant to this exercise—between owning and renting, consuming and investing, on-site and off-site factors, factors under the household's control and those beyond the household's control, tides and spillovers. Figure 8-1

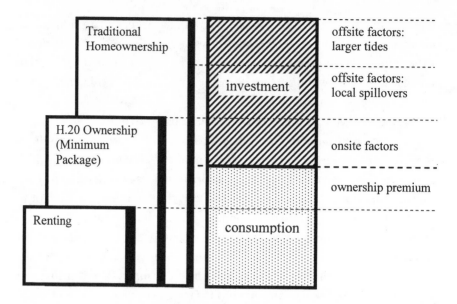

Figure 8-1. Components of homeownership

makes a start at showing how these factors relate to each other and to the construction of a new form of homeownership.

Figure 8-1 begins with the well-established observation that traditional homeownership is made up of both consumption and investment components. Although these two categories are presented as distinct blocks, there is actually some overlap between them. Until the owner dies or moves out, some of her housing consumption will be in the future, representing a form of savings.[51] The value of those savings—that is, the enjoyment that the owner will realize through future consumption of housing—can fluctuate. In this sense, at least, even an intensely consumption-minded homeowner who plans to live in her home for the rest of her life is nevertheless an investor. Still, it is possible to draw at least a rough distinction between the investment value of the home and its consumption value. As Figure 8-1 shows, each of these components can then be subdivided further.

The dashed line cutting through the "consumption" box distinguishes between elements of consumption achievable through renting and those unique to homeownership. The latter elements of consumption represent a type of "ownership premium." If leaseholds were improved in certain ways, this dashed line (and the top edge of the "renting" box) would move upward. The distinction would not disappear entirely, however, at least to the extent that "ownership" continues to carry some consumption cachet by conferring higher status and other benefits. Some elements of this ownership premium may require a certain degree of investment. In other words, there may be no conceptually coherent tenure form that would snap off cleanly at the top edge of the consumption box; to get all of those benefits, one must pick up more of the homeownership bundle.

The dashed lines running through the "investment" box indicate that the investment portion of homeownership comprises several categories of risks. The lower portion of the box contains risks associated with on-site factors. Most of these on-site factors lie within the household's direct control, but some do not—for example, a fire caused by a lightning strike. Nonetheless, households are in a good position to procure insurance against such events, because they will play out (or not) on the household's individual parcel. The balance of the investment box is split into two categories of off-site factors: local spillovers and larger tides. While this dichotomy is something of a simplification, I mean to distinguish here between the sorts of impacts with an identifiable local source that would be amenable to control by homeowners acting collectively and larger social and economic forces that lie beyond the capacity of local homeowners, even acting collectively, to control.

Comparing the bar marked "traditional homeownership" in Figure 8-1 with the one marked "renting" reveals a large gap in housing bundles. One must choose between the level of consumption available through renting or accept the full array of investment risks through traditional homeownership. Andrew Caplin and his coauthors capture the dilemma well: "The 'all or nothing' constraint on home ownership forces households to make the stark choice between rental accommodations' disadvantages and complete ownership's harsh financial realities."[52] To address this gap, Figure 8-1 depicts a third, intermediate choice—H2.0 ownership. The next chapter explores this proposed new tenure form in more detail. In brief, homeowners would be offered a default package that would include, at a minimum, investment risk associated with on-site factors. They could then customize their housing bundles by selectively adding in investment risk associated with off-site factors to the extent desired.

H2.0, as depicted in Figure 8-1, is not the only possible way of responding to the existing gap between renting and owning. Two alternatives raised by the categories presented in Figure 8-1 deserve special consideration. First, we might imagine reforming leaseholds and changing other elements of social policy (including tax policy) so that the ownership premium is minimized. Indeed, leases could even be constructed in such a manner as to give tenants some stake in the investment returns associated with the households' acts and omissions on the premises. Moral hazard issues with leaseholds remain difficult to address, however, and political and cultural obstacles loom even larger.[53] Longer and better leaseholds and reform of homeownership's tax advantages are worthy goals, and ones that might in the long run help to produce a society that is less enamored of ownership. But taking the world as we find it, with strong social and governmental pressures pushing households toward ownership, improved leaseholds are not the most promising answer for filling the existing gap on the tenure spectrum.

A second possibility would include in the new tenure form's minimum bundle not only the risks associated with on-site factors but also the risks attributable to one subset of off-site factors—local spillovers amenable to collective control by homeowners. Homeowners as a group wield significant control over block-level, neighborhood, and local conditions through the use of norms, politics, exit options, and direct participation in the collective production of local public goods. Indeed, homeowners might be instrumental in crafting and implementing some of the innovative responses to externalities that we explored earlier in the book. We might wonder, then, whether our new tenure form should leave homeowners exposed to investment risks associated with local spillovers, to ensure that they do not become less effective as citizens and neighbors. Although I ultimately answer the question in the negative, it is a difficult one that requires thinking through the implications of moving local risks from homeowners to other investors.

Risk Exposure, Local Participation, and Politics

Transferring investment risk associated with local factors from homeowners to investors would be expected to produce a number of changes in local participation and politics. It is helpful first to consider the impacts on homeowner incentives, and then turn to some larger implications of having investors as local stakeholders.

Homeowner Behavior: The Good, the Bad, and the Ugly

If homeowners' concerns about resale values motivate much of their local collective behavior, scaling back their risk exposure should dampen their incentives to act collectively through formal and informal channels to maintain and enhance property values. These incentive changes would have a variety of effects. At present, homeowners act collectively both for good (resolving local collective action problems or building bonds among neighbors in ways that are socially valuable on net) and for ill (excluding outsiders or offloading externalities onto them in ways that are socially costly on net). Based on the net impacts, we can refer to these two categories of collective control as "value enhancing" and "value reducing," respectively. Historically, a good deal of the behavior in the latter category has been not only bad but also ugly, the product of biases and prejudices. We must consider the impact of changes in homeownership on behavior falling in both broad categories.

In *The Homevoter Hypothesis*, William Fischel explores some of the more desirable facets of homeowners' intense interest in their homes' values.[54] Fischel observes that a desire to maximize home values underlies local political behavior, and he suggests that homeowners' politics generally inure to the benefit of the community and society at large. For example, Fischel observes that even a homeowner without children (or any prospect of children) will nonetheless be concerned about the quality of the local public schools, given the expected impact of school quality on her home's resale value.[55] More generally, we might expect homeowners with a financial stake in a given community to do more to advance the fortunes of that community—perhaps by participating in neighborhood watches, or otherwise helping to police and enforce behavioral and aesthetic norms.

While these arguments are important ones, they do not support forcing homeowners to accept investment risks associated with local conditions. Indeed, Fischel himself has advocated the use of home equity insurance to reduce fear-driven behavior by homeowners.[56] H2.0 as formulated here would leave the homeowner exposed to risks to the consumption stream itself, whether emanating from on-site or off-site factors. Thus, we would expect H2.0 homeowners to continue to make localized investments in the community that will pay dividends in kind through the flow of housing services they consume. For example, homeowners will want to keep the neighborhood clean and crime-free for their own consumption reasons, even if they will not bear the downside loss on resale associated with the neighborhood's deterioration. It is true that the exit option becomes less costly to the homeowner who becomes dissatisfied with her neighborhood, because she will not bear the full loss associated with a downward trend in prices. But the protection against downside loss on resale also makes staying less risky, and hence less costly.

It is also important to note that H2.0 would be expected to attract some households that would otherwise choose to rent, as well as some households that would otherwise opt for traditional homeownership. If tenants are deemed to be less engaged neighbors and community members than owners (on average), the move from tenancy to H2.0 would be an improvement.[57] Even though H2.0 owners will not own all of the risk associated with their investment, they hold an option to stay in the community as long as they wish, and would therefore not be discouraged (as tenants presumably are) from making site-specific investments in the community.

We must also consider the effects of diminished investment stakes on value-reducing behavior. Buffering home investment risk may protect society from the socially damaging actions that homeowners driven by unchosen risk might undertake. This was the impetus behind the early versions of home equity insurance, and it explains recent efforts to use such insurance to stem "not-in-my-backyard" (NIMBY) impulses. Free of the fear accompanying undiversified home value risk, the argument runs, homeowners will no longer pursue socially costly collective actions.[58] While this is an extraordinarily important potential benefit, it is subject to two important qualifications.

First, the consumption interest that H2.0 homeowners would continue to have in their homes might still cause them to undertake socially costly collective actions. But, importantly, it would alter the rhetoric surrounding such actions. Currently, homeowners can justify positions on local issues that would otherwise appear indefensible on the grounds of "preserving property values." For example, a homeowner who maintains that she does not personally mind having a homeless shelter or low-income housing project in her neighborhood may nonetheless oppose the shelter or project on the grounds that prospective buyers to whom she will need to resell her home several years hence may be less enlightened.[59] A homeowner who is exposed only to consumption stream effects from such developments, and not to the chance of resale value diminution, could no longer blame her actions on the supposed prejudices of others.

There is a second qualification, however. H2.0 lets homeowners shift risk onto investors who are in a position to diversify that risk away, but it does not eliminate the investors' incentives to avoid taking losses on the investment. In other words, granting households the capacity to transfer unwanted investment risk elsewhere does not eliminate financial stakes in the community but instead merely creates a new class of stakeholders. Will these new stakeholders behave any better than the old ones? This question, and the broader implications of risk reallocation, can best be approached by revisiting some ideas introduced earlier in the book.

Risk Reallocation, Tragedies, and the Semicommons

The tragedies of the commons and anticommons that were the focus of earlier chapters would not evaporate just because homeowners scale back their investment risk. Actors will still have incentives to undertake actions that are individually profitable but collectively harmful, and efforts to counter those tendencies—themselves capable of producing further tragedy—will not disappear. Reallocating risk would, however, change the identities of the parties who stand to gain and lose the most when things go wrong in neighborhoods, municipalities, and metropolitan areas. This change in identity could alter both incentives and behavior, as I will explain. But one important element would not change: investors, like homeowners, are not keen on suffering losses.

At least in theory, investors can do a better job of pooling and diversifying away risk than can individual households. For investors, the fact that particular housing markets exhibit high variance in possible outcomes should not be problematic, whereas it may be decidedly so for risk-averse homeowners. However, no amount of pooling and diversifying can transform a low expected value event into a high expected value event. If a particular change or practice in a local area would unambiguously reduce property values, an investor would be no happier with the prospect of that occurrence than would a homeowner.

Thus, we might expect investors, just like homeowners, to demand land use controls designed to preserve property values. While investors may not be able to vote locally, they can express their demands through price signals to homeowners who wish to purchase protection against downside risk or to sell upside potential. These price signals could even reintroduce the phenomenon of homeowners distancing themselves rhetorically from the positions that they take on local matters—instead of referring to a risk to property values, homeowners might refer to risk of unfavorable price changes in their dealings with investors.[60] Alternatively, as special interests with a high stake in a community's future, investor groups might be able to wield political power to obtain these results directly, notwithstanding their inability to vote locally.

Would we expect the rigidity of land use controls critiqued in Part II to continue unabated, or perhaps even be worsened, by the involvement of investors? Would we also expect the same kinds of socially damaging exclusionary measures that were the focus of Part III? In short, would anything change for the better? Although any answers must be tentative at this stage, there are several reasons why reallocating risk might reduce certain kinds of problematic land use actions. First, as Fischel has suggested, homeowners may oppose projects because of the high variance in outcomes, not because of low expected value.[61] Diversification works well when the real problem is risk aversion, rather than a desire to avoid an occurrence with a negative expected value. Second, investors are at a physical and emotional remove from the local neighborhood and have consciously chosen to take on a certain level of risk. Hence, they should be less vulnerable to overblown fears or group hysteria about changes that are actually unlikely to produce negative results. Third, and perhaps most important, investors are more likely than individual homeowners to hold offsetting interests in other properties or entities. If the mark of NIMBY-ism is narrow self-interest that pushes externalities onto others, investors who also hold positions in nearby neighborhoods, localities, and entities would be less inclined toward such behaviors.

The resulting benefits can be best understood through the lens of the semicommons. As Henry Smith has explained, medieval grazing and farming arrangements constituted a semicommons; the land was shared in common for purposes of grazing, but farming strips were individually owned. The farming strips held by a given owner were scattered throughout the grazing field. The scattered arrangement has been attributed to various purposes, such as diversification of risk, but Smith emphasizes its role in controlling strategic behavior. Spatially interspersing the holdings of many different owners neutralizes each owner's temptation to use the commons in a way that would selectively offload costs onto the farmland of others or selectively direct benefits to her own land.[62]

Neighborhoods, localities, and metropolitan areas can similarly be viewed as semicommons regimes. Individual households own parcels of land, but many elements of value are held in common by a larger group. These semicommons regimes largely lack the protection against strategic behavior that marked medieval grazing and farming arrangements. The politically powerless and impoverished are likely to be spatially concentrated, enabling wealthier and more powerful citizens to selectively burden, or fail to benefit, those areas. Although subject to debate, concerns about geographic targeting have arisen in contexts involving the siting of locally undesirable land uses, the provision of public goods and services, and, of course, the exercise of eminent domain.[63]

Slicing up interests in owner-occupied property and dispersing the slices among investors helps to sever the link between self-interest and geography. It is at least possible that the result will be a better-functioning political process in which a larger percentage of the population holds interdependent residential interests. I do not want to overstate this point. The interests of investors may diverge from those of homeowners in many ways, and making interests more diffuse may dilute incentives to become involved in any particular dispute. Yet, intertwining interests seem likely to ease the isolation and powerlessness of the most vulnerable communities.

An important empirical question is whether investments would actually tend to take this scattered form, or whether investors would instead attempt to acquire heavily concentrated interests in particular communities so as to wield more power in the local political process. If investor capture were viewed as a sufficient threat to local governance, it could be countered through regulatory policy. For example, limits might be placed on the fraction of holdings within a given jurisdiction that could be held by a single investor, or H2.0 investments above a given dollar amount might automatically bundle together geographically disparate holdings that represent substantively similar types and levels of housing risk.[64]

We know that homeownership has come unbound from the edges of the owned parcel. Finding better tools for reaching outward to control spillovers constitutes only one approach, however. Another tack, which has been explored in a preliminary way here, is to scale back the homeowner's exposure so that it better aligns with the factors under her control.

If unwanted elements of risk could be perfectly filtered out of homeownership, what homeowners paid at the time of purchase would be net of the expected value of those elements, and what they received on resale would be net of the actual impact of those elements on the resale price. Accomplishing such filtering with a reasonable degree of accuracy presents practical difficulties that are considerable, although probably not insurmountable. In addition, a reduced-risk version of homeownership can only take hold if formidable cognitive and cultural obstacles to altering homeownership investment arrangements can be surmounted. People bring entrenched sets of expectations to the institution of homeownership, and changing familiar features of the arrangement is likely to generate suspicion and resistance. The next chapter examines the possibility of a new form of homeownership in greater depth, addressing these and other concerns.

9

HOMEOWNERSHIP, VERSION 2.0

Altering the risks associated with homeownership is no mere thought experiment. The idea has been around for decades, but academic and popular interest in realizing it on a broader scale has greatly intensified in recent years.[1] The introduction of derivatives markets based on local housing market indexes should soon make it feasible for homeowners to shield themselves from off-site threats to home values and to alienate the appreciation potential attributable to off-site factors. The previous chapter offered a theoretical account of how these sorts of changes in risk-bearing might fit together with this book's thesis and with other mechanisms for managing extraparcel effects on home values. In this chapter, I explore the potential for a reduced-risk form of homeownership in greater detail. After outlining the basics of a new form of tenure—Homeownership 2.0, or "H2.0"—I turn to its cognitive and social implications.

H2.0 Basics

H2.0 is built around a distinction between two kinds of influences on home values: on-site factors (such as remodeling, maintenance, and landscaping choices) and off-site factors (occurrences, events, and conditions beyond the four corners of the parcel, such as housing market fluctuations). Just like traditional homeownership, H2.0 assigns all the gains and losses associated with on-site factors to the homeowner. But H2.0 differs radically in its treatment of off-site influences on home values. At closing, a homebuyer is metaphorically presented with two dials that represent his ownership of the upside and downside components, respectively, of off-site price volatility. Under traditional homeownership, all of the downside risk and upside potential is assigned to the homeowner; in other words, both dials are stuck at 100 percent and do not adjust. Under H2.0, both dials are reset to 0 percent (or some other value) by default with respect to off-site factors, but the homeowner can adjust them.[2] In economic substance, the move from 100 percent to 0 percent means that the homeowner compensates an investor to take on off-site downside risk, while an investor compensates the homeowner and receives the off-site upside potential. Under the default arrangement, however, the homeowner would simply encounter an interface that repriced the home to take these changes into account. He could then twist either or both dials to selectively add back in as much upside and downside risk relating to off-site factors as he wished to accept.

Allowing a homebuyer to transfer off-site factor volatility to an investor who can hold it as part of a diversified portfolio offers an untapped opportunity to produce Pareto improvements.[3] Potential advantages for homeowners would include reduced risk, increased housing affordability, and greater portfolio choice.[4] For investors, H2.0 offers the chance to purchase a stake in owner-occupied housing without consuming that housing. Significantly, H2.0 would achieve these advantages not through a stand-alone product that chips away at homeownership but rather through a new and theoretically well-grounded alternative form of tenure. Such a new version of homeownership represents a broad-spectrum response to a central tension emphasized throughout this book—between a boundary-oriented understanding of ownership and the reality of homeownership as it exists on the ground.

This is an apt historical moment for such a proposal. Home values have shown themselves to be vulnerable to downside risk, while lending practices, especially in the subprime market, have injected high levels of price instability into repayment schedules.[5] With millions of U.S. homeowners facing foreclosure, the wisdom of the national obsession with homeownership has been called into question.[6] The answer is not to ditch homeownership, I suggest, but rather to reconfigure it to deliver on its promises.

Looking under the Hood

The moving parts inside H2.0—market mechanisms for offloading homeownership risk—are the ongoing work of others. My focus here is not on perfecting the technical elements of these underlying risk transfer mechanisms but rather on explaining how a reformulated tenure package could deliver the benefits of these innovations to ordinary homeowners in a manner congruent with property theory, human cognition, and the social goals of communities. Nonetheless, we must look behind H2.0's user-friendly dials to understand a little more about how risk transfers themselves would work. A stylized example will help to illustrate the basic mechanics behind H2.0, as well as some of the design challenges that such a program would have to confront.

Agatha, a homeowner who lives in the town of Doldrums, fears declining home values. Her house is currently appraised at $200,000, and she would like to be sure she can sell it for at least $200,000 five years from now, when she plans to move. One way to do this would be to buy a "put option" on her house that gives her the right to force a sale at the price of $200,000 in five years' time. However, such put options do not exist, for good reason—the problem of moral hazard. Nobody is willing to promise to buy Agatha's house for $200,000 five years from now, because Agatha can directly affect her home's value through her own choices.[7] At the right price, however, an investor would be willing to sell her the right to receive, five years hence, a percentage of $200,000 that is proportionate to any general decline in housing values within Doldrums.

Suppose Agatha buys such an instrument, a put option keyed to a housing index for Doldrums, from Blake. Following a spate of local plant closings, Doldrums experiences a 10 percent decline in home values. Agatha should still be able to sell her home for $180,000, assuming that she has not made any unfortunate decorating choices or failed to maintain the property (factors under her own control). In addition, Agatha can exercise her put option and receive $20,000, an amount that represents the drop in home values attributable to market risk. The $180,000 sales price added to the $20,000 in insurance proceeds amounts to the $200,000 she originally paid for the house; she has been able perfectly to hedge the risk of a market decline (setting aside the problem of inflation).

It would also be possible for Agatha to transact with an investor with respect to the home's upside potential. Suppose Cody believes that the housing prices will rise in Doldrums, and is willing to bet on it. Instead of going to Doldrums, buying a house, and waiting for it to appreciate, Cody might instead buy a call option from Agatha that gives him the right to receive, say, $2,000 for each percentage point increase in home values that Doldrums experiences over the next five-year period. Assuming Agatha's house value moves in concert with the housing market as reflected in the Doldrums housing index, she will realize enough from her home's sale to cover the required payout to Cody. Meanwhile, she can use the money Cody pays her for the call option to invest in more diversified holdings or reduce her mortgage balance. Indeed, she may use some of the proceeds from her sale of the call option to Cody to finance her purchase of a put option from Blake that will pay out if home values drop in Doldrums.

Agatha might also transact with the same investor (say, Blake) as to both the call option and the put option. Such an arrangement would be identical to Blake buying futures in the local housing market from Agatha. I break apart the two transactions here to emphasize the flexibility of financial instruments to transfer risk selectively. It is precisely this flexibility that would enable an H2.0 homebuyer to independently adjust the upside and downside dials of her home investment. Assuming robust trading in the local housing market, information about expected price movements should be efficiently aggregated, and each of these options priced accordingly.

Of course, most homeowners do not plan a move on a date certain in the future but rather wish to be protected against price fluctuations over the entire (unknown) period that they will own the house, however long or short it turns out to be. Short-term calls and puts might either be made available on a rolling basis or triggered by life events (such as sale of a home) that are unpredictable in the individual case but predictable in the aggregate.[8] With a few such modifications, instruments that are used to hedge risk could be marketed directly to homeowners.

Some important design challenges remain. As the example above suggested, housing indexes can work well in theory to separate off-site factors from on-site factors. But designing such indexes is not easy. The more thinly an index is sliced, the more capable it will be of drawing fine distinctions among homes, but the less well it will work as a basis for trading. The smaller the number of observations in a particular index and the fewer the market participants trading on that index, the less liquid and accurate it will be.[9] The same design tension surfaces in efforts to disaggregate on-site and off-site influences on value. An index that perfectly tracked one particular home would of course reintroduce full consideration of on-site factors. At the other extreme, a nationwide housing index that aggregated all owner-occupied housing would do a poor job of capturing regional and local off-site influences. In between these extremes, there are questions about whether any given housing index will pick up too much of what owners are doing on their own parcels (such as a rash of home improvements within a particular neighborhood) or too little of what is happening outside the parcel (such as highly localized undesirable land uses).[10]

These concerns illustrate "basis risk," which Shiller and Weiss define "as the risk that fluctuations in the home price index will not match up well with fluctuations in the price of the home that are beyond the homeowners' control."[11] Basis risk is a real concern, because it could keep H2.0 from working as advertised for homeowners. First, consider a household that purchases downside protection only. Assume the home's value falls for reasons that have nothing to do with the household's parcel-specific actions or omissions. Ideally, the index would fall by the same amount. But if it did not, and if payouts were made based on the index alone, the difference between the loss (if any) shown by the index and the actual loss the household experienced on reselling its home would amount to a failure in the product's protection.

Basis risk takes on an even more worrisome cast when the household sells upside potential, either alone or in combination with the purchase of downside protection. Consider a scenario in which the index reflects a larger gain than is experienced by the homeowner, and the difference between the resale price as actually experienced and as predicted by the index is an artifact of imprecision in the index rather than the result of any actions or omissions on the part of the household. If settlements were determined by the index alone, the householder would have to pay out the share of gains reflected in the index even though he did not realize those gains. An even more catastrophic manifestation of basis risk would occur if the index showed a gain while the home itself actually sold at a loss. Not only would an index-based payout system fail to protect against downside loss, it would add insult to injury by requiring someone in a loss position to make a payout for gains.

Because of these problems, index use would require supplementation in order to avoid anomalous results. One approach would use local housing indexes to generate raw payoff figures that could then be adjusted as needed to address basis risk. An additional layer of insurance might be used to accomplish this, as Shiller and Weiss have suggested.[12] Payouts on the "basis" insurance could be contingent either on verification of differential local conditions or on an investigation that rules out the possibility that negative on-site factors—such as neglect, destruction, an extraordinarily rapid sale, or a sale that was not conducted at arm's length—were responsible for the outcome. The insurer in this story could even develop schedules of recommended maintenance and acceptable sales practices, which the homeowner might be required to follow (and document) in order to make out a basis risk claim. As an alternative method for dealing with moral hazard at the time of sale, recovery under the insurance policy could be made contingent on a right of first refusal. The homeowner might, for example, be required to extend the insurer a put option to acquire the home at a price slightly higher than the proposed sales price during, say, a ten-day window. The reason for the premium and the short time fuse would be to avoid discouraging buyers from writing a contract on an H2.0 home.[13]

These design issues are only a few of the many that would have to be confronted in translating the H2.0 concept into a workable policy. Myriad technical factors go into constructing a workable local housing index.[14] Similarly, many other crucial operational details—from the timing of payouts to the income tax and property tax treatment of H2.0 homeownership—would require close attention. I leave these important matters undiscussed here to focus on the broader theoretical, cognitive, and societal implications of introducing a new tenure form.[15] I do so in part because the sophisticated work that others have conducted (and continue to conduct) on these questions suggests that the technical and operational sticking points are not, ultimately, insurmountable.

Off the Rack or Build from Scratch?

If shifting risk from homeowners to investors can produce important gains, the question remains how best to go about accomplishing those transfers. Innovative tools such as housing market derivatives could be used to reach the target that property theory suggests is the right one—narrowing homeowner investment risk to on-site factors, which are either under the homeowner's control or efficient for the homeowner to insure against. What, then, would be the point of introducing a new tenure form like H2.0? If we already have (or will soon have) the technical capacity to reshape home investment risk in endlessly flexible ways, why not let the market supply an assortment of products for modifying traditional homeownership, and let consumers choose exactly which ones they wish to use? In theory, the raw materials of risk transfer could be used to build from scratch something that resembles my idea of H2.0 as well as any number of alternatives. My case for the H2.0 package as a new starting point for homeownership is based on three considerations: its compatibility with property theory, its ability to serve as a focal point for the further development of law, and its cognitive role in facilitating widespread acceptance of new risk allocation arrangements.

First, introducing H2.0 as a new starting point is theoretically more coherent than altering, piecemeal, a homeownership form that no longer serves the needs of most households. To see this point, consider a fictitious municipality, Stockville, where land buyers are required to purchase one share of stock in the county's largest enterprise (say, a sock factory) for each square foot of land they purchase. As long as the stock purchase adds little cost or risk to the real estate package, it might be tolerated. But if the company's stock begins to skyrocket and fluctuate wildly, we would expect bright minds to seize quickly on the idea of separating the investment in socks from the investment in Stockville real estate.

In this case, it is easy to see that scaling back the Stockville real estate bundle so that it no longer includes a stock purchase requirement would be a more coherent approach than leaving the bundle unchanged and inventing elaborate devices to alter it after the fact. Of course, unbundling off-site risks from homeownership is not as simple as suspending a senseless stock purchase requirement. But from a theoretical perspective, the goal should be the same—a sensibly configured bundle delivered seamlessly to the purchaser without extraneous risk attached. Risk transfer mechanisms should serve only as a means to accomplishing that end.

Second, a new tenure form solves a coordination problem by providing a focal point around which law and shared social and cultural understandings can evolve.[16] Most immediately, the existence of such a focal point would facilitate debate about the merits of changing the risk allocation that accompanies homeownership. To date, the numerous existing and proposed models that change how homeownership risk is allocated are difficult even to converse about in an efficient way because they all have different names and often different purposes as well. A theoretically coherent bundle with well-known default settings can offer a more unified springboard for public discourse. Moving forward, a single focal point would facilitate the orderly evolution of law. Just as condominiums, cooperatives, and homeowners associations have become comprehensible legal categories around which law has developed, so too could a new version of homeownership serve as a center point around which new legal understandings could develop. In addition, providing a unified label for a new tenure regime will have significant advantages in terms of consumer comprehension.

Third, and most important, without a new paradigm for homeownership, the widespread adoption of mechanisms designed to alter home value risk seems unlikely. Having a comprehensive new mental template as a starting point will be crucial to effecting such a paradigm shift. Cognitive features relating to the processing of risks, gains, and losses pose significant obstacles to incremental do-it-yourself changes in risk-bearing. Creating a new default package with pricing that already reflects the shedding of investment risk is likely to be essential in making an alternative to traditional homeownership cognitively viable.

But what, exactly, would it mean to cast H2.0 as a new tenure form? Carol Rose has suggested that one of the roles government performs with respect to property involves "defining off-the-rack versions of entitlements that individuals (or at least their lawyers) can understand."[17] Hence, I contemplate governmental involvement in formulating and defining this property form within a regulatory framework that will, among other things, enable consumers to readily distinguish H2.0 from other arrangements.

Such definitional and regulatory steps would be crucial in reducing the risk of consumer confusion.[18] It is not necessary, however, to add a new possessory estate to the slate of property forms in order to provide a standardized, recognizable package. For example, common interest communities combine existing property forms—the fee simple and the servitude—to create a familiar set of arrangements that is nonetheless quite complex and transformative.[19] H2.0 could similarly work with elements in the existing property lexicon to produce a new default bundle.[20]

Cognitive Implications

One aspect of human psychology, loss aversion, suggests that H2.0's replacement of risky prospects with surer ones would be attractive.[21] But other cognitive features present obstacles to H2.0's adoption.[22] Cognitive biases also might lead people to misuse a new tenure form like H2.0. Thus, we might worry both that people would not use H2.0 when it would benefit them and that they would make use of H2.0 in ways that would harm them. I will address these concerns in turn. My focus here is only on the perceptions of homeowners, not those of the investors who would be necessary to the successful operation of a program for reassigning homeownership risk. Although resistance to (and misuse of) novel financial arrangements might not come exclusively from the consumer side, investors as a group may have more sophisticated views of money and risk and may be relatively less burdened by cognitive biases.

Barriers to Acceptance

Two features of human cognition, overoptimism and regret avoidance, might keep homeowners from using H2.0 when it would be in their best interests to do so. Because framing is central to how payoffs are viewed, the introduction of a new default point could help to address these concerns.

OVEROPTIMISM People tend to be more optimistic about many aspects of their lives and finances than is objectively justified.[23] This overoptimism extends to investments generally and to home values specifically. For example, an April 2007 poll that reflected "widespread unease about the U.S. economy" nonetheless found that only 16 percent of respondents predicted a decline in their home's value during the next six months, notwithstanding significant slowdowns in sales and mounting inventories.[24] If people believe their homes will not lose value, then purchasing downside risk protection will seem unnecessary. Likewise, if people hold unrealistic beliefs about their home's upward value trajectory, then the price at which an investor would be willing to buy the upside potential will seem too low. Thus, a valid initial question is whether overoptimism would make H2.0 a nonstarter.

There are a few reasons why this might not be the case. Significantly, H2.0's target audience includes not only current homeowners but also those who are not yet homeowners. Optimism and confidence among current homeowners as to the predicted future value of their homes thus does not capture the mental states of all those who might employ H2.0. Because homeowners are a self-selected group who chose to buy notwithstanding the cost and risks involved in existing institutional arrangements, we would expect their ranks to contain disproportionate numbers of people who are optimistic about home values. Tenant households may include more of those who are less optimistic about home price movements, and who would therefore find value in H2.0's risk buffering.

In addition, some homeowners may espouse optimism and confidence as a defense against cognitive dissonance and buyer's remorse. Having made the purchase, a homebuyer will resist any suggestion that he has made a horrible mistake. This does not necessarily mean that he would not have chosen differently at the time of purchase if a lower-risk alternative had been available. Some support for this thesis is found in the anecdotal evidence that homeowners tend to be rather fretful participants in local government.[25] If they truly believed that they had no chance of suffering a decline in home values and that fabulous returns awaited them on resale, then this fear-driven behavior would be difficult to explain.

To look at the question from a slightly different angle, the fact that people tend to be optimistic about their own investment choices does not mean that optimism dictates making any particular set of investment choices. H2.0 would facilitate investing less in local housing markets and more in other enterprises about which homeowners might be equally or more optimistic. In addition, H2.0 leaves the homeowner exposed to that subset of gains and losses that are under his control—especially attractive outlets for optimism.[26] To the extent that indexes are used to determine payouts, for example, homeowners can channel their optimism into their own home's outperformance of the index. While some homeowners would undoubtedly be disappointed on this front (not every home can outperform the index, just as not everyone can be above average), screening out the volatility associated with off-site factors will reduce the variance in outcomes, and actions taken in an effort to beat the index may be socially valuable.

Finally, it is important to keep in mind that H2.0 is not only a tool for overcoming risk but also an affordability tool. For this reason, H2.0 might be attractive even to those who are quite sanguine about home prices.

REGRET AVOIDANCE Another reason that consumers might steer clear of H2.0 is regret avoidance.[27] Attempts to avoid future regret, coupled with a cognitive apparatus that causes actions to be regretted more than omissions, can lead people to favor the status quo.[28] Daniel Kahneman and Amos Tversky present an example comparing the regret attributed to two actors. The first of them (George) sells stock in one company to purchase stock in another company and is worse off as a result. The second actor (Paul) is worse off by the same dollar amount because he stuck with the stock he owned and did not switch to a different company's stock. Kahneman and Tversky distinguish between acts and omissions in explaining the higher levels of regret attributed to George: "Apparently it is easier for George to imagine not taking an action (and therefore retaining the more advantageous stock) than it would be for Paul to imagine taking the action."[29] To the extent that choosing H2.0 is coded as an act, it may be more likely to produce regret, and its anticipation.

People are also more likely to anticipate regret when they know that, after making their choice, they will obtain full knowledge not only about the outcome chosen but also about the outcome not chosen.[30] Because many paths not taken involve significant uncertainty, people are often protected from regret (and hence from its anticipation) by an inability to fully assess what would have happened in the counterfactual state.[31] Even when it is possible to determine the value of an unchosen alternative, such as a stock one did not buy, people usually devote limited attention to tracking the progress of every alternative that was not selected. In contrast, if one elects H2.0 over traditional homeownership when purchasing a particular home, the counterfactual alternative (owning the home's full upside and downside) remains continually in view as one follows neighborhood housing trends; it stands starkly at the center of one's attention when the home is eventually sold. On average, houses will appreciate over time. Hence, it might seem that regret would not be a rare occurrence for H2.0 owners but rather the typical state of affairs.

In assessing the significance of regret avoidance for the viability of H2.0, it is helpful to separate downside protection from the transfer of upside potential. People frequently buy insurance without anticipating or experiencing any regret if no covered event occurs; on the contrary, insurance may be purchased precisely to avoid the regret that would result from a failure to insure against a low-probability but severe event.[32] Regret avoidance seems more clearly implicated when people contemplate alienating the home's upside potential. There are some additional factors that might attenuate this anticipated regret, however, at least for some homeowners. For example, consider a homeowner who uses H2.0 to get into a more expensive home than he could otherwise qualify to finance. The appropriate point of comparison on resale is not what the homeowner's house would have netted him had he not alienated equity rights, because that particular house would have been out of his reach. Rather, the appropriate comparison would be the gains on resale from the less-expensive house that he could have afforded without altering equity arrangements, less the disutility from having to live in that house rather than in the one he actually occupied.

Typically, there will be a much greater degree of uncertainty about the returns that the homeowner would have received had he opted for a house in a different price range than there will be about the returns on the house that he actually purchased. But even if the returns on a cheaper alternative could be known with certainty (suppose the homeowner had previously identified a specific house in that less-expensive price range, knew exactly the price at which he could have purchased it, and observed it being resold at precisely the same time as the house that he ended up buying), the counterfactual state of the world in which the owner bought the cheaper house is not directly comparable with the owner's actual outcome. The consumption streams from the two homes involve experiential elements that cannot be easily reduced to a common metric like money. Moreover, the consequences of the counterfactual state of living in a different house in a different neighborhood will often be both uncertain and difficult to compare. For example, it is hard to know whether one's child would have done as well in school or whether one would have felt less safe.

When the counterfactual and actual outcomes are not directly comparable, regret (and the anticipation of regret) is diminished.[33] Eric van Dijk and Marcel Zeelenberg studied this effect by asking subjects to imagine choosing between two scratch cards and finding, on the one they selected, either a €15 coupon for liquor or (in a different condition) a €15 coupon for books. They were then told that the unchosen scratch card would have yielded them a €50 prize—in different conditions, either a €50 book coupon or a €50 liquor coupon. When the forgone €50 card was for a product category different from the €15 prize given to the subject (for example, the subject received a €15 book coupon and the forgone prize was a €50 liquor coupon), reported regret was lower than when the actual prize and the forgone prize were from the same product category.[34]

Lack of comparability may, therefore, dilute expected and actual regret for people who use H2.0 to access better housing stock than they could otherwise afford. Not everyone will want to use H2.0 in this way, however. People may use the benefits provided by H2.0 to pay down or avoid debt, or to make other investments. Assuming that buyers in this category occupy the same homes they would have occupied under traditional homeownership, the relevant comparison is the H2.0 payoff plus or minus the gains or losses on the homeowner's other investments (or debt reduction). Because these elements can be reduced to dollars, there is no lack of comparability. When viewed ex ante, however, the house might be either a better or worse investment than the alternatives, making regret imaginable either way. What may be most important, then, is which choice is viewed as the status quo arrangement and which is viewed as an active investment decision.

FRAMING AND DEFAULTS Because people dislike losses much more than they mind failures to achieve gains, the implicit baseline from which changes are measured matters a great deal.[35] The baseline is also important to regret avoidance because it determines which choices will be coded as commissions and thus especially likely to trigger regret. Because traditional homeownership has long been the pervasive model in the United States, it is inevitable that consumers will measure payoffs against that baseline, at least in part, for the foreseeable future. However, H2.0's default package could eventually represent a new baseline against which action or inaction could be assessed.

Behavioral research shows that defaults can have a powerful influence on choices, drawing as they do on inertia, and perhaps also on the consumer's faith in those who have designed the institutional interface.[36] Defaults accompanied by open-ended (and hence procrastination-inducing) windows for making changes are especially potent, as seen in the context of 401(k) retirement plan choices.[37] This aspect of default "stickiness" would not apply in the H2.0 context, assuming the relevant decisions would be made concurrently with the home purchase transaction. But defaults work in another way that is directly relevant here—by requiring action to move away from a given baseline.[38]

Because H2.0's default settings reflect the removal of off-site volatility, the homebuyer must consciously choose to add in risk factors that lie outside his parcel and over which he has no direct control. If a homeowner adds in only the downside risk, he will save some money, but loss aversion is likely to steer him away from this move. If he adds in the right to upside potential, his net outlay for the home increases. He must ask himself whether he wants to invest in his local neighborhood housing market with that extra outlay, or whether he would rather invest in something else, like a stock index fund, a larger home, or debt reduction. Framed in this manner, the choice to stick with the default arrangement may seem unexceptional. Because the homeowner does not have to take any action to keep the defaults in place, the choice may be less likely to induce regret.

Of course, H2.0 will not be the only game in town. Thus, it will not represent "the" default arrangement for homeownership but rather only a new, competing paradigm for homeownership. The question is whether this new paradigm can be made attractive and familiar enough to gain the attention of consumers. Home sellers and realtors, who have an intense interest in moving homes into the hands of buyers, might be the natural parties to launch a publicity campaign.[39] H2.0's use of a single default setting would facilitate the easy communication of an "H2.0

price" along with the regular price. Multilist software could be upgraded to permit home hunters to search within regular or H2.0 price ranges. As homes that previously seemed out of reach begin to show up on home seekers' radar screens, we might expect significant consumer interest in the H2.0 alternative.

Potential for Misuse

At least as worrisome as the cognitive barriers just discussed is the possibility that cognitive biases might cause people to use H2.0 in ways that are ultimately self-defeating. The largest concern in this regard relates to time-inconsistent preferences. Many people behave myopically at times, heavily discounting the future.[40] Because the sale of upside potential under H2.0 would provide immediate consumption opportunities funded by a delayed payment (in the form of foregone appreciation on resale), it might seem poised to exploit myopic individuals. Currently, people aware of their own self-control problems may use their mortgage payments as a form of forced savings.[41] Of course, a volatile asset is hardly an ideal savings instrument.[42] Moreover, the ease with which households can tap into their home equity undermines its utility as a forced savings vehicle.[43] Nonetheless, if the wealth-building potential of the home is reduced, then people might end up saving even less than they do now.

There are several responses. First, not all decisions to consume now and pay later are irrational. The typical breadwinner's earning profile takes an inverted-U shape over the life cycle, rising with age and then falling in retirement. Under the permanent income hypothesis and the related life-cycle hypothesis, people are expected to consume in each period based on lifetime income, rather than on income received during that period alone.[44] But spreading lifetime earnings optimally across the life cycle is not easy, in part because it is so difficult to borrow against future earnings.[45] Permitting people to tap into future home appreciation could make consumption smoothing easier to accomplish.[46]

Even apart from these liquidity issues, it is difficult to establish that any particular trade-off between current and future consumption should be objectively regarded as a mistake. An individual's marginal utility of consumption might vary over time, making consumption now more worthwhile than consumption later. In addition, considerations like the interest rate, uncertainty about future events, and differing degrees of connectedness to other selves might rationally influence one's temporal preferences.[47] What are easier to identify as mistakes are *inconsistent* time preferences.[48] Where an individual's long-run plans are vulnerable to short-run impulsiveness, it is helpful to have mechanisms in place that allow the earlier self to precommit to a more patient choice.[49] To the extent a homebuyer views H2.0 as a too-tempting impulse purchase that would interfere with his long-run wealth-building agenda, the opportunities for advice and reflection that ordinarily accompany the purchase of a home should be helpful.[50]

Perhaps most important to keep in mind, however, is the fact that innumerable opportunities already exist for myopic individuals to act in a manner that is counter to their own long-run interests. Adjustable rate mortgages that can escalate out of the borrower's affordability window represent just one example. Similarly, home equity loans that allow homeowners to extract most of the home's equity during market peaks can set the stage for financial disaster if prices fall at a later time. It would be inaccurate to predict that a program like H2.0 would never get in the way of wealth building or cause any households to make choices that they will later view as ill advised. But given the many ways in which people can already thwart their own long-run interests, H2.0 seems like a relatively innocuous instrument. Indeed, mild forms of myopia might actually act to counterbalance other cognitive biases that would cause people to forgo the benefits of H2.0 (although it would be mere happenstance if they did so perfectly).

Societal Effects

Because nothing like H2.0 has ever been implemented on a broad scale, its larger societal effects cannot be fully predicted. In the previous chapter, I discussed some possible effects on local participation and politics of shifting local off-site risks from homeowners to investors. Homeowners who are relieved of irrational fears about falling property values will not feel compelled to push for socially harmful measures that benefit their locality at the expense of other parts of the metropolitan area. This advantage works together with an increased level of interdependence—

what we might term the "semicommons effect"—that derives from investors holding stakes in many different communities. Although concerns about excessively concentrated investor interests might require regulatory attention, the potential exists for a less provincial and more interdependent approach to local governance. I trace here some additional benefits and concerns that might accompany H2.0's change in the meaning and content of homeownership.

More Stability, Less Stickiness

Under traditional homeownership, downward-trending housing markets can suffer from inertia: current owners refuse to accept prices that are any lower than the property could command at its most recent peak, while would-be buyers refuse to pay anywhere near that amount.[51] Sales volume plummets, inventory piles up, but prices do not respond accordingly, at least in the short run. The result is diminished mobility among homeowners. This stickiness may be driven in part by liquidity constraints (the need to pay off an existing mortgage or the desire to walk away with sufficient equity to make a down payment on a new home), but loss aversion is strongly implicated as well. For example, an empirical study of condominium sales in Boston between 1990 and 1997 showed that sellers facing a loss from the benchmark of the nominal price paid for the home chose higher asking prices and took longer to sell their homes than other sellers.[52] Because accepting a price below that benchmark would be framed as a loss, homeowners are willing to take risks—refuse to drop the asking price or turn down offers—to avoid it.[53] Their risk-seeking behavior resembles that of people who continue placing risky bets in the wake of a gambling loss in an attempt to break even.[54]

H2.0 could help in a number of ways. First, sellers who are protected against downward price trends would be more willing to sell. Second, buyers who can purchase protection against future price drops would be less reluctant to buy. Third, to the extent that equity financing (selling off upside potential) begins to take the place of debt financing, the liquidity problems that produce lock-in effects would become rarer. In combination, these advantages would be expected to dampen the feedback effects of declining market conditions on mobility choices. Widespread risk buffering through H2.0 therefore benefits housing consumers in general, not just those who have opted for H2.0. Because of its potentially favorable societal and macroeconomic effects, the risk buffering aspects of H2.0 have some of the characteristics of a public good.[55]

One concern is whether such a program would increase mobility overall and thereby destabilize neighborhoods. If homeowners' reluctance to take losses on their homes makes them stick around (and perhaps, while there, exercise political "voice"), we might worry that buffering those losses would increase resort to "exit."[56] But downward price protection could also reassure homeowners when price downturns threaten, encouraging them to stay put and ride out changes in the neighborhood.[57] Another way that H2.0 might deliver greater stability is simply by encouraging more homeownership.[58] Data on mobility show that homeowners move significantly less frequently than tenants.[59] These data may be picking up on some of the stickiness that H2.0 would alleviate, but it is likely that much of the effect is attributable to transaction costs associated with buying and selling a home. While it cannot be said with much certainty which of several mobility related effects will dominate, there is at least the potential for less stickiness in housing markets without any loss in stability.

Competitive Consumption

Robert Frank has suggested that people engage in competitive consumption in their efforts to attain relative standing. Homes are one of the primary vehicles through which such competition is carried out. It is not just a matter of outdoing the Joneses with respect to square footage or fancy trim. Rather, people bid against each other for homes in particular neighborhoods and school districts because those neighborhoods and school districts are better, in relative terms, than other neighborhoods and school districts.[60] With so much riding on the choice of a home, people often stretch themselves quite thin to get a foothold in a premier neighborhood, even when it means placing themselves at risk of foreclosure and bankruptcy. It is worth thinking about how H2.0 might affect incentives in this regard.

By adding a new financing mechanism, H2.0 makes housing more affordable. But if homebuyers simply follow the heuristic of buying as much house as they can afford, an upward shift in affordability would merely produce an upward shift in housing consumption rather than a change in relative housing consumption. H2.0's effects on affordability would not operate uniformly throughout the income distribution—not all households face a binding constraint on home consumption that H2.0 would loosen—but it could affect a large proportion of households.[61] Even if the houses people buy are objectively larger or nicer, adaptation effects and a focus on relative standing might leave many individuals no happier and no more diversified than before.[62]

Interestingly, inertia could prove helpful in avoiding this cycle of increased consumption. If most people continue to live in their current homes, at least in the short run, any upward shift in housing consumption would be gradual and perhaps concentrated toward the lower portions of the income continuum. Socioeconomic mixing that occurred during the early (inertial) stage of H2.0 could also perform an educative function, again reducing the perceived need to get into a more exclusive setting. If diminished concerns about resale values softened the exclusionary policies of local governments, this could help reduce stratification and lower the pressure to get into a particular neighborhood or school district. Ultimately, however, larger reforms aimed at altering the incentives toward socioeconomic stratification might be necessary to prevent competition in housing consumption from eroding the advantages of H2.0.

Atrophy and Conformity

Another concern is that investor pricing practices could interact with a competitive consumption dynamic to pressure H2.0 households to relinquish many of the prerogatives that have traditionally accompanied homeownership. I have mentioned already that, notwithstanding their risk tolerance, investors want to avoid losses. They may therefore send price signals to homeowners about the kinds of land use restrictions that must be in place in order to receive top dollar for upside potential or the best deal on downside protection. In concept, this is no different than an insurer offering a discount for features like fire extinguishers and deadbolts. However, the restrictions that would maximize investment returns might not always optimize the homeowner's consumption experience. To be sure, we would generally expect the investment returns—the home's resale value—to be tightly linked to consumption value. If restrictions on autonomy are aversive, then the price that future homebuyers are willing to pay should drop accordingly. This might not happen, however, if homebuyers misgauge the significance of these restrictions or if competitive pressures overwhelm such concerns.

If getting one's child into the best school means buying in the most exclusive neighborhood, and if buying in the most exclusive neighborhood means surrendering large measures of control over one's home, then we might begin to see an overall reduction in the autonomy that homeowners enjoy. The fact that any such effects would stem from individual households choosing to make bargains does not provide a full answer. If ceding autonomy represents a competitive strategy that everyone undertakes, then everyone loses autonomy and gains nothing in relative position. Instead, these concessions merely enable households to keep their previous places in the neighborhood (and public school) hierarchy. There could also be society-wide externalities associated with many or most households giving up the personal autonomy that goes with homeownership.[63] The sense of individual responsibility and self-direction that may currently accompany homeownership could begin to atrophy, and society as a whole might become more conformist than anyone would prefer.

These concerns are not unique to H2.0, however. Land use controls, including stringent rules in common interest communities, can present much the same dynamic.[64] The possibility that H2.0 could intensify what many already see as a very troubling trend toward residential conformity must be taken seriously. What may be needed, though, is not a ban on innovation in homeownership but a broader pushback against undue intrusions on personal liberty in housing.

Homeownership currently requires households to take on a large and undiversified dose of investment risk, much of which relates to off-parcel factors. I have sketched here how a new version of homeownership could help bring the homeowner's risk exposure into line with his effective scope of control. By allowing owners to alienate both upside and downside risk, homeownership can be made more stable and less expensive, homeowners more secure and less fearful, and local governmental decisions less narrow and exclusive.

H2.0 is no magic bullet. It cannot solve underlying problems of economic inequality and socioeconomic stratification.[65] The cognitive and societal implications of changing the investment structure of homeownership also require careful consideration, as I have emphasized in this chapter. But homeownership, as currently configured, falls far short of its promise for many households. By thinking creatively about what is and is not essential to the institution, it becomes possible to identify a gap in the tenure menu and to devise an alternative version of homeownership capable of filling it. By presenting H2.0, I do not mean to suggest that it is the only possible model for reform. Instead, I hope to advance a conversation about how the future of homeownership might best proceed.

CONCLUSION

This book has attempted to shed light on the modern meaning of property ownership by examining its most familiar and contentious manifestation—the home. Interdependent, urban residential life drives a wedge between boundary-focused property templates and the reality of homeownership. With much of the home's value bound up in off-site factors, homeowners seek ways to expand their sphere of control, even as they resist any diminution in their right to control what happens on their own parcels. The trade-offs are difficult ones for which homeowners have been given neither a useful theoretical framework nor the right practical tools. I have tried to make a start toward providing both of these missing elements.

As the analysis here has shown, tragedies of the commons and anticommons may play out at different geographic and political scales. While neighbors share an aesthetic commons at the block level, private neighborhoods and local governments share an associational commons at the metropolitan level. Self-serving conduct and efforts to constrain it occur in both types of commons, with implications for the entire system. By examining various pieces of this complex puzzle in turn, the book has illuminated some of the shortcomings of the conventional impulse to approach these problems through blunt-force land use controls. It has also recommended two alternatives: finer-grained devices for managing spillovers at all scales, and changes in the homeownership bundle itself. Both of these approaches consciously expand the choice sets with which policymakers confront metropolitan problems.

Many of the existing legal arrangements that we have surveyed represent binary choices: either a land use is prohibited by regulation or it is allowed without restraint. Either a particular form of associational exclusion is outlawed or it is freely permitted. Either a homeowner must take on all of the risk associated with owning a home or she must remain a tenant. Throughout this book, I have sought to add "middle ways" to the menu—options that fall between prohibition and permission, between renting and owning. In designing such alternatives, we should not be afraid to adapt design elements drawn from other contexts. For example, as in other settings, substantial gains may be achieved by using alienable entitlements to facilitate value-enhancing trades. No such trades can occur, however, until we define the entitlement in question, which in turn requires an explicit recognition of the interest at stake—whether aesthetics, association, or risk. Thus, part of my project here has been to develop a way of thinking and talking about the dilemmas of homeownership that will facilitate entitlement-based solutions.

The literature on entitlement design teaches us that transferable instruments can be configured in virtually limitless ways to achieve efficiency and fairness. For example, entitlements that can be unilaterally transferred can facilitate efficient results in high-transaction-cost contexts—such as those involving multiple players in a neighborhood or metropolitan area. Concerns about undercompensation and loss of autonomy associated with such unilateral transfers can be minimized through the use of self-assessed valuation techniques that effectively require parties to write options for each other. Similarly, reconfiguring the homeownership bundle itself may offer an important additional approach to the tensions that currently accompany homeownership. Changing the nature and magnitude of the risks accepted by homeowners would not eliminate the need for well-designed instruments to manage spillovers, but it could reduce some of the pressures that are currently the product of homeowner fear.

Notwithstanding my enthusiasm for innovative approaches to the challenges of metropolitan residential life, I have tried to flag potential drawbacks and obstacles. Two deserve special mention. First, people do not always behave in accordance with the dictates of rationality, and any solutions to collective action problems must be devised with a careful eye to how human cognition operates on the ground. An important corollary to this point is that we can gain policy traction by consciously recognizing and leveraging features of cognition, as by transforming the default selection for homeownership's risk allocation. Second, a great deal of cultural and emotional baggage surrounds the concept of homeownership as it exists in the United States, and making changes will require moving beyond entrenched and perhaps deeply internalized understandings. Nonetheless, such changes are already under way as the demands of interdependent metropolitan life put pressure on the popular visions of ownership. This book has endeavored to outline specific ways in which these clashing forces can be accommodated through the use of new property tools.

The ideas pursued in this book also have broader significance for property theory, beyond the residential context. I have advanced here a functional vision of property as an institution for regularly collecting inputs and outcomes and charging them to the same owner—in short, a bucket of gambles. As with any bucket, we can expect a certain amount of sloshing and leaking. But when spillovers become so pervasive that more is sloshing out of the bucket than is remaining inside, we should begin to question whether we have configured property appropriately. Perhaps owing to its historical roots, property is a notoriously slow-changing institution; it does not deftly shapeshift to accommodate new circumstances and conditions. While some degree of inertia in property forms is desirable in fostering settled expectations, property theorists must also be ready to diagnose shortcomings and call for reconfigurations of outmoded property forms (or the development of complementary instruments that can keep old forms working better for longer). This book has focused on shortcomings in homeownership, but the theoretical model of property I have advanced could be used to detect and address similar shortfalls in other forms of property.

At bottom, property is nothing more than a social invention for ordering our actions. It does so by granting a large degree of control to parties over specific resources, in exchange for requiring those parties to accept exposure to risk related to those resources. When exposure and control fall out of alignment, as has happened in the case of homeownership, a societal response is necessary. That response, as I have suggested, can involve both an expansion of control through appropriately designed entitlements and a contraction of exposure through new versions of property. By judiciously adjusting policy instruments along these two dimensions, we can build a homeownership worthy of the new century.

NOTES

Introduction

1. U.S. Bureau of the Census, *Urban/Rural and Metropolitan/Nonmetropolitan Population: 2000;* U.S. Bureau of the Census, *Population: 1790 to 1990, United States, Urban and Rural.* The Census Bureau began using a new definition of "urban" in 1950, which somewhat increased (in that year, from 59.6 to 64.0) the percentage reported as falling in that category.

2. In 1900, fewer than half of the householders in the United States owned their own homes. U.S. Bureau of the Census, *Historical Census of Housing Tables: Homeownership.* In 2007, 68.1 percent of householders owned their own homes, including 66.8 percent of householders inside metropolitan statistical areas. U.S. Bureau of the Census, *Housing Vacancies and Homeownership, Annual Statistics: 2007.* The subprime crisis has produced some slippage in homeownership rates, however. See Swarns, "Rise in Renters" (reporting a drop to 67.8 percent in the first quarter of 2008, down from a high of 69.1 percent in 2005); U.S. Bureau of the Census, "Census Bureau Reports," 1 (reporting a homeownership rate of 67.9 percent for the third quarter of 2008).

3. See, e.g., Singer, "Ownership Society" (discussing the "castle model" of ownership).

4. See Fischel, *Homevoter Hypothesis,* 9 (referencing homeowner risk aversion driven by the dominance of the home in the household's portfolio).

5. See, e.g., Shiller, *Macro Markets;* Case, Shiller, and Weiss, "Index-Based Futures and Options"; Caplin et al., *Housing Partnerships.*

Chapter One. Beyond Exclusion

1. Economists have given increased attention to this question in recent years. See, e.g., Shiller, *Macro Markets;* Case, Shiller, and Weiss, "Index-Based Futures and Options"; Caplin et al., *Housing Partnerships.* This topic is taken up in Part IV.

2. See, e.g., Grey, "Disintegration."

3. Blackstone, *Commentaries,* 2:2. Sources characterizing Blackstone's description as hyperbolic include Merrill and Smith, "What Happened," 362; R. Ellickson, "Property in Land," 1362, n. 237.

4. See, e.g., Schorr, "How Blackstone Became a Blackstonian."

5. For example, Joseph Singer has identified the "core conception" that people hold about property as "absolute control . . . the ability to do what you like with your own, without having to account to anyone else for your actions." Singer, *Entitlement,* 29.

6. The metaphor of a bundle of sticks or bundle of rights was introduced by the legal realists. See Singer, *Entitlement,* 9–10. It has been associated with the work of Tony Honoré and Wesley Hohfeld, among others. See Honoré, "Ownership"; Hohfeld, *Fundamental Legal Conceptions,* 36–42. For discussion of the development and implications of this metaphor, see generally Penner, "'Bundle of Rights.'"

7. "Granny flat" is a colloquial term for an "accessory dwelling unit" that can be rented out by the owner of the main dwelling unit. See Van Hemert, "Time to Update."

8. See, e.g., Merrill and Smith, "What Happened"; Smith, "Property and Property Rules"; Penner, *Idea of Property,* 71–72. In some contexts, exclusion might be undertaken to deprive competitors of access to resources rather than to make use of those resources oneself. Here, the value of the exclusion would come from its impact on the excluder's return on activities undertaken on or with *other* property. I thank Jonathan Nash for discussions on this point.

9. As Henry Smith has put it, law "delegates" the choice of uses to the property's owner by granting her exclusive rights to the property. Smith, "Exclusion and Property Rules," 974–75; 978–85.

10. Ibid.

11. See Cane, *Anatomy of Tort Law,* 142.

12. Property law's *ad coleum* doctrine (*cujus est solum, ejus est usque ad coelum et ad infernos*—whoever owns the soil owns also to the sky and to the depths) is not taken literally in the case of ordinary overflights. See Dukeminier et al., *Property,* 126. In a case addressing the interaction between property law and federal statutory provisions governing navigable airspace, the Supreme Court concluded that "[f]lights over private land are not a taking, unless they are so low and so frequent as to be a direct and immediate interference with the enjoyment and use of the land." United States v. Causby, 328 U.S. 256, 266 (1946). See also Heller, *Gridlock Economy,* 27–29.

13. Under existing tort doctrines, this would be an abnormally sensitive use that would not give rise to a cause of action. For example, *Amphitheaters, Inc. v. Portland Meadows,* 198 P.2d 847 (Or. 1948), affirmed a directed verdict for a defendant whose race-track lights interfered with plaintiff's drive-in movie operation. There, the court discussed and applied the rule that "a man cannot increase the liabilities of his neighbor by applying his own property to special and delicate uses." Ibid., 854.

14. Cf. Kennedy and Michelman, "Are Property and Contract Efficient?" 760 (presenting "The Law of Conservation of Exposures").

15. See Grey, "Disintegration"; Merrill and Smith, "What Happened."

16. See Markby, *Elements of Law*, 158 (asserting that ownership "is no more conceived as an aggregate of distinct rights than a bucket of water is conceived as an aggregate of separate drops"), quoted in Smith, "Property and Property Rules," 1760.

17. Smith, "Property and Property Rules," 1760.

18. This characterization seems to follow from Markby's discussion of the bucket analogy. See Markby, *Elements of Law*, 158–59 (characterizing the alienation of specific use privileges, such as to walk on land or graze cattle on it, as withdrawing drops from the bucket).

19. See Smith, "Property and Property Rules," 1729 ("[O]wners make bets in situations of uncertainty and are rewarded or punished depending on how those bets turn out later when the uncertainty is resolved.").

20. See Harris, *Property and Justice*, 33–34 (discussing "property-independent prohibitions").

21. See R. Ellickson, "Property in Land," 1322–35 (examining how the scale of occurrences unfolding on property relates to the placement of boundaries and the choice of ownership form).

22. Calabresi and Melamed, "Cathedral."

23. See Coase, "Problem of Social Cost," 2 (emphasizing the reciprocal nature of causation).

24. Ibid., 15; see Calabresi and Melamed, "Cathedral," 1094–97.

25. See Calabresi and Melamed, "Cathedral," 1092, 1106, 1116 (discussing property rules); ibid., 1092, 1108–9 (discussing liability rules). Calabresi and Melamed also discussed a third category of entitlements, those that are inalienable. Ibid., 1111–15. Calabresi and Melamed did not include a grid in their article, but their successors derived one from their textual discussion. See ibid., 1115–18; Michelman, "There Have to Be Four," 142–46.

26. See Calabresi and Melamed, "Cathedral," 1116. The approach suggested by Calabresi and Melamed's fourth rule had made an earlier appearance in a student note. Atwood, "Land Use Conflicts," 315, cited in Calabresi, "Simple Virtues," 2204 and n. 10.

27. Spur Indus. v. Del E. Webb Dev. Co., 494 P.2d 700 (Ariz. 1972).

28. For an overview of the literature employing the Calabresi and Melamed framework, see Smith, "Property and Property Rules," 1720–22.

29. Building on the Calabresi and Melamed framework, Saul Levmore identified sixteen ways that remedies might be structured, and Madeline Morris presented fourteen different entitlement forms. See Levmore, "Unifying Remedies"; Morris, "Structure of Entitlements." Other examples of work expanding and elaborating on the original set of entitlements include Ayres, *Optional Law;* Coleman and Kraus, "Rethinking the Theory of Legal Rights," 1347–52; Krier and Schwab, "Another Light," 470–75; Polinsky, "Resolving Nuisance Disputes, 1087–88.

30. This input/outcome distinction tracks a number of distinctions that have been drawn in the law and economics literature—between ex ante and ex post approaches, between risk-based and harm-based approaches, and between regulation and liability. See, e.g., Wittman, "Prior Regulation versus Post Liability"; Porat and Stein, *Tort Liability under Uncertainty*, 103–10 (comparing "risk-based liability" and "damage-based

liability"); Shavell, "Liability for Harm versus Regulation of Safety"; Innes, "Choice between Ex-Post Liability and Ex-Ante Regulation."

31. See, e.g., Cane, *Anatomy of Tort Law,* 217; Coleman and Kraus, "Rethinking the Theory of Legal Rights," 1370–71.

32. Rose, "Shadow," 2181–82.

33. See Cooter, "Unity in Tort, Contract, and Property," 14 (explaining how invariant damage awards (such as liquidated damages in contract) can induce efficient behavior).

34. See ibid., 3–4 (explaining how compensation externalizes costs).

35. See, e.g., *Economist,* "Come Rain or Come Shine"; CME Weather Products, http://www.cme.com/trading/prd/weather/.

36. Boomer v. Atlantic Cement Co., 257 N.E.2d 870, 876 (N.Y. 1970) (Jasen, J., dissenting).

37. See R. Ellickson, "Property in Land," 1400 ("A land regime that is efficient for a small group might conceivably cause significant extraterritorial spillover effects that harm outsiders so much that the regime is undesirable from a broader social perspective.").

Chapter Two. Constructing the Home

1. The elements bundled together in the home purchase, although variously delineated, have been well noted in the literature. See, e.g., Rose-Ackerman, "Beyond Tiebout," 74; Jackson, "Public Needs," 6; Walters, *Noise and Prices,* 29; Pozdena, *Modern Economics of Housing,* 43–44, 82; The Kaiser Committee, "A Decent Home," 186; Fox, *Conceptualising Home,* 142–77. Richard Thompson Ford has made the related point that "political geography" is itself a bundled product whose components are not necessarily those that residents would choose "if they could order à la carte." Ford, "Geography and Sovereignty," 1411–12. See also Logan and Molotch, *Urban Fortunes,* 103–10 (cataloguing six aspects of neighborhood "use values").

2. Quadeer, "Nature of Urban Land," 171–72.

3. Tiebout, "A Pure Theory of Local Expenditures."

4. For a discussion of agglomeration benefits and associated tradeoffs with congestion costs, see, e.g., R. Ellickson, "Suburban Growth Controls," 442–43. Technological and social changes affect the need for, as well as the nature and cost of, agglomeration. See, e.g., Glaeser, Kolko and Saiz, "Consumers and Cities"; Webber, "Order in Diversity," 37.

5. Tiebout, "A Pure Theory of Local Expenditures," 422 ("Spatial mobility provides the local public-goods counterpart to the private market's shopping trip.").

6. See Yinger, "Capitalization and the Median Voter," 101. My discussion will be limited to home purchases; leaseholds raise somewhat different issues. See Ross and Yinger, "Sorting and Voting," 2020.

7. Figure 2-2 was inspired by a similar figure in R. Ellickson, "Property in Land," that was used to illustrate the impact of events of different scales on decisions about property ownership regimes. Ibid., 1325, fig. 2. See also Buchanan and Flowers, *Public Finances,* 438 fig. 36-1; 441 fig. 36-2 (illustrating through sets of concentric shapes the spillover range of various goods provided privately and at various governmental levels).

8. See, e.g., Schelling, "Dynamic Models," 145; Rothenberg, "Redevelopment Benefits," 218.

9. The term "local public good" has two overlapping meanings. In economic literature, the term refers to goods that, within a localized area, meet the criteria of public goods—they are nonrival and nonexcludable. See, e.g., Cornes and Sandler, *Theory of Externalities*, 6–7, 24. The phrase is also used to reference goods that are provided by local governmental entities to their citizens, whether or not those goods meet the economic criteria of public goods. See, e.g., Stretton and Orchard, *Public Goods*, 54. My usage corresponds to the latter definition, although the goods I discuss also exhibit some of the economic characteristics of public goods.

10. The people in Tiebout's stylized model live off dividend income and therefore do not have workplaces to which they must commute. Tiebout, "A Pure Theory of Local Expenditures," 419.

11. See Ladd and Yinger, *America's Ailing Cities*, 145–66 (discussing "overlying jurisdictions").

12. See Gillette, "Regionalization and Interlocal Bargains," 203–4; Hunter, *Symbolic Communities*, 67–77.

13. See Tilly et al., "Space as a Signal" (exploring employers' perceptions of different neighborhoods and the impact of those perceptions on hiring practices, based on in-depth interviews with a sample of firms in Atlanta, Boston, Detroit, and Los Angeles).

14. Changes in the perceived boundaries of neighborhoods are also a matter of potential interest. Those just outside high-status enclaves have an incentive to claim the place name as their own, while residents of the neighborhood can be expected to resist any boundary shifting that would "dilute" the place name. Logan and Molotch, *Urban Fortunes*, 44. See also Hunter, *Symbolic Communities*, 77–89 (discussing changes in community names and boundaries). For a recent example of the significance of neighborhood names to community identity, see Leovy, "Community Struggles in Anonymity" (noting the impact on the area once known as South Central L.A. of the city's decision to discontinue use of the place name).

15. See, e.g., Stiglitz, "Theory of Local Public Goods," 41–42 (observing that capitalization follows from "free migration" among jurisdictions); Fischel, *Homevoter Hypothesis*, 45–51 (discussing the empirical literature on capitalization).

16. Fischel, *Homevoter Hypothesis*, 40–45 (presenting an example involving adjoining towns in different municipalities—Bow and Concord, NH—to demonstrate capitalization of tax differences into home prices), 148–55 (arguing that capitalization of school quality, as reflected in test scores, influences homeowner voting behavior).

17. See ibid., 47–51. For an argument that features of the local legal environment can be capitalized into home values (as well as into wages), see Malani, "Valuing Laws as Local Amenities."

18. Risk aversion as to home values can be attributed in part to the fact that the home is the single largest financial investment for most homeowners. See Fischel, *Homevoter Hypothesis*, 4–5, 8–10 (noting the relative size of the home investment in homeowners' portfolios and resulting risk aversion); Bucks, Kennickell, and Moore, "Recent Changes," A22–23 (noting that "housing wealth is typically the largest component of families' fungible wealth").

19. See Barzel, *Economic Analysis of Property Rights*, 93–94 (noting that features like salt and the space that one occupies while dining are effectively placed in the "public domain" by restaurant owners).

20. Hamilton, "Zoning and Property Taxation," 205.

21. See, e.g., Buchanan and Flowers, *Public Finances*, 438–39 ("For the great bulk of private goods and services, the actions of the individual do not externally affect the utility of any other individual or family . . . there are no spillover effects beyond the ordinary market mechanism."). Some exceptions to this principle are discussed in Sunstein and Ullmann-Margalit, "Solidarity Goods." For discussion of goods for which co-consumers play a large role, see, e.g., Becker and Murphy, *Social Economics*, 4 (addressing various forms of "group consumption"); Rothschild and White, "Analytics," 574 (discussing group consumption experiences, including sporting events, amusement parks, restaurants, and the like, for which "the other customers partially determine the quality of what each customer consumes").

22. See, e.g., Hamilton, "Review," 101 (observing that "the public service must be consumed in concert with those who share residence in a jurisdiction"); Diamond and Tolley, "Urban Amenities," 6 (contrasting "location-specific" goods with other goods).

23. See, e.g., Ross and Yinger, "Sorting and Voting," 2038–40 (reviewing literature establishing the link between community characteristics and the production and cost of local public goods); Schwab and Oates, "Community Composition"; Oates, "Population Flows"; Diamond and Tolley, "Urban Amenities," 6. Work focusing on the significance of population characteristics for education includes Manski, "Educational Choice," 356; Dynarski, Schwab, and Zampelli, "Local Characteristics." My focus here is on the impact of consumers on the production of publicly supplied goods and services. Members of a community can also consciously undertake coproduction of a particular local public good, such as community day care. See Pestoff, "Citizens as Coproducers," 163–65.

24. Clotfelter, "Private Life of Public Economics," 582–84.

25. Tiebout, "A Pure Theory of Local Expenditures," 419–20.

26. Ibid.; see Oates, "On Local Finance," 95 (discussing the "U-shaped cost curve" that Tiebout posited, in which the low point of the curve "served to define optimal community size").

27. See Becker, "Restaurant Pricing" (analyzing why restaurants, theaters, and other venues might not raise prices when excess demand produces queues).

28. Hirschman, *Exit, Voice, and Loyalty*, 15–20 (explaining how the quality-control mechanisms of exit and voice relate to economics and politics, respectively).

29. Tiebout's "consumer-voter" formulation emphasizes the resident's dual role. Tiebout, "A Pure Theory of Local Expenditures." See also Rose-Ackerman, "Beyond Tiebout," 55; Ross and Yinger, "Sorting and Voting," 2003; B. Ellickson, "Jurisdictional Fragmentation," 335.

30. See, e.g., Schelling, *Micromotives and Macrobehavior*, 150 ("Everybody who selects a new environment affects the environments of those he leaves and those he moves among. There is a chain reaction.").

31. Strahilevitz, "Rights to Exclude," 1850–53.

32. See Alamo Drafthouse Cinema, http://www.drafthouse.com/lakecreek/shows.php?id=88.

33. Oakerson, *Governing Local Public Economies,* 110–11.

34. See Yinger, "Capitalization and the Median Voter," 101.

35. See, e.g., Henderson and Ioannides, "Housing Tenure Choice," 102; Brueckner, "Consumption and Investment Motives."

36. On consumer decision-making across multiple attributes, see, e.g., Korobkin, "Bounded Rationality," 1227–29; Malhotra, "Information Load." Bundled products containing all of one's preferred components may be unavailable, see, e.g., Kelman, *Critical Legal Studies,* 108, or impossible to negotiate given attentional limits, see, e.g., Alexander, "Freedom, Coercion," 894–95.

37. This point is examined in greater depth in Part III, as well as in Fennell, "Properties of Concentration."

38. See, e.g., Delafons, *Land-Use Controls,* 28–29; Poindexter, "Legal Framework," 12–14. Reduced uncertainty may be especially valuable to early entrants to a community who cannot determine anything about the likely future of land use by scanning the area. See Epple, Romer, and Filimon, "Community Development," 133.

39. For discussions of the multiple motivations for zoning, see, e.g., Bogart, "Big Teeth"; Dietderich, "Egalitarian's Market," 31; Ellickson and Been, *Land Use Controls,* 769–70.

40. See Bogart, "Big Teeth."

41. Hamilton, "Zoning and Property Taxation," 205.

42. Ibid.

43. See Hamilton, "Capitalization," 744; Rubinfeld, "Economics of the Local Public Sector," 591–94 and nn. 22, 25.

44. See Fischel, *Homevoter Hypothesis,* 69; Fennell, "Homes Rule," 640.

45. See Heilbrun, "Poverty and Public Finance," 538 (suggesting that moves to the suburbs may be substantially influenced by a household's "being able to receive back as service benefit most of what it pays out to the local tax collector, instead of seeing a substantial part of its tax payments to provide services for the poorer families that do not 'pay their way' in the tax expenditure calculus"); cf. Barzel and Sass, "Allocation of Resources by Voting," 763–64 (results in a study of voting rules in private communities were consistent with the prediction that "votes will be assigned in order to conform to owners' gains and costs from new projects").

46. White, "Fiscal Zoning." For a concise overview of land use exactions, see Been, "'Exit' as a Constraint," 478–83.

47. See, e.g., White, "Fiscal Zoning," 73–74; Epple, Romer, and Filimon, "Community Development," 155.

48. For discussion of how land use controls allocate rights between individual landowners and the community, see, e.g., Nelson, *Zoning and Property Rights,* 1, 15–18; Fischel, "Equity and Efficiency," 302. On the potential for shifts in control to produce net gains and net losses, see generally Fischel, "Equity and Efficiency."

49. On the impact of homogeneity in tastes on the consumption and production of

public goods, see, e.g., Nelson, *Zoning and Property Rights,* 39–40; Sugden, "Reciprocity," 783; Musgrave, *Fiscal Systems,* 299.

50. See Frug, "City Services," 31. Frug notes that sources of immobility other than poverty may contribute to reduced choice. Ibid., n. 31.

51. For further discussion see Fennell, "Beyond Exit and Voice," and the discussion in my Part III. Economic models examining the impact of population characteristics often use such simplifying dichotomies. See, e.g., Schwab and Oates, "Community Composition," 220–30 (types A and B); Ross and Yinger, "Sorting and Voting," 2044 (type-1 and type-2).

52. For discussion of how zoning can screen out low-income families, see, e.g., Span, "Exclusionary Zoning," 8–9.

53. See, e.g., Fischel, *Homevoter Hypothesis,* 87–89.

54. See Rose-Ackerman, "Beyond Tiebout," 65 (illustrating this point with an example).

55. I am grateful to Bill Fischel for discussions on this point. For a brief overview of some of the literature on such "political economic zoning," see Bogart, "Big Teeth," 1672. For a discussion of the converse strategy of adopting policies designed to drive higher-income constituents out of the jurisdiction, see Glaeser and Shleifer, "Curley Effect."

56. See Ford, "Boundaries of Race," 1871 (noting this "self-perpetuating quality" of exclusionary zoning).

57. Frank, *Choosing the Right Pond.*

58. See Riccardi, "Leveling Restrictions."

Chapter Three. The Commons and the Anticommons

1. Mishan, *Costs of Economic Growth,* 71.

2. Ibid.

3. Buchanan, "Institutional Structure of Externality," 73–74.

4. G. Hardin, "Tragedy of the Commons," 1244.

5. The literature on resource dilemmas is vast. For some examples, see Ostrom, Gardner, and Walker, *Common-Pool Resources,* 14–15 (discussing underprovision and underuse problems); Libecap and Smith, "Petroleum Property Rights" (overextraction of oil); Thompson, "Tragically Difficult," 250 ("overdrafting" of water); R. Ellickson, "Property in Land," 1326 (shirking in communal farming); Eggertsson, "Open Access," 77 ("supply side" effects of open access regimes, such as the disincentive to invest).

6. I am using the term "inefficient" here in the Kaldor-Hicks sense; efficient arrangements are those that produce gains sufficient to enable the winners to compensate the losers—even though no compensation need actually be paid. See, e.g., Cooter and Ulen, *Law and Economics,* 48.

7. See, e.g., Dukeminier et al., Property, 44–45.

8. See, e.g., ibid.; Buchanan and Stubblebine, "Externality," 380–81; Haddock, "Irrelevant Externality Angst."

9. See, e.g., De Alessi, "Gains from Private Property," 91; Epstein, "Optimal Mix," 28.

10. See, e.g., Buchanan and Stubblebine, "Externality," 380–81. The fact that the choice is efficient does not necessarily make it normatively desirable as a distributive matter. See, e.g., Dukeminier et al., *Property,* 43–44.

11. See, e.g., Cooter, "Cost of Coase," 16 (describing zero-sum games); Landes and Posner, "Indefinitely Renewable Copyright," 486 (distinguishing between "pecuniary" externalities that alter wealth distributions and "technological" externalities that lead to a net reduction in overall utility). See also Ostrom, Gardner, and Walker, *Common-Pool Resources,* 15–16 (observing that situations involving common-pool resources only present dilemmas when two conditions are present: "suboptimal outcomes" and "institutionally feasible alternatives" that offer room for improvement).

12. See, e.g., Posner, *Economic Analysis of Law,* 493–94.

13. See, e.g., R. Ellickson, "Property in Land," 1332 and n. 62 (noting the inverse relationship between tract size and the per-acre cost of fencing or monitoring the perimeter); Cohen, "Holdouts and Free Riders" (presenting a land assembly example that assumes that scale economies will be realized); Heller, "Tragedy of the Anticommons" (discussing assembly problems produced by fragmented entitlements).

14. See Anderson and McChesney, "Economic Approach to Property Rights," 5 (discussing costs of competition); cf. Posner, *Economic Analysis of Law,* 36–37 (explaining why excessively costly recovery efforts may be expended to recover treasure from a shipwreck).

15. See, e.g., Dagan and Heller, "Liberal Commons," 582 (referencing the "wasteful struggles regarding the fruits and revenues that a commons may produce").

16. See, e.g., Baird, Gertner, and Picker, *Game Theory,* 33; Goetz, *Law and Economics,* 8–17.

17. See, e.g., Baird, Gertner, and Picker, *Game Theory,* 33.

18. See R. Ellickson, *Order without Law,* 161–64 (applying the Prisoner's Dilemma structure to fence building between neighbors, and elaborating a game-theoretic variation).

19. Baird, Gertner, and Picker, *Game Theory,* 33–34 (discussing the Prisoner's Dilemma); ibid., 19–22 (describing and discussing the Nash equilibrium).

20. See, e.g., Elster, *Cement of Society,* 27–28 and fig. 1.3 (presenting a multiparty Prisoner's Dilemma, using a graph type introduced by Thomas Schelling).

21. The structural equivalence between the tragedy of the commons and the Prisoner's Dilemma has been well noted. See, e.g., Baird, Gertner, and Picker, *Game Theory,* 34; Dagan and Heller, "Liberal Commons," 555 and n. 12; Ostrom, *Governing the Commons,* 3.

22. See, e.g., Ostrom, *Governing the Commons,* 35–37, 88–89, 205–7 (stressing the role of norms in managing common-pool resources); Schlager and Ostrom, "Property-Rights Regimes" (discussing de jure and de facto rights to common property). A large literature exists on the impact of norms on incentive structures. For a recent overview, see McAdams and Rasmusen, "Norms and the Law."

23. See, e.g., Ullmann-Margalit, *Emergence of Norms,* 37 (describing how factors like

esteem and dishonor alter payoffs for soldiers confronting a strategic dilemma).

24. Dagan and Heller, "Liberal Commons," 552 (noting that in some commons settings "the social gains from cooperation are not just fringe benefits, but instead are a major part of what people seek").

25. See Rousseau, *Origin of Inequality,* 349, quoted in Ullmann-Margalit, *Emergence of Norms,* 121 n. 15.

26. See Ullmann-Margalit, *Emergence of Norms,* 121.

27. The Assurance Game closely resembles the Stag Hunt, despite minor differences. See Baird, Gertner, and Picker, *Game Theory,* 277 n. 14, 301, 315; see also Lewinsohn-Zamir, "Consumer Preferences," 392 nn. 39–40 (discussing variations of the Assurance Game); Sen, "Isolation," 114–15 (presenting the "assurance problem").

28. See, e.g., R. Ellickson, *Order without Law,* 55 (characterizing relationships among rural residents as "multiplex" rather than "simplex" and citing sociological literature on the distinction); ibid., 177–83 (discussing norms within "close-knit" groups).

29. Ostrom, *Governing the Commons,* 8–15.

30. G. Hardin, "Tragedy of the Commons," 1247.

31. See Ostrom, *Governing the Commons,* 12–13; Smith, "Exclusion versus Governance" (comparing exclusion-based private property approaches with governance strategies).

32. See R. Ellickson, "Property in Land," 1388–92.

33. See G. Hardin, "Tragedy of the Commons," 1244 (inviting the reader to "[p]icture a pasture open to all").

34. See, e.g., Ciriacy-Wantrup and Bishop, "'Common Property' as a Concept," 715 (arguing that the term "common property" itself implies some institutional arrangement that would exclude nonowners); Eggertsson, "Open Access," 75–76 (noting confusion in the literature between "open access" and "common property" regimes and clarifying the distinction between these arrangements).

35. Ostrom, *Governing the Commons.*

36. Rose, "Several Futures of Property," 155.

37. See Ostrom, *Governing the Commons,* 14 (noting that institutions for successfully managing common-pool resources often constitute "rich mixtures of 'private-like' and 'public-like' institutions defying classification in a sterile dichotomy"); ibid., 20 (discussing the role of local knowledge in institutional arrangements).

38. See Eggertsson, "Open Access," 76 (observing that outsiders, even if granted access to a community resource, "often are excluded by transportation costs").

39. Michelman, "Ethics, Economics," 6, 9; see also Heller, "Tragedy of the Anti-commons," 667–68 (tracing the evolution of the anticommons idea and its original "thought experiment" quality).

40. Michelman, "Ethics, Economics," 6, 9; see R. Ellickson, "Property in Land," 1322 n. 22 (discussing Michelman's "anticommons" idea); Dukeminier et al., *Property,* 48–49.

41. See Heller, "Tragedy of the Anticommons," 667–69.

42. Ibid.

43. Ibid., 633–40.

44. See, e.g., Heller, "Tragedy of the Anticommons"; Heller and Eisenberg, "Can Patents Deter Innovation?"; Heller, *Gridlock Economy.*

45. Buchanan, "Institutional Structure of Externality," 73–74.

46. Arrow, "Property Rights Doctrine," 24–26.

47. Demsetz, "Toward a Theory of Property Rights," 354–55; see Krier, "Part Two," 335–36.

48. See, e.g., Buchanan and Yoon, "Symmetric Tragedies," 1; Heller, "Tragedy of the Anticommons," 624; Hsu, "Two-Dimensional Framework," 814.

49. See Heller, "Tragedy of the Anticommons," 673–75; see also Bell and Parchomovsky, "Of Property and Antiproperty" (arguing that bargain-impeding fragmentation can sometimes be efficient).

50. Parchomovsky and Siegelman, "Selling Mayberry," 128–29 (defining "holdins"); see also Rose, "Servitudes, Security, and Assent," 1412 (explaining that "[s]ometimes that purported holdout has a genuine interest in his property right, however irrationally inflated that interest may seem to the world at large").

51. For discussions of holdout strategies and resulting bargaining problems, see, e.g., Cohen, "Holdouts and Free Riders," 362; Stake, "Touch and Concern," 936; Arrow, "Property Rights Doctrine," 24–26.

52. See, e.g., Cohen, "Holdouts and Free Riders," 352–53; Lewinsohn-Zamir, "Critical Observations," 226 n. 25; Polinsky, "Resolving Nuisance Disputes," 1077–78.

53. See, e.g., Krier and Schwab, "Another Light," 466–67.

54. See, e.g., Cohen, "Holdouts and Free Riders," 359; R. Ellickson, "Suburban Growth Controls," 445 n. 167; Heller and Hills, "Land Assembly Districts." For a recent economic analysis of assembly problems that emphasizes the negative returns that a partial assembly might produce, see McDonald, "What Is Public Use?" 14–22 and figs. 1–2.

55. See, e.g., Buchanan and Yoon, "Symmetric Tragedies," 4; Parisi, Schulz, and Depoorter, "Duality in Property," 579–80.

56. See, e.g., Goetz, *Law and Economics,* 35 (associating land assembly problems with the Chicken Game); Heller and Hills, "Land Assembly Districts," 1469 (observing that an anticommons problem can thwart land assembly).

57. See, e.g., Heller and Hills, "Land Assembly Districts," 1473–74; Dibadj, "Regulatory Givings," 1050 n. 42, 1114.

58. See Baird, Gertner, and Picker, *Game Theory,* 43–45 (modeling a labor negotiation as a Chicken Game); Farnsworth, *Legal Analyst,* 130–32 (applying the Chicken model to a variety of bargaining situations); see also Cooter, "Cost of Coase," 20 (presenting a bargaining model "in which everyone has an interest in avoiding the worst outcomes, but the outcome which is best from one player's viewpoint is not best from another's").

59. See, e.g., Jolls, Sunstein, and Thaler, "Behavioral Approach," 21–26 (surveying empirical studies of ultimatum games).

60. To address this difficulty, Robert Nelson has proposed legal changes that would permit the establishment of covenant-bound private communities on less than unanimous consent. See Nelson, *Private Neighborhoods,* 265–73.

61. See Smith, "Semicommon Property Rights."

62. For an overlapping but somewhat broader use of the term "neighborhood commons," see Karkkainen, "Zoning," 25–26.

Chapter Four. Managing the Neighborhood Commons

1. R. Ellickson, "Unpacking the Household," 277–87; 319–20; see also R. Ellickson, *The Household*.

2. See Karkkainen, "Zoning," 26. Whether something counts as a "draw" against ambience depends, of course, on societal judgments, which are mutable. See Mahoney, "Perpetual Restrictions," 759–63; cf. Bruegmann, "Urban Density," 177.

3. See Ostrom, *Governing the Commons*, 8–13. Ostrom critiques this dichotomous thinking and examines successful local institutional arrangements that do not fit neatly into either model. See ibid., 13–23.

4. See Pogodzinski and Sass, "Economic Theory of Zoning," 295 (distinguishing between "direct effects" of zoning and "effects via mobility"); my Chapter 6 (elaborating on the distinction between compliance effects and membership effects).

5. Nelson, *Zoning and Property Rights*, 15–18.

6. See, e.g., Dana, "Land Use Regulation," 1286–99; Rose, "Planning and Dealing."

7. Euclid v. Ambler Realty, 272 U.S. 365 (1926); see Ellickson and Been, *Land Use Controls*, 74–75.

8. See, e.g., Nelson, *Zoning and Property Rights*, 22–83; Ellickson and Been, *Land Use Controls*, 74–76.

9. See, e.g., Nolon, "*Golden* and Its Emanations," 31 (observing that "[d]espite its promise and growing relevance in an environmentally challenged society, performance zoning has not gained wide acceptance"). For background on performance zoning, see, e.g., ibid., 30–32; Kendig, *Performance Zoning;* Acker, "Performance Zoning." See also Jacobs, *Dark Age Ahead*, 153–56 (discussing advantages of a "performance code" over prohibitions on uses).

10. See, e.g., Ellickson and Been, *Land Use Controls*, 90–91. For example, under cumulative zoning, an R-1 zone might permit single-family homes on lots of at least a quarter acre, an R-2 zone might additionally permit single-family homes on smaller lots as well as duplexes and triplexes, and an R-3 zone might permit apartment buildings in addition to the uses permitted in R-2 and R-1.

11. See Callies, Freilich, and Roberts, *Land Use*, 48–49 (explaining that under cumulative zoning, "the heavy industrial zone—typically at the bottom of the zoning 'pyramid,' would permit just about anything").

12. See, e.g., Ellickson and Been, *Land Use Controls*, 92–94.

13. Nollan v. Cal. Coastal Comm'n, 483 U.S. 825, 837 (1987); Dolan v. City of Tigard, 512 U.S. 374, 391 (1994).

14. Fennell, "Hard Bargains and Real Steals." During my tenure as associate counsel at the State and Local Legal Center, I worked on an amicus brief that was filed in *Dolan v. City of Tigard* on behalf of the National Association of Counties et al.—a fact

I mention only in the interest of full disclosure. My academic work on land use exactions began more than five years later and, of course, has always reflected only my own views.

15. Monetary impact fees and development agreements may escape the heightened exactions scrutiny outlined in the *Nollan* and *Dolan* cases, although the law is not entirely clear on these points. See, e.g., Fenster, "Regulating Land Use," 753–758 (analyzing the impact of the Supreme Court's decision in *Lingle v. Chevron,* 544 U.S. 528 (2005), on the impact fee question); ibid., 747 n. 111 (collecting citations to literature on the development agreement question). See also Dana, "Land Use Regulation," 1286–99 (analyzing the role of repeat play in circumventing the *Nollan* and *Dolan* constraints).

16. See Fischel, "Equity and Efficiency," 304 fig. 1; Fischel, *Regulatory Takings,* 343 fig. 9.1.

17. See Fischel, "Equity and Efficiency," 316.

18. See Nelson, *Zoning and Property Rights,* 2 (noting that zoning rights have been established without "any effective mechanism for transferring" them); O'Flaherty, *City Economics,* 182–85 (discussing various forms of agreements relating to zoning and observing that "none of them resembles a Coasian bargain"); see also Fischel, *Economics of Land Use Exactions,* 104 (observing that "[s]everal legal doctrines discourage exchanges of land use controls").

19. Nelson, *Zoning and Property Rights,* 105; see also Clawson, "Why Not Sell Zoning and Rezoning?" 9 (questioning lack of free alienability in zoning); Fischel, "Equity and Efficiency," 321–29 (presenting a proposal for salable zoning).

20. Calabresi and Melamed, "Cathedral," 1092.

21. See ibid., 1092–93 (discussing "inalienability rules"); Nelson, *Zoning and Property Rights,* 84 (noting inconsistency of salable zoning with police powers and planning justifications for zoning).

22. Fischel, "Equity and Efficiency," 327; see generally ibid.

23. See, e.g., Dana, "Land Use Regulation," 1286–99; Rose, "Planning and Dealing"; Fischel, *Homevoter Hypothesis,* 278. For a recent investigation into zoning practices in Chicago, for example, see Mihalopoulos, Becker, and Little, "Cash, Clout."

24. See, e.g., Posner, *Economic Analysis of Law,* 13 (explaining that under Kaldor-Hicks efficiency, "[t]he winners *could* compensate the losers, whether or not they actually do").

25. See, e.g., Fischel, "Equity and Efficiency," 326 (discussing bargaining dynamics); my Chapter 3 (considering the role of strategic holdout behavior in negotiations).

26. See Nelson, *Zoning and Property Rights,* 87; Siegan, *Land Use without Zoning,* 196; R. Ellickson, "Alternatives to Zoning," 701.

27. See Fischel, "Equity and Efficiency," 307 (explaining why barter arrangements may be inefficient).

28. Nollan v. Cal. Coastal Comm'n, 483 U.S. 825, 837 (1987); Dolan v. City of Tigard, 512 U.S. 374, 391 (1994).

29. For discussion of rezoning see, e.g., Ellickson and Been, *Land Use Controls,* 302–352; Rose, "Planning and Dealing."

30. The Community Associations Institute estimated that there were 300,800 community associations in the United States in 2008, housing approximately fifty-nine and a half million people. Community Associations Institute, "Industry Data: National Statistics."

31. See, e.g., McKenzie, *Privatopia,* 186–87.

32. Amenity-related motivations are discussed in, e.g., *Restatement (Third) of Property: Servitudes,* ch. 6, introductory note; Brower, "Communities within the Community," 205; Nelson, "Privatizing the Neighborhood," 832. Social and associational preferences are noted in, e.g., Brower, supra, 206; Gillette, "Courts, Covenants, and Communities," 1396–97. Sources that focus on the capacity of private communities to regulate the neighborhood environment or interactions between neighbors include *Restatement,* supra, introductory note; R. Ellickson, "Alternatives to Zoning," 712–13; Reichman, "Judicial Supervision of Servitudes," 144. See also Rosenblum, *Membership and Morals,* 117, 148–57 (discussing environmental, associational, and amenity-related aspects of residential community associations).

33. See, e.g., Rosenblum, *Membership and Morals,* 112 (noting that 70 percent of new housing in Los Angeles and San Diego counties is within residential community associations and that such communities "make up more than 50 percent of new home sales in the fifty largest metropolitan areas").

34. Such requirements might be viewed as backdoor methods for selling development rights, given that the private community will provide services that otherwise would have to be paid for through tax revenues. Nelson, "Double Taxation," 359–60.

35. See, e.g., Reichman, "Judicial Supervision of Servitudes," 279–80, 303 n. 192.

36. See G. Hardin, "Tragedy of the Commons," 1244–45.

37. See Reichman, "Judicial Supervision of Servitudes," 281 ("By purchasing a home in a residential private government community, the owner waives part of the incidents of his title; he is compensated for this diminution of his rights, however, by the generally improved living conditions and the extra services provided for all the members of the community."). See also Libecap, *Contracting for Property Rights* ("Capturing a portion of the aggregate gains from mitigating common pool losses is a primary motivating force for individuals to bargain to install or to modify property rights arrangements.").

38. See Epstein, "Covenants and Constitutions," 914–15.

39. For a general discussion of the anticommons dilemma, see Chapter 3. Michael Heller connects the idea to the problem of covenants in private communities in Heller, "Boundaries of Private Property," 1185. See also Elberg, "Remedies," 1981–83 (noting difficulty in assembling covenant releases); cf. Buchanan, "Institutional Structure of Externality," 179 (giving an example in which too many veto rights could result in too little of an "externality-generating good or service").

40. The two kinds of fragmentation are mirror images of each other; one can only be overcome at the expense of the other. See Fennell, "Common Interest Tragedies," 966–71.

41. See, e.g., Reichman, "Judicial Supervision of Servitudes," 274; Nelson, *Private*

Neighborhoods, 94–95 (noting and discussing the range of supermajority vote requirements for amending a private community's constitution).

42. See Buchanan and Tullock, *Calculus of Consent,* 68–72.

43. See, e.g., Licker v. Harkleroad, 558 S.E.2d 31, 34–35 (Ga. Ct. App. 2001) (invalidating an attempted covenant amendment that would release only some of the lots in a private development from residential use, and collecting cases from other jurisdictions supporting that outcome); *Restatement (Third) of Property: Servitudes* § 6.10 (stating that nonuniform amendments are ineffective without the consent of negatively affected parties, except where purchasing parties receive notice of potential for such amendments). For further discussion and citations, see, e.g., Randolph, "Changing the Rules," 1092, 1103–4; Reichman, "Judicial Supervision of Servitudes," 158 and n. 54; Weiser, "Real Estate Covenant as Commons," 310 and n. 162.

44. In recent years, the Community Associations Institute has urged private communities to exercise greater discretion in rule enforcement. Stabile, *Community Associations,* 192–93, 215 (describing Community Association Institute's shift, starting around 1995, from advocating strict enforcement of rules to emphasizing flexibility).

45. See, e.g., Hyatt and French, *Community Association Law,* § 8.04(A)–(C) (presenting materials on defenses of arbitrary application, selective enforcement, and waiver); Weiser, "Real Estate Covenant as Commons," 288–89 (discussing doctrines that create pressure toward rigid covenant enforcement); Elberg, "Remedies," 1987 and n. 170 (examining the possibility that nonenforcement will lead to waiver, and citing cases). But see Rosenberry, "Trends in Covenant Enforcement," 477–78 (observing that courts are less likely to find waiver when unenforced violations are few or distinguishable, especially if a provision in the governing documents recites that nonenforcement does not constitute waiver); Elberg, supra, 1987 n. 170 (noting that waiver is alleged much more often than it is found).

46. See, e.g., Bounds, "'Green' Lawns."

47. See ibid.

48. See, e.g., Winokur, "Choice, Consent, and Citizenship," 99 and n. 32 (collecting cites indicating that "few prospective owners intelligently review the restrictions to which they subject themselves upon acceptance of a deed to land burdened by servitudes"). In evaluating the enforceability of covenants against subsequent purchasers, scholars have emphasized that a covenant is only one part of a bundled decision and may not have received individualized attention from the buyer. See Alexander, "Freedom, Coercion," 894–95; Kelman, *Critical Legal Studies,* 108–9.

49. See Miller and Page, *Complex Adaptive Systems,* 17–20.

50. In this connection, Miller and Page note the value of mechanisms that would shake up the system and offer new opportunities for re-sorting. See ibid., 18–25 (presenting "the idea that well-structured noise can jolt a system out of inferior equilibria and lead it toward superior ones, and that choice mechanisms can be designed to introduce noise in a decentralized way"); see also Kollman, Miller, and Page, "Political Institutions and Sorting."

51. See Fennell, "Contracting Communities," 866–67 (developing this adverse selection argument).

52. See Gillette, "Courts, Covenants, and Communities," 1395 (discussing covenants as signals).

53. See, e.g., Ladd and Yinger, *America's Ailing Cities*, 293–94 (noting household and societal costs of mobility).

54. See, e.g., R. Ellickson, *Order without Law*, 164–66, 225–29 (noting the role of repeat play in strategic interactions); Keser and van Winden, "Conditional Cooperation," 31–33 (presenting empirical results showing that subjects' expectations about future interactions influence cooperation levels in experimental public goods games).

55. See, e.g., Mishan, "Pareto Optimality and the Law," 259–61 (illustrating this point with a numeric example); Heymann, "Problem of Coordination," 840–42 (discussing Mishan's example and its implications for general rules). Alternative voting systems that might better incorporate preference intensities have received some attention. See, e.g., Fenster, "Community by Covenant," 13–14 (explaining how consensus-based voting models work); R. Ellickson, "Cities and Homeowners Associations," 1546–47 (referencing voting models in which dollars can be used to indicate preference strength); Levmore, "Voting with Intensity" (examining the implications of allowing vote-selling); Tideman and Tullock, "Social Choices" (discussing and extending the literature on voting procedures designed to elicit honest valuations of alternatives).

56. See, e.g., Gillette, "Courts, Covenants, and Communities," 1403–4 (observing that the property-based voting rules typically used in private communities disenfranchise renters). For discussion of voting based on property ownership, see Nelson, *Private Neighborhoods*, 403–22.

57. See, e.g., Weiser, "Real Estate Covenant as Commons," 287 n. 69; 295; Elberg, "Remedies," 1970–76. Legal fees assessed against noncompliant owners can also significantly increase the total penalty associated with a violation. For example, see Rich, "Homeowner Boards," A1 (reporting that one individual who violated a community's rule regarding trash can placement was ordered to pay nearly $12,000 in fines and legal fees).

58. Cf. Been, "'Exit' as a Constraint," 506–28 (building on Tiebout's theory of local government competition).

59. See, e.g., Hyatt, "Reinvention Redux," 53 (observing role of "institutional inertia" in common interest communities).

60. See Abramowicz and Duffy, "Intellectual Property for Market Experimentation," 366–71 (examining the risks associated with the launch of new products and services and analyzing the potential role of intellectual property protection in providing adequate incentives for market experimentation); see also Weiser, "Real Estate Covenant as Commons," 299 (discussing some of the potential barriers to developer innovation).

61. See, e.g., Nelson, *Private Neighborhoods*, 94–95.

62. See Buchanan and Tullock, *Calculus of Consent*, 68–72 (examining the trade-offs between the costs of decision-making and the costs of adverse decisions in selecting a voting rule). Private communities could add "private taking clauses" to their governing documents that would require compensation to those harmed by changes. See, e.g., R. Ellickson, "Cities and Homeowners Associations," 1535–39.

63. See, e.g., Rose, "Planning and Dealing" (examining piecemeal land use changes and the controversies surrounding them).

64. See Nelson, *Private Neighborhoods,* 370–73 (discussing land use bargains in the private development context, building on ideas in R. Ellickson, *Alternatives to Zoning*).

65. See, e.g., Epstein, "Clear View," 2095 (identifying "undercompensation" as the "signature risk[ ]" of liability rules).

66. Calabresi and Melamed, "Cathedral," 1092.

67. See, e.g., R. Ellickson, "Adverse Possession," 724; Morris, "Structure of Entitlements," 842; see also Christman, *Myth of Property,* 19, 167 (associating liability rules with a lack of control, and explaining that "control rights serve autonomy interests").

68. See, e.g., Epstein, "Clear View," 2096–99 (discussing the dominance of property rules); Smith, "Property and Property Rules," 1724 (explaining "[t]he preference for property rules" in terms of "information costs").

69. See, e.g., Model Penal Code § 221.2 (1962) (classifying trespasses under particular circumstances as misdemeanors or petty misdemeanors).

70. Jacque v. Steenberg Homes, 563 N.W.2d 154 (Wis. 1997).

71. Evangelical Lutheran Church of the Ascension of Snyder, N.Y. v. Sahlem, 172 N.E. 455, 456 (N.Y. 1930).

72. Ibid., 457; see also Rick v. West, 228 N.Y.S.2d 195 (Sup. Ct. 1962) (deciding an analogous case in a similar manner, and quoting from Judge Cardozo's opinion in *Evangelical Lutheran*).

73. See, e.g., Kelo v. City of New London, 545 U.S. 469 (2005).

74. See Bell and Parchomovsky, "Pliability Rules," 59–64. Scholars have questioned how compensation interacts with political incentives. See, e.g., Levinson, "Empire-Building," 969–71; Farber, "Public Choice," 294–98.

75. Parchomovsky and Siegelman allude to this point when they discuss differences between "[c]lassic holdout settings," in which all properties must be acquired, with situations in which something less than a unanimous buyout is sufficient. Parchomovsky and Siegelman, "Selling Mayberry," 128; see Depoorter and Vanneste, "Humpty Dumpty," 3–8, 15–16 (studying the effects of altering the degree of complementarity).

76. These land assembly examples and the figures accompanying them (Figures 4-3 and 4-4) are drawn from Fennell, "Taking Eminent Domain Apart."

77. See, e.g., Merrill, "Economics of Public Use," 75 (discussing the example of a pipeline for which "only one feasible pipeline route exists").

78. See, e.g., R. Hardin, *Collective Action,* 55–61 (analyzing step goods).

79. See Merrill, "Economics of Public Use," 75–76 (noting the potential efficiency of eminent domain for resolving "assembly problems" and addressing other "thin market" situations); Posner, *Economic Analysis of Law,* 56–57.

80. For examples of construction around holdouts, see Alpern and Durst, *Holdouts!;* see also Cohen, "Holdouts and Free Riders," 358–59.

81. Some alternative approaches to the holdout problem associated with land assembly have received recent attention. See, e.g., Heller and Hills, "Land Assembly Districts."

Chapter Five. Adaptive Options

1. My description of general average contribution is based on Epstein, "Holdouts, Externalities, and the Single Owner," 582–84; Levmore, "Self-Assessed Valuation Systems," 860 n. 214. See also Barnard v. Adams, 51 U.S. 270 (1850) (discussing and applying the doctrine of general average contribution).

2. Discussions of self-assessed valuation mechanisms include, for example, Abramowicz, "Law-and-Markets Movement," 364–73, 389–93; Bell and Parchomovsky, "Takings Reassessed," 300–306; Bell and Parchomovsky, "Taking Compensation Private"; Chang, "Self-Assessment"; Epstein, "Holdouts, Externalities, and the Single Owner," 582–84; Fennell, "Revealing Options"; Levmore, "Self-Assessed Valuation Systems"; Holland and Vaughn, "Evaluation of Self-Assessment," 112–15; Tideman, "Three Approaches," 52–69; Plassmann and Tideman, "Accurate Valuation." See also Tideman and Tullock, "Social Choices" (discussing voting procedures that incorporate valuation mechanisms).

3. Scholars have long recognized that traditional liability rules amount to call options. See, e.g., Morris, "Structure of Entitlements," 852–54; Ayres, *Optional Law*, 14–15. But see Rose, "Shadow," 2181–82 (suggesting that the "option" metaphor breaks down in contexts where specificity and advance planning are absent).

4. Madeline Morris observed that property entitlements could be conceptualized and formulated as "put options" in Morris, "Structure of Entitlements," 854–56. Later work on structuring entitlements as put options includes, for example, Ayres, *Optional Law*, 11–38; Ayres, "Protecting Property with Puts"; Krier and Schwab, "Another Light."

5. See Epstein, "Protecting Property Rights," 844 (pointing out the perverse incentive to pollute under a Rule 5 regime that allows polluters to receive payment when they stop polluting). Similar issues have been raised in the context of measures to buy back old, polluting cars; there, the fear is that people will get junked cars running solely to claim the credit. Requiring a period of ownership and registration that significantly predates the announcement of the put option would help, assuming the put option were wholly unanticipated. See Blinder, "Eco-Friendly Stimulus." The importance of this element of surprise, however, limits the long-term sustainability of such policies.

6. See Internal Revenue Service, *Summary of the Credit for Qualified Hybrid Vehicles*. If most people are already engaging in a particular desirable behavior, penalizing the few who are not may be less administratively costly than rewarding all who are. See Levmore, "Carrots and Torts," 206–7.

7. On the potential for subsidies to produce unintended incentive effects, see Levmore, "Carrots and Torts," 208 (presenting an example in which granting rewards to drivers found wearing seatbelts could induce additional driving (with seatbelts on) and thereby perversely increase the number of accidents). On the potential for monetary compensation to "crowd out" intrinsic motivations under some circumstances, see, for example, Frey, *Not Just for the Money*.

8. Francesco Parisi first brought this possibility to my attention. Cf. Merges, "Contracting into Liability Rules" (discussing the possibility, in the intellectual property

realm, that parties could choose to "contract into" organizations that would be governed by liability rules).

9. See, e.g., Winokur, "Choice, Consent, and Citizenship," 100–101 (discussing the possibility that homebuyers who enter common interest communities expect that any problems presented by the restrictions can be amicably worked out with their neighbors).

10. As Ian Ayres points out, it makes sense to assign an option to the party with the "higher variance of potential values." Ayres, "Protecting Property with Puts," 819. In this case, the community's valuation may be as variable as that of the individual homeowner.

11. See Krier, "Marketable Pollution Allowances," 453 (explaining that under tradable allowance programs, policymakers manipulate the quantity of pollution while leaving price to the market).

12. See Nash, "Trading Species," 13–19.

13. Various approaches to spatial and temporal issues in tradable permit systems are discussed in, for example, Baumol and Oates, *Theory of Environmental Policy,* 182–88; Nash and Revesz, "Markets and Geography"; Nash, "Trading Species."

14. Salzman and Ruhl, "Currencies," 645; see also Rose, "Expanding the Choices," 59–62 (analyzing tensions between increasing complexity in tradable schemes to account for factors like nonfungible pollution and the simplicity and transparency that facilitate the definition, trading, and monitoring of entitlements).

15. See, e.g., Ayres and Balkin, "Legal Entitlements as Auctions."

16. See, e.g., ibid., 733–34 (describing a "sealed bid" procedure that would make use of the parties' valuations in determining damages); Knysh, Goldbart, and Ayres, "Instantaneous Liability Rule Auctions," 3 (describing a mechanism that contemplates submission of valuations by the two parties, an award of the entitlement to the higher valuer, and selection of damages from a curve based on their two reports).

17. The traditional understanding of liability rules as involving prices set by third parties stems from Calabresi and Melamed, "Cathedral." See, e.g., ibid., 1092 (explaining that a liability rule allows for the transfer or destruction of an entitlement "on the basis of a value determined by some organ of the state rather than by the parties themselves"); see also Polinsky, "Property Rules and Liability Rules," 233 ("What distinguishes the liability rule is that the amount of compensation is determined by the collective authority, rather than by negotiation between the parties."). As the sources cited in my note 16 indicate, however, it is possible to formulate liability rules that draw on valuations set by the parties themselves. For further discussion, see Fennell, "Revealing Options."

18. See sources cited in note 2, supra.

19. This entitlement form is introduced in Fennell, "Revealing Options." Cf. Rose, "Shadow," 2179 (observing that a liability rule creates a "property right subject to an option (or easement)"—that is, a "PRSTO (or PRSTE)").

20. See Epstein, "Clear View," 2091–95 (discussing the need to balance the risks of "undercompensation" and "expropriation" in structuring entitlements).

21. See, e.g., ibid., 2093 (observing that liability rules necessitate "some level of state

intervention in *each and every* transaction to set the appropriate value for the parties"); Calabresi and Melamed, "Cathedral," 1092 (because of the need to set values, "liability rules involve an additional stage of state intervention" compared with property rules).

22. See, e.g., Farrell, "Information and the Coase Theorem," 117 (observing that where private valuations are involved, "[u]nless everyone shares the same goals, people typically have incentives to lie"); Ayres and Talley, "Solomonic Bargaining," 1030 (noting that "self-interested bargainers have a strong incentive to misrepresent their private valuations so as to capture a larger share of the bargaining 'pie'"). On the impact of self-serving biases on reservation prices and perceptions of fairness, see, for example, Babcock and Loewenstein, "Explaining Bargaining Impasse."

23. See, e.g., Polinsky, "Resolving Nuisance Disputes," 1092 and n. 37 (discussing the risk of bargaining breakdown as well as the costs associated with unnecessary bargaining).

24. See Ayres and Talley, "Solomonic Bargaining," 1030 (noting the impact of this sort of "identity crisis" on statements during bargaining); see also Abramowicz, "Law-and-Markets Movement," 370–71 (discussing pairing calls with puts to elicit honest self-assessed valuations); Levmore, "Unifying Remedies," 2169–70 (noting the constraints on misstatements of value that would be provided by a system in which a judge could use a party's valuation either as the basis of a damage award to that party for harms suffered from the other party's operations or as the basis for a payment that the other party could collect if it chose to shut down its operations).

25. See Brooks and Spier, "Trigger Happy or Gun Shy?" (presenting a formal analysis of the technique and discussing work on this mechanism and related approaches); see also Levmore, "Self-Assessed Valuation Systems," 838–43 (examining the potential for self-assessed valuation in partnership dissolution cases).

26. See Brooks and Spier, "Trigger Happy or Gun Shy?" 2; Levmore, "Self-Assessed Valuation Systems," 838–40.

27. This is not to say that the partner making the valuation will always honestly reveal her reservation price. See Plassmann and Tideman, "Accurate Valuation," 350–51 (stating that "shotgun" partnership dissolution provisions do not generally induce truthful self-assessments and presenting a mathematical proof of the proposition); Brooks and Spier, "Trigger Happy or Gun Shy?" 12–13 (modeling the incentive effects of the Texas Shootout and discussing when it would induce the assessing partner to "tell the truth"). The point is simply that the valuer's uncertainty about her role places useful upward and downward pressure on the valuation. See Levmore, "Self-Assessed Valuation Systems," 838–40 (discussing the advantages of this approach as well as some complications and drawbacks).

28. See, e.g., Baumol, *Superfairness*, 15–16 (describing solutions to cake-division problems); Brams and Taylor, *Fair Division*, 8–29 (discussing cake-cutting and other cut-and-choose games); Rawls, *A Theory of Justice*, 85 (describing a cake-divisionexercise in which the person cutting will receive the last slice); Ayres and Talley, "Solomonic Bargaining," 1034, 1072 and n. 133 (discussing cake-cutting examples).

29. See, e.g., Holland and Vaughn, "Evaluation of Self-Assessment" (describing and discussing self-assessed property tax proposals by Arnold Harberger, Nicholas Kaldor,

and others); Levmore, "Self-Assessed Valuation Systems," 778–83 (discussing literature on property value self-assessment); Ulen, "Public Use of Private Property," 182–83; Tideman, "Three Approaches," 52–69; Bell and Parchomovsky, "Taking Compensation Private"; Fennell, "Taking Eminent Domain Apart," 995–1002; see also Chang, "Framework" (presenting a taxonomy and critical analysis of self-assessment models).

30. See, e.g., Plassmann and Tideman, "Accurate Valuation," 355 n. 1 (noting past use of self-assessment mechanisms for real property in the Dutch colony of New Amsterdam (now New York), as well as in New Zealand, India, Korea, Spain, and Taiwan); Chang, "Self-Assessment," 6–8 (describing self-assessment system employed in Taiwan between 1954 and 1977). An empirical analysis of Taiwan's self-assessment system found patterns of underassessment. Chang, "Self-Assessment."

31. See, e.g., Boyle and Boyle, *Derivatives*, 5 ("The owner of the option has the right—but not the obligation—to buy (or sell) the asset.").

32. See, e.g., Brealey and Myers, *Principles of Corporate Finance*, 564–68 and figs. 20.1, 20.2 (discussing and illustrating this point). As a result, options are more valuable under conditions of greater volatility. See, e.g., ibid., 579–81 and fig. 20.11.

33. See Ayres, "Protecting Property with Puts," 819 (observing that the party with the greater degree of variation in potential valuations should hold the option).

34. The idea of iterated takings is explored in, e.g., Ayres and Balkin, "Legal Entitlements as Auctions."

35. See Abramowicz, "Law-and-Markets Movement," 429 (observing that "small-scale testing" of different mechanisms could help to avoid jarring systemwide changes).

36. Options in private law provide analogous levels of flexibility. See Goldberg, *Framing Contract Law*, 313–24 (explaining that the termination clause at issue in *Wasserman's v. Township of Middletown*, 645 A.2d 100 (N.J. 1994), can be understood as an option that afforded the lessor flexibility to respond to changes that might occur over the thirty-year lease period).

37. For example, perhaps the process required to produce them causes environmental damage, so that each flamingo represents a particular amount of harm inflicted on the community. See Bergstrom and Miller, *Experiments with Economic Principles*, 155–56 (presenting a hypothetical in which factories generate pollution in creating lawn ornaments, so that each ornament represents a particular increment of pollution cost).

38. See, e.g., Polinsky, "Property Rules and Liability Rules," 234 (explaining that "all of the 'gains from trade' from moving from the entitlement point to the efficient outcome are obtained by the party subject to the liability rule"). Property rules allow the surplus to be divided between the parties in any manner but can also generate strategic behavior that dissipates surplus or blocks efficient deals. Ibid., 235, 238.

39. For discussion of these points, see, e.g., Godsil and Simunovich, "Just Compensation in an Ownership Society," 21–24; Levmore, "Self-Assessed Valuation Systems," 781.

40. ESSMOs are not always structured on this "full value payment" model, as demonstrated by examples such as assessment for purposes of property tax payment or general average contribution in admiralty. In these instances, however, the reason for

inducing valuations is merely to spread burdens fairly, rather than to internalize externalities. For analysis of how relating the tax rate to the probability that property will be taken at various valuation levels induces honest valuations, see Plassmann and Tideman, "Accurate Valuation."

41. Scholars have observed that developers would be expected to select only those restrictions that add net value for buyers. See, e.g., Barzel, *Economic Analysis of Property Rights*, 115; R. Ellickson, "Alternatives to Zoning," 713.

42. See, e.g., Fennell, "Contracting Communities," 851 n. 95; Weiser, "Real Estate Covenant as Commons," 299–300 (discussing impediments to developer innovation).

43. See Weiss and Watts, "Community Builders and Community Associations," 101–2 (explaining that "[d]evelopers creating associations increasingly are responding to local governments' subdivision regulations rather than to the home buyers' interests," diluting the "market-driven rationale").

Chapter Six. Association and Exclusion

1. See Pogodzinski and Sass, "Economic Theory of Zoning," 295 (similarly distinguishing "direct" effects of land use controls from those effects that are produced by mobility).

2. Strahilevitz, "Exclusionary Amenities" (analyzing amenity choice as an exclusionary mechanism); ibid., 464–76 (examining the golf example).

3. See, e.g., Stiglitz, "Theory of Local Public Goods," 46; Pozdena, *Modern Economics of Housing*, 53.

4. See, e.g., Schelling, *Micromotives and Macrobehavior*, 137–66; Schelling, "Dynamic Models."

5. Cf. Cook and Ludwig, "Assigning Deviant Youths," 29–31 (distinguishing "system-level" studies from "mover" studies that look only at the impact of a grouping change on those experiencing the change).

6. The example is not a fanciful one: many common interest communities limit exterior paint colors, and some municipalities, such as Coral Gables, Florida, do so as well. See City of Coral Gables, "So You Want to Paint Your House."

7. See, e.g., Schwab and Zampelli, "Disentangling the Demand Function," 246–47; cf. Réaume, "Rights to Public Goods," 15 (discussing goods, such as culture, that "unite production and consumption").

8. See Oates, "Population Flows," 205 (noting that "characteristics of the individuals of the community are themselves a critical determinant of the level of local services"); Manski, "Educational Choice," 356 (addressing the role of student interactions in the production of education); Schwab and Oates, "Community Composition," 218 (referencing studies that support the idea "that the level of attainment in a school system or the level of safety in a neighborhood depends not so much on the instructional staff or frequency of police patrols as on the characteristics of the residents of the jurisdiction"); Schwab and Zampelli, "Disentangling the Demand Function," 254 (noting the role of the income level of residents in the demand and supply of public safety).

9. See, e.g., Chubb and Moe, *America's Schools*, 119 ("Researchers have found that

student achievement is influenced by the attitudes and behavior of other students in a school—by the pressures from student peer groups.") (citations omitted); Henderson et al., "Educational Production Functions," 97 (finding "that the principal variable or effect which is at the potential disposal of policy makers and which has a consistent and strong impact on the achievement of individual students is the quality (characteristics) of the typical or average student in a class"); Hoxby, "Peer Effects in the Classroom" (finding peer effects after controlling for selection biases).

10. Hoxby, "Peer Effects in the Classroom," 5–6; see also Manski, "Educational Choice," 356 (noting that in addition to direct student interactions, students may indirectly influence the production of education by affecting such things as teachers' instructional decisions, teacher recruitment, and course offerings).

11. Nechyba, "Public and Private School Competition."

12. The recent Moving to Opportunity studies have generated new insights on this question (and many others) by offering an experimental design that avoids the usual selection effect problems through random assignment of families to treatment and control groups with respect to housing vouchers. See Ludwig and Kling, "Is Crime Contagious?" (presenting and discussing findings suggesting that violent crime "contagion" is a less important explanatory factor than previous studies had indicated, and noting other possible mechanisms through which neighborhood effects might operate, such as the prevalence of local drug markets).

13. See, e.g., Case and Katz, "Company You Keep" (finding evidence of neighborhood effects for criminal activity and drug and alcohol use among youth); but see Kling, Liebman, and Katz, "Neighborhood Effects," 103–7 (finding beneficial effects for teenage girls and adverse effects for teenage boys on measures like risky behavior and substance use for families randomly chosen through the Moving to Opportunity program to receive housing vouchers for use in low-poverty neighborhoods).

14. Jacobs, *Death and Life of Great American Cities*, 35; see ibid., 35–42. Empirical work has challenged Jacobs's supposition that increased opportunities for informal observation would translate into better order maintenance and lower crime rates in mixed-use neighborhoods as compared with purely residential districts. See, e.g., Taylor et al., "Street Blocks"; Wilcox et al., "Busy Places." For an excellent discussion of this literature and its implications for policy, see Garnett, *Ordering the City*, ch. 3.

15. Jacobs, *Death and Life of Great American Cities*, 30.

16. Sampson and Raudenbush, "Systematic Social Observation," 612.

17. Ibid.

18. See Venkatesh, *American Project*, 29–34, 77–83.

19. Models analyzing group effects often specify two types of individuals, but migration between the categories is not typically contemplated. See, e.g., Schwab and Oates, "Community Composition," 220–30 (1991) (dividing population into types A and B); Ross and Yinger, "Sorting and Voting," 2044 (dividing the population into type-1 people and type-2 people).

20. Other scholars have taken related approaches in applying common-pool resource analysis to social issues. See, e.g., Foster, "City as an Ecological Space" (conceptualiz-

ing social capital within cities as a common resource with spatial dimensions and discussing strategies for protecting that resource, including the use of property rights). My use of the phrase "associational commons" should be distinguished from its usage in P. Levine, "Building the Electronic Commons," 1, 8 (using "associational commons" to refer to voluntary associations that operate in common resource settings).

21. See, e.g., Putnam, *Bowling Alone,* 18–24 ("social capital"); Downs, *Opening Up the Suburbs,* 61 ("social linkages"); Clotfelter, "Private Life of Public Economics," 582–84 ("participation effects"). Analogous ideas are discussed in, for example, R. Ellickson, "Unpacking the Household," 245 ("household surplus"); Wax, "Egalitarian Marriage," 529 n. 40 ("marital surplus"). Association may produce a deficit rather than a surplus. See, e.g., Becker and Murphy, *Social Economics,* 12 (discussing "negative capital").

22. These are the same criteria for tragedy that were specified in Chapter 3; see also Ostrom, Gardner, and Walker, *Common-Pool Resources,* 15–16 (noting conditions that lead to common-pool resource dilemmas).

23. For a discussion of linearity and the possible effects of nonlinearity, see, for example, Jencks and Mayer, "Social Consequences," 122.

24. See, e.g., Bénabou, "Equity and Efficiency," 248 (discussing possible shapes of a production function for surplus associated with the percentage of rich households in a community); Cook and Ludwig, "Assigning Deviant Youths," 17–38 (examining the significance of "the shape of what might be called the 'social contagion function'"); Marwell and Oliver, *Critical Mass in Collective Action,* 58–100 (exploring "the dynamics of production functions"); ibid., 59, fig. 4.1 (showing a variety of different production functions)

25. See, e.g., Oliver, Marwell, and Teixeira, "Theory of the Critical Mass," 527–28, fig. 1(a) (presenting and discussing S-shaped production functions); Schelling, *Micromotives and Macrobehavior,* 94–102 (applying the notion of "critical mass" to a variety of social phenomena).

26. See Oliver, Marwell, and Teixeira, "Theory of the Critical Mass," 525–27, fig. 1 (discussing and illustrating different production function shapes). My Figure 6-3 represents an "accelerating" production function. See ibid., 527, fig. 1(c).

27. Empirical work on the impact of choice on cooperation suggests some interesting complexities. Esther Hauk and Rosemarie Nagel found that players who are forced into a Prisoner's Dilemma game when they would prefer not to play will usually defect. Hauk and Nagel, "Choice of Partners," 772, 778, and tbl. 1. However, arrangements that allowed the game to proceed without the consent of one or both players also increased *overall* cooperation rates over arrangements where mutual consent was required for the game to proceed. Ibid., 778 and tbl. 1. When matches could be forced, would-be defectors could not remove themselves from the game. Yet, some of those forced to play cooperated (even though most defected), yielding an increase in overall cooperation. Ibid., 780, 784, 786–88. See also Hauk, "Leaving the Prison," 65–68 (demonstrating through simulations that stable cooperation in Prisoner's Dilemma interactions can be achieved if players employ a rule of thumb for choosing and for refusing partners that rewards cooperation and punishes defection).

28. Some recent work has examined how the threat of exclusion might motivate group members to contribute to the production of a local public good. See Brekke, Nyborg, and Rege, "Fear of Exclusion," 2–4; Cinyabuguma, Page, and Putterman, "Threat of Expulsion," 1422–23; see also Charness and Yang, "Endogenous Group Formation" (examining contributions to pubic goods within an experimental setting which allows groups to grow, shrink, and merge, and in which groups can exclude uncooperative members but excluded members have a chance at "redemption" through later cooperation).

29. Heck and Fowler, "Friends, Trust, and Civic Engagement."

30. Rosenblum, *Membership and Morals,* 47–50.

31. For a fascinating classroom experiment examining investment changes in response to decisions based on imperfect proxies and resulting feedback effects on decision-making, see Fryer, Goeree, and Holt, "Experience-Based Discrimination." This experiment is based on a model of statistical discrimination developed in Arrow, "Theory of Discrimination," 23–32.

32. See Dickerson, "Caught in the Trap" (proposing that school attendance be delinked from residence and that households making "integrationist" residential choices be given priority in school choice).

33. See Moe, *Schools, Vouchers,* 288 (explaining that parents making judgments about vouchers "appear to be combining two roles: they are consumers, concerned about their own personal interests, and they are citizens, concerned about society as a whole"); Sunstein, "Social Norms and Social Roles," 923–25 (positing that individuals may desire different outcomes and follow different norms when occupying the roles of citizens and consumers, respectively). See also Lewinsohn-Zamir, "Consumer Preferences" (examining the consumer-citizen distinction).

34. See Fennell, "Beyond Exit and Voice," 34–35. The two-part payoff discussed in the text is a bit of a simplification, because some households do not directly consume a particular good (such as education) but instead receive a benefit in the form of an increased home value based on the capitalized consumption value that purchasers can expect to receive. See Fischel, *Homevoter Hypothesis,* 150–52.

35. Abraham Bell and Gideon Parchomovsky similarly used two-person game matrices to model the "stay/leave" decision in the context of housing segregation. Bell and Parchomovsky, "Integration Game," 1991–93; see also Dagan and Heller, "Liberal Commons," 576–77 (discussing strategic interactions between "stay-putters" and "foot-out-the-door folks").

36. Nothing in my analysis turns on where the relatively advantaged and disadvantaged areas lie geographically; I use the admittedly stereotypical contrast between an inner-city neighborhood and a wealthy suburb for simplicity. Nor does my analysis of the choice situation depend on whether the residents of Optoutia have actually fled the city or even see themselves as having consciously opted out of it. See Garnett, "Suburbs as Exit," 279 (observing that many residents of suburbs have never lived in, and do not identify with, the city at the center of their metropolitan area).

37. Robert Putnam has recently suggested, based on an empirical study of homogeneous and heterogeneous census tracts, that "people living in ethnically diverse settings

appear to 'hunker down'—that is, to pull in like a turtle." Putnam, *"E Pluribus Unum,"* 149. Interestingly, the findings did not show any out-group hostility—subjects living in diverse settings distrusted members of their own ethnic group just as much as they distrusted members of other groups—but rather a more general inclination "to withdraw from collective life" altogether. Ibid., 150.

38. See, e.g., Frank, *Falling Behind,* 2–3 (defining "positional" and "nonpositional" goods); ibid., 66–67 (discussing the "highly positional" nature of children's education and the resulting competition for homes in better school districts). Frank adopts the term "positional goods" from Hirsch, *Social Limits to Growth,* 11, 27–31. Frank, "Nonpositional Goods." Like Hirsch, Frank emphasizes that relative status flowing from these goods may be sought not as an end in itself but rather as a way of achieving other valued outcomes, such as well-paid jobs, in a competitive environment. Ibid., 103.

39. These game structures are discussed in Chapter 3.

40. See note 27, supra.

41. See, e.g., Ullmann-Margalit, *Emergence of Norms,* 37 (explaining how norms relate to the "Mortarmen's Dilemma"); McAdams and Rasmusen, "Norms and the Law," 1578–81 (examining how norms might create incentives through mechanisms like guilt, esteem, and shame).

42. Buchanan, "Urban Fiscal Strategy," 4. Of course, times have changed; central cities (or at least portions of them) have recently become much more attractive to the well-off. But the essential dilemma of jurisdictional choice to which Buchanan was responding has not disappeared.

43. Much of the discussion has revolved around subsidizing inclusive choices. See, e.g., Silverman, "Subsidizing Tolerance," 377 (presenting a proposal that would include payments to local governments accepting low-income entry, individuals residing in inclusive communities, and certain migrating households); Bell and Parchomovsky, "Integration Game," 2011–15 (proposing "institutional subsidies" for communities); Yinger, "Prejudice and Discrimination," 460 (critiquing proposals to offer communities or individuals "desegregation bonuses").

44. I refer here to the vast literature building on the framework presented in Calabresi and Melamed, "Cathedral."

45. The idea that people have "entitlements" or "property interests" that relate to association has appeared in, for example, Hersey, "Fractured Paean," 62 (using the phrase "familial associational entitlements" in connection with the Supreme Court's decision in *Moore v. City of East Cleveland,* 431 U.S. 494 (1977)); Singer, *Entitlement,* 39–44 (observing that civil rights laws might be viewed as granting an easement to enter private property).

Chapter Seven. Property in Association

1. See Schelling, "Dynamic Models," 145 ("To choose a neighborhood is to choose neighbors.").

2. Spatially concentrated poverty, in particular, has been associated with a range of adverse consequences, even though the mechanisms producing these consequences

are not well understood. See, e.g., Jencks and Mayer, "Social Consequences." The re-cent Moving to Opportunity studies, which made moves to lower-poverty areas ran-domly available to eligible households, offer new insights into this set of questions. See, e.g., Kling, Liebman, and Katz, "Neighborhood Effects" (finding significantly improved outcomes on adult mental health measures but no statistically significant impact on adult economic self-sufficiency, and finding beneficial behavioral effects on teenage girls but negative effects on teenage boys); Moving to Opportunity Research, online at http://www.nber.org/~kling/mto/ (collecting research papers and briefs based on this set of studies). The mixed results found in those studies offer important cautions about the ability to engineer improvements across all life domains by moving families from high-poverty neighborhoods to lower-poverty neighborhoods, but do not negate the body of work establishing that negative consequences are associated with growing up in conditions of concentrated poverty. The positive effects of moves to lower-poverty neighborhoods on measures of adult mental health are especially in-teresting, and could produce intergenerational effects over time.

3. See, e.g., J. Levine, *Zoned Out* (providing an extended analysis of the nonmarket character of zoning).

4. On the limits of "property," see, for example, Penner, "Misled by 'Property,'" 76–77 (suggesting that the "property" label should be reserved for interests that are not central to identity within a given normative system); Young, *Justice and the Poli-tics of Difference,* 25 ("Rights are not fruitfully conceived as possessions.").

5. For the view that the right to exclude is the defining attribute of property see, for example, Merrill, "Right to Exclude"; Merrill and Smith, *Property,* v. For a recent ex-ploration of the mechanisms of exclusion in property, see Strahilevitz, "Rights to Ex-clude." Exclusion incorporates the right to selectively include. See, e.g., Merrill, "Right to Exclude," 740 (characterizing the property owner as a "gatekeeper"); Penner, "'Bundle of Rights, '" 744 (explaining that property rights operate "like a gate, not a wall," and permit others to be selectively included and excluded).

6. Reich, "The New Property," 771.

7. See, for example, Singer, *Entitlement,* 43–44 (discussing privacy-based distinc-tions between homes and places of business with respect to the applicability of public accommodations law); Emerson, "Freedom of Association," 20 (explaining that prob-lems involving prohibited or required associations "must be framed in terms of draw-ing the line between the public and private sectors of our common life").

8. See Markovits, "Quarantines and Distributive Justice," 323 (discussing the choice between vaccinations and quarantines); Cook and Ludwig, "Assigning Deviant Youths," 14–15 (discussing the "Good Behavior Game" used in elementary school classrooms, which has been characterized by one scholar as a "behavioral vaccine").

9. Calabresi, *The Costs of Accidents,* 136–38.

10. A primary tool for fighting housing discrimination is the federal Fair Housing Act, 42 U.S.C. §§ 3601 et seq. Other protections include state and local legislation that is modeled on, but sometimes goes beyond, the federal statute. 42 U.S.C. § 1982 (a pro-vision of the Civil Rights Act of 1866) forbids both public and private racial discrimi-

nation in property rights.) See Jones v. Alfred H. Mayer Co., 392 U.S. 409 (1968). The Fourteenth Amendment's equal protection clause also addresses housing discrimination. See, e.g., Shelley v. Kraemer, 334 U.S. 1 (1948).

11. Other scholars have also applied the Calabresi and Melamed framework to social problems. See, e.g., Godsil, "Behind the Color Line."

12. Calabresi and Melamed, "Cathedral."

13. Table 7-2 is adapted from Fennell, "Revealing Options," 1447 fig. 6, which was in turn based on Ayres, "Protecting Property with Puts," 798 tbl. 3.

14. Calabresi and Melamed briefly discussed variations involving a "compelled buyer," which corresponds to the "put options" represented by what are now known as Rules 5 and 6. Calabresi and Melamed, "Cathedral," 1122 n. 62. Subsequent work developing and discussing these rules includes, for example, Krier and Schwab, "Another Light"; Morris, "Structure of Entitlements," 854–56; Ayres, "Protecting Property with Puts," 796. Rules 5 and 6 appear at some points in the literature with the numbers reversed from what is shown in Table 7-2. See Ayres and Goldbart, "Optimal Delegation," 7 n. 13.

15. See Ayres and Goldbart, "Optimal Delegation," 6.

16. This latitude is not unlimited, however, and varies depending on state law. See, e.g., Ellickson and Been, *Land Use Controls,* 710, 783–88.

17. Mills, "Urban Land-Use Controls," 537.

18. R. Ellickson, "Suburban Growth Controls," 410–14, 436–38, 467–70, 505–10.

19. White, "Liability Rules and Pigovian Taxes." Pigovian taxes attempt to align incentives by requiring a party whose activities generate costs for others to pay a tax "equal to marginal social damage." Cropper and Oates, "Environmental Economics," 680; see Pigou, *The Economics of Welfare,* 172–203.

20. Buchanan, "Urban Fiscal Strategy."

21. Ibid., 1. Variations on this theme are discussed in, for example, Gewirtz, "Remedies and Resistance," 652–56; Gillette, "Opting Out of Public Provision," 1204–5.

22. See Frug, "City Services," 31 n. 31.

23. E.g., Silverman, "Subsidizing Tolerance," Bell and Parchomovsky, "Integration Game."

24. Title I of the Elementary and Secondary Education Act of 1965 is codified at 20 U.S.C.A. 6333 (West Supp. 2002). For discussion of school subsidization approaches, see, e.g., Ryan and Heise, "Political Economy of School Choice."

25. See, e.g. Fischel, *Homevoter Hypothesis,* 279–81.

26. See Dickerson, "Caught in the Trap," 1288–94.

27. S. Burlington County NAACP v. Township of Mt. Laurel, 336 A.2d 713 (N.J. 1975) (Mount Laurel I).

28. S. Burlington County NAACP v. Township of Mt. Laurel, 456 A.2d 390 (N.J. 1983) (Mount Laurel II).

29. Hills Dev. Co. v. Township of Bernards, 510 A.2d 621 (N.J. 1986) (known as Mount Laurel III). The New Jersey Fair Housing Act established the Council on Affordable Housing (COAH) to administer local governments' "fair share" obligations under the state constitution and provided for RCAs. See ibid. RCAs were eliminated in

2008. See NJ Stat Ann § 52:27D-329.6. Scholarship on RCAs includes, for example, Hughes and McGuire, "Market for Exclusion"; McDougall, "Regional Contribution Agreements"; Field, Gilbert, and Wheeler, "Trading the Poor." A student note published before RCAs were developed had anticipated the idea. "Zoning for the Regional Welfare"; see McDougall, "Regional Contribution Agreements," 681–82.

30. Hughes and McGuire, "Market for Exclusion," 213. The COAH, which administers New Jersey's Fair Housing Act, maintains a list of approved RCAs. See http://www.state.nj.us/dca/affiliates/coah/reports/.

31. See Field, Gilbert, and Wheeler, "Trading the Poor," 25–26.

32. Hughes and McGuire, "Market for Exclusion," 216.

33. The COAH set a minimum per-unit transfer price and was required to approve all transactions, but appears to have played a relatively minor role in the negotiations. See Field, Gilbert, and Wheeler, "Trading the Poor," 10 and n. 38, 28–29.

34. For discussion of the bargaining dynamics, see, e.g., ibid., 3; Hughes and McGuire, "Market for Exclusion," 215–16; McDougall, "Regional Contribution Agreements," 686–88. See also Ford, "Boundaries of Race," 1900–1903 (discussing possible reforms that would respond to shortcomings of RCAs, including unequal bargaining power).

35. See, e.g., Field, Gilbert, and Wheeler, "Trading the Poor," 3.

36. See McDougall, "Regional Contribution Agreements," 683–84.

37. As discussed in Chapter 5, the law of general average contribution used a similar approach to deter underassessments and overassessments. Close parallels can also be found in auction proposals for siting locally undesirable land uses. See, e.g., Been, "What's Fairness Got to Do With It?" 1052–55 (discussing and critiquing proposals that would allow neighborhoods to bid for veto rights); Inhaber, "Market-Based Solution," 812–15 (proposing use of a reverse Dutch auction for siting waste); O'Hare, "Facility Siting," 438–56 (analyzing auction approaches to facility siting).

38. Cf. Nash and Revesz, "Markets and Geography" (presenting a proposal that would make marketable permit schemes sensitive to spatial and temporal nonlinearities).

39. 42 U.S.C. § 3603(b)(2) contains the exemption from Fair Housing Act liability colloquially known as the "Mrs. Murphy exemption." This provision does not exempt actors from liability for violations of Section 3604(c), which prohibits discriminatory advertisements, notices, and statements. See ibid., § 3603(b). Housing discrimination based on race, whether by public or private actors, is categorically prohibited by the Civil Rights Act of 1866, 42 U.S.C. § 1982, notwithstanding the exemption in the Fair Housing Act. Section 3604(c)'s limits on speech about legal conduct arguably raise first amendment issues, given developments in the protection afforded commercial speech. Compare United States v. Hunter, 459 F.2d 205, 214 (4th Cir. 1972) ("[n]or is there any constitutional requirement that sellers or lessors of otherwise exempted dwellings be permitted to advertise their intent to discriminate") with Chicago Lawyers' Committee for Civil Rights Under Law v. Craigslist, 519 F.3d 666, 668 (7th Cir. 2007) ("any rule that forbids truthful advertising of a transaction that would be substantively lawful encounters serious problems under the first amendment").

40. See Schwemm, "Discriminatory Housing Statements," 249–51.

41. For a discussion of the links between norms and shame, see, e.g., McAdams, "Regulation of Norms." As for the possibility that payment might be viewed as sufficiently compliant with an anti-exclusion norm within a regime that provides for such payments, an analogy might be found in Gneezy and Rustichini, "A Fine Is a Price" (study of private day care centers in Israel showed that late pickups increased when parents were charged for each instance).

42. Oates, "From Research to Policy," 138–39; see also Been, "What's Fairness Got to Do With It?" 1040–42 (discussing "moral objections" to compensation schemes for the siting of locally undesirable land uses).

43. As Michael Walzer has emphasized, much of associational life is unchosen. Walzer, *Politics and Passion*, 2–3.

44. I thank Robert Post and Jerry Mashaw for discussions on this point.

45. See, e.g., Stoll, *Sets, Logic, and Axiomatic Theories*, 14 (defining a "partition of set X" as a "disjoint collection . . . of nonempty and distinct subsets of X such that each member of X is a member of some (and, hence, exactly one) member" of the collection of subsets).

46. The textual point is distinct from the argument about associational preferences that was famously and controversially put forward in Wechsler, "Toward Neutral Principles," 34. Wechsler focused on the conflict between those desiring an association and those not desiring it. In the context in which he wrote (racial integration), principles of equality would clearly trump any preference not to associate. See, e.g., Black, "Segregation Decisions," 429. But in many other contexts (like choosing friends) this type of conflict can be readily resolved by applying a rule of mutual consent that allows any party to the would-be association to veto it. The discussion in the text references cases in which the principle of mutual consent fails—not because of trumping normative principles but simply as a matter of logic. Some settings are structured such that some nonconsensual associations will inevitably result, regardless of the rules governing grouping.

47. Korematsu v. United States, 323 U.S. 214 (1944).

48. Ibid., 320 (Roberts, J., dissenting). The exclusion order was promulgated pursuant to President Franklin D. Roosevelt's Executive Order 9066, which authorized the Secretary of War and his designees "to prescribe military areas . . . from which any or all persons may be excluded."

49. Koramatsu, 323 U.S. at 231–33 (Roberts J., dissenting); ibid., 242–44 (Jackson, J., dissenting).

50. See, e.g., Schuck, *Diversity in America*, 21 (observing that group boundaries are often unclear or overlapping); Young, *Justice and the Politics of Difference*, 238–39 (discussing advantages of ambiguity in neighborhood boundaries).

51. See, e.g., Sommer, *Personal Space*, 153; R. Ellickson, "Suburban Growth Controls," 450.

52. On the implications of the reduced mobility of low-income people for residential patterns, see Frug, "City Services," 27, 31 n. 31.

53. I thank Bruce Ackerman for discussions relating to the points in this paragraph.

54. I thank Jed Rubenfeld for helpful comments on this point.

55. The argument that localities should internalize the effects of their exclusion is interestingly explored in Schragger, "Paying for Our Localism." For discussion and citations on the competitive use of exclusion, see Fennell, "Exclusion's Attraction." Competitive exclusion need not involve excluding uses from the whole jurisdiction; it can also be pursued through intrajurisdictional zoning choices. See, e.g., Ford, "Boundaries of Race," 1854.

56. For analysis of the implications of these sorts of assemblies, see, e.g., Peñalver, "Property as Entrance," 1940–44; Hills, "Constitutional Rights of Private Governments," 218–29; Stolzenberg, "He Drew a Circle That Shut Me Out," 588–98.

57. Strahilevitz, "Rights to Exclude," 1850–53.

58. On the many motives behind exclusion, see, e.g., Dietderich, "Egalitarian's Market," 31; Bogart, "Big Teeth," 1671–72; Oates, "On Local Finance," 96; Hansmann, "Theory of Status Organizations," 119.

59. Under the federal Fair Housing Act, as under Title VII of the Civil Rights Act of 1964, discrimination can be established through disparate impact analysis without the need to show discriminatory intent. See, e.g., Huntington Branch NAACP v. Town of Huntington, 844 F.2d 926, 933–41 (2d Cir 1988), aff'd 488 U.S. 15 (1988) (per curiam). However, it is relatively difficult for plaintiffs to prevail under this standard, and it has produced limited results. See generally Selmi, "Was the Disparate Impact Theory a Mistake?"

60. See Selmi, "Was the Disparate Impact Theory a Mistake?" 767–82 (suggesting that the disparate impact theory of discrimination may have been counterproductive to the extent that it impeded the development of a more robust understanding of intentional discrimination).

Chapter Eight. Breaking Up the Bundle

1. Caplin et al., *Housing Partnerships,* 80.

2. See, e.g., Fischel, *Homevoter Hypothesis,* 9–10, 268; Shiller, *Macro Markets,* 78.

3. See, e.g., Fischel, *Homevoter Hypothesis,* 4; Bucks, Kennickell, and Moore, "Recent Changes." On human capital, see R. Ellickson, "Property in Land," 1353.

4. See, e.g., Fischel, "Why Are There NIMBYs?" 146 (likening a home purchase to the investment of nearly all one's assets in "a single firm that produce[s] one product in a single location").

5. See, e.g., ibid.

6. As a result of excesses in lending practices in recent years, millions of U.S. homeowners have mortgages that they cannot afford to repay; with refinancing out of reach due to declining home values, and loan restructuring inhibited by securitization, default rates have skyrocketed. Research firm Moody's Economy.com projects that mortgage foreclosures could reach 7.3 million between 2008 and 2010, with as many as 4.3 million American homeowners losing their homes. Crittenden and Holzer, "Relief Nears." Governmental efforts to respond to the housing crisis are ongoing as of this writing. See, e.g., Phillips and Simon, "Mortgage Bailout."

7. The costs of foreclosure extend beyond the defaulting household. In addition to the financial losses that have fueled the current economic downturn, nondefaulting households in neighborhoods with high concentrations of foreclosures may suffer spillover effects, including negative impacts on property values. See, e.g., Bostic and Lee, "Mortgages, Risk," 311, 313–14 (noting the potential for concentrated foreclosures to generate negative externalities for neighborhoods); Schuetz, Been, and Ellen, "Concentrated Mortgage Foreclosures" (finding some evidence, based on regression analysis, that proximate foreclosures above a certain threshold reduce home prices).

8. See, e.g., Krugman, "Home Not-So-Sweet Home" (arguing that "homeownership isn't for everyone" and that "we should drop the obsession with ownership"); Streitfeld and Morgenson, "Building Flawed American Dreams" (quoting former HUD secretary Henry Cisneros as saying that "people came to homeownership who should not have been homeowners").

9. See Caplin et al., "Facilitating," 5, 13–14 (recommending use of a type of shared appreciation mortgage to forestall an "affordability crisis" following the current housing crisis).

10. See, e.g., Hagerty, "Mortgage Woes," A2; Case and Shiller, "Mortgage Default Risk," 245.

11. See Shiller and Weiss, "Moral Hazard," 3, 13–14; Leland, "Facing Default."

12. A reverse mortgage draws down the equity in the home through a lump sum or stream of monthly payments. When the owner dies or moves away, the loan is repaid from the home's sales proceeds, and the reverse mortgagee has no recourse against the owner's other assets. See, e.g., Tergesen, "Reverse Mortgage Fees Drop."

13. See ibid.

14. See, e.g., Banks et al., "Housing Ownership over the Life Cycle," 10; Sinai and Souleles, "Hedge Against Rent Risk."

15. The Oak Park program would pay homeowners for 80 percent of any loss on resale after five years of enrollment in the plan if the house sold below its appraised value and the drop in value was not attributable to metropolitan-area value changes or to damage or loss to the individual property. See McNamara, "Homeowner's Equity Assurance," 1468–69. Oak Park has not experienced a significant home price decline since the program was implemented, and no claims have been made under the program. See Shiller and Weiss, "Home Equity Insurance," 33.

16. Home equity programs similar to the one in Oak Park have been adopted in a number of other communities. See Shiller and Weiss, "Home Equity Insurance," 32–33; Shiller, "Radical Financial Innovation," 316; Caplin et al., "Pilot Project." William Fischel has argued for an expansion of home equity insurance as a way to address the "NIMBY" ("not in my backyard") problem. See, e.g., Fischel, "Economic History," 335–36.

17. See CME Group, "S&P/Case-Shiller Home Price Indices Futures and Options," 3; see also Macro Markets, "S&P/Case-Shiller Home Price Indices." These housing market derivatives grew out of many years of work by Robert Shiller, Karl Case, and Allan Weiss. See, e.g., Shiller, *Macro Markets*, 78–87; Shiller, *New Financial Order,*

118–20; Shiller and Weiss, "Home Equity Insurance"; Case, Shiller, and Weiss, "Index-Based Futures and Options." For a recent discussion of the history and future prospects of housing derivatives, see Shiller, "Derivatives Markets."

18. For background on shared-appreciation mortgages and shared-equity mortgages, see, e.g., Caplin et al., "Shared-Equity Mortgages"; Caplin et al., "Facilitating." Work on limited-equity cooperatives and related arrangements for delivering affordable housing includes, e.g., Davis, "Shared Equity Homeownership," 2–3; Byrne and Diamond, "Matrix Revealed," 541–51; Kennedy, "Limited Equity Coop"; Stone, "Social Ownership"; see also Caplin et al., "Innovative Approaches." An extensive analysis of housing partnerships is provided in Caplin et al., *Housing Partnerships*.

19. For discussion of some recent examples, see Wilmot, "Radical Thinking"; Coy, "SwapRent"; Hagerty, "Product Taps Home Equity"; Tergesen, "Trading on the Future"; Ayres and Nalebuff, "Equity Kicker." See also Ayres and Nalebuff, "Price-Protect Your Home"; Christie, "New Way to Bet on Real Estate."

20. Public Law 110-289, Title IV, § 1402 (k); see also Caplin et al., "Facilitating," 5–6; Ayres and Nalebuff, "Equity Kicker."

21. See Demsetz, "Toward a Theory of Property Rights," 350 ("property rights develop to internalize externalities when the gains of internalization become larger than the costs of internalization").

22. See, e.g., Davis, "Shared Equity Homeownership," 65 (observing that "the bulk" of home appreciation "is usually caused by societal factors outside of the homeowner's control, including public investment in the city as a whole, private investment in the surrounding neighborhood, changes in the regional economy, and changes in the way that residential real estate is regulated, financed, and taxed").

23. See, e.g., Brueckner, "Consumption and Investment Motives"; Henderson and Ioannides, "Housing Tenure Choice," 102.

24. See Sinai and Souleles, "Hedge against Rent Risk."

25. See, e.g., Radin, "Residential Rent Control"; Smithsimon, "Rent Regulation."

26. See, e.g., Gramlich, *Subprime Mortgages*, 17–18.

27. The concern here is with price movements in the homeowner's current housing market that are not matched by correlated price changes in the market to which the homeowner is moving. To the extent that prices in the new and old housing markets move in tandem, investment risk is reduced accordingly. See Sinai and Souleles, "Hedge against Rent Risk," 764.

28. For a discussion of legal reforms directed at providing greater security of tenure to tenants, see generally Roisman, "Right to Remain."

29. Kelo v. City of New London, 545 U.S. 469 (2005) (holding that the "public use" requirement of the Fifth Amendment's Takings Clause was met where private residences were condemned to redevelop an economically distressed area). The decision generated widespread public backlash. See, e.g., Cole, "Not Good News," 819–24; see also Nadler and Diamond, "Psychology of Property Rights" (presenting experimental studies probing the reasons for the public's outrage).

30. The federal Fair Housing Act protects families with children against discrimination, and thus would typically protect the right of parents to add their own children,

or children who have been placed in their custody, to the household. See 42 U.S.C. §§ 802(k), 804.

31. See, e.g., Franzese, "Does It Take a Village?" 555–56 (providing examples of restrictions placed on property owners in common interest communities governing such matters as landscaping, exterior aesthetic choices, and even some aspects of dress and conduct); Rawling, "Reevaluating Leasing Restrictions" (examining restrictions on leasing properties in common interest communities to tenants).

32. 2005 American Housing Survey data indicate that 88.15 percent of the nation's single-family detached homes occupied year round are owner occupied; the figure is 86.24 percent when all-year-round-occupied one-unit homes, both detached and attached, are included. See U.S. Bureau of the Census, *American Housing Survey for the United States: 2005,* tbl. 1A1 (providing data from which the percentages above were calculated). The data also indicate that owner-occupied homes that are on the market are far more likely to be listed "for sale only" than to be available for rent; even vacant single-family homes on the market are about one and one-half times as likely to be "for sale only" as to be listed for rent. See ibid.

33. Chau, Firth, and Srinidhi, "Double Moral Hazard," 1391; see also Henderson and Ioannides, "Housing Tenure Choice" (describing and modeling the "rental externality").

34. See Akerlof, "Market for 'Lemons.'"

35. See Dietz and Haurin, "Social and Micro-Level Consequences," 422 (citing Henderson and Ioannides, "Housing Tenure Choice"); see also Akerlof, "Market for 'Lemons'" (examining analogous dynamics in a number of contexts).

36. Internal Revenue Code §§ 163(h); 164; see Gale, Gruber, and Stephens-Davidowitz, "Encouraging Homeownership." Imputed rent is taxed in some other countries, such as Italy, Norway, and Denmark. See, e.g., Gale, Gruber, and Stephens-Davidowitz, "Encouraging Homeownership," 1172–73 and n. 3; see also Chatterjee, "Taxes, Homeownership" (discussing the significance of the nontaxation of imputed rent).

37. Subject to various limitations, an individual can receive up to $250,000 in tax-free gains ($500,000 for a married couple) from the sale of a primary residence. Internal Revenue Code § 121.

38. The potential for homeownership's tax benefits to be capitalized into home prices introduces some complexities. See Chatterjee, "Taxes, Homeownership" (explaining how the capitalization of tax benefits might affect the relative attractiveness of owning a home, and concluding that tax advantages are capitalized into home prices "[t]o some extent, but not fully for all types of housing").

39. See ibid.

40. See, e.g., Gale, Gruber, and Stephens-Davidowitz, "Encouraging Homeownership"; McKinnon and Vaughan, "Tax Hikes" (Obama proposals).

41. See Follain and Melamed, "False Messiah of Tax Policy"; Chatterjee, "Taxes, Homeownership" (providing an example illustrating this point).

42. See, e.g., Perin, *Everything in Its Place,* 53.

43. See, e.g., Fischel, *Homevoter Hypothesis,* 4; Bucks, Kennickell, and Moore, "Recent Changes."

44. See, e.g., Cauley, Pavlov, and Schwartz, "Homeownership as a Constraint," 309;

Brueckner, "Consumption and Investment Motives"; Henderson and Ioannides, "Housing Tenure Choice," 111.

45. Barzel, *Economic Analysis of Property Rights,* 78–79; see also Smith, "Property and Property Rules," 1795–96 (applying and explaining the idea of a property owner as "the holder of the residual claim"); Markby, *Elements of Law* (explaining that even though specific rights may be removed from ownership, "[h]owever numerous and extensive may be the detached rights, however insignificant may be the residue, it is the holder of this residuary right whom we always consider as the owner").

46. Smith, "Property and Property Rules," 1795–97.

47. See, e.g., Shiller and Weiss, "Moral Hazard," 5–11.

48. Cf. Demsetz, "Toward a Theory of Property Rights" (explaining how changes in the relative costs and benefits of internalizing externalities cause property rights to evolve). The role of housing indexes in offloading off-site risk is taken up in Chapter 9. For a detailed discussion of how indexes can be used to transfer risk, as well as many technical issues surrounding their use, see Shiller, *Macro Markets.*

49. See, e.g., Chau, Firth, and Srinidhi, "Double Moral Hazard," 1391; Henderson and Ioannides, "Housing Tenure Choice," 104 and n. 3.

50. The term "Homeownership 2.0" appeared independently in an online newslist heading posted after I began work on this project under this name; others may have employed this formulation as well. See posting of National Housing Institute/Shelterforce, nhi_press@nhi.org, to colist@comm-org.wisc.edu (May 4, 2007), http://comm-org.wisc.edu/pipermail/colist/2007-May/004667.html.

51. Durable goods are commonly understood to contain such a savings component. See Speight, *Consumption, Rational Expectations, and Liquidity,* 10.

52. Caplin et al., *Housing Partnerships,* 6.

53. See Fischel, "Economic History," 334 (observing the impracticality of attempting to address homeowners' exclusionary tendencies by "[r]educing homeownership").

54. See generally Fischel, *Homevoter Hypothesis.*

55. Ibid., 149–51.

56. See, e.g., ibid., 268–70; Fischel, "Economic History"; see also Fischel, "Voting, Risk Aversion," 886–90 (suggesting that both Shiller's home equity insurance proposal and Caplin et al.'s housing partnership idea could reduce harmful NIMBY behaviors).

57. A variety of positive social effects have been associated with homeownership in the theoretical and empirical literature, although selection biases present difficult challenges. See, e.g., DiPasquale and Glaeser, "Incentives and Social Capital"; Haurin, Dietz, and Weinberg, "Neighborhood Homeownership Rates."

58. See, e.g., Fischel, "Economic History."

59. Such political behavior is one implication of the fact that the home is an investment as well as a source of consumption value. See Brueckner and Joo, "Voting with Capitalization," 464 (explaining that "the voter's ideal public spending level reflects a blend of his own preferences and those of the eventual buyer of his house"); see also Fennell, "Homes Rule," 647–49.

60. I thank Eduardo Peñalver for discussions on this point.

61. See Fischel, *Homevoter Hypothesis,* 9–11.

62. Smith, "Semicommon Property Rights," 146–54. For an illustration of an open field village, see R. Ellickson, "Property in Land," 1389 (providing an image adapted from maps dated 1719 appearing in Homans, *English Villagers,* 88–89).

63. For discussions of locational equity issues, see, e.g., Been, "What's Fairness Got to Do With It?" (raising questions about causality); Pritchett, "'Public Menace.'"

64. For further treatment of this point, see Fennell, "Homeownership 2.0," 1104–07. I am grateful to Lior Strahilevitz for helpful discussions on the potential political power of investors.

Chapter Nine. Homeownership, Version 2.0

1. For example, a proposal for government-provided home equity insurance appeared nearly forty years ago. See Marcus and Taussig, "Government Insurance of Home Values." While some homeownership risk-reallocation programs have been employed in limited ways over the years, there has been a marked uptick in interest and activity in the field over the past few years, and especially since the onset of the present housing crisis. See Chapter 8.

2. For simplicity, my discussion here will ignore the impact of inflation, although H2.0's design would need to account for it. See, e.g., Shiller, *Macro Markets,* 96–98; Shiller and Weiss, "Home Equity Insurance," 31–32.

3. See Caplin et al., *Housing Partnerships,* 89. A Pareto improvement "makes at least one person better off and no one worse off." Posner, *Economic Analysis of Law,* 12.

4. These advantages have been emphasized in the literature on reallocating homeownership risk. See, e.g., Shiller and Weiss, "Home Equity Insurance"; Caplin et al., *Housing Partnerships,* 90. H2.0 would also reduce the substantial risk for lenders that price downturns present, making loans more affordable—especially for the credit-challenged. See Syz, Vanini, and Salvi, "Index-Linked Mortgages"; see also Case and Shiller, "Mortgage Default Risk" (discussing potential for lenders themselves to purchase home equity insurance products).

5. See, e.g., Gramlich, *Subprime Mortgages,* 17–18 (explaining that subprime mortgages are typically adjustable rate mortgages); ibid., 6 (observing that subprime mortgage originations grew from $35 billion in 1994 to $625 billion in 2005, representing a shift from less than 5 percent of all mortgage originations to 20 percent of all mortgage originations).

6. See, e.g., Krugman, "Home Not-So-Sweet Home."

7. See, e.g., Shiller and Weiss, "Moral Hazard," 5–11 (discussing moral hazard with respect to multiple decisions about the home, including maintenance, improvement, and marketing and sale of the home).

8. See Shiller and Weiss, "Home Equity Insurance," 38–44.

9. This issue affects the design of markets in many areas. See, e.g., Abramowicz and Henderson, "Prediction Markets," 1352 (noting the concern that some prediction markets will have too few participants, "resulting in low liquidity and therefore lower reliability," and discussing how to address that concern); Salzman and Ruhl, "Currencies,"

645–48 (exploring the trade-off between making tradable environmental currencies "fat and sloppy" and "thin and bland").

10. See, e.g., Shiller, *Macro Markets*, 166–68 (discussing the concern that home improvements could affect the housing index, but concluding that this factor would not be very significant given the dollar value of home improvements relative to home values generally); Hilber, "Neighborhood Externality Risk," 218 (suggesting, given the role of neighborhood externality risk, that a real estate price index of the sort advocated by Shiller and Weiss "ought to be neighborhood specific if it is to be successful").

11. Shiller and Weiss, "Moral Hazard," 2.

12. Shiller and Weiss, "Home Equity Insurance," 26 (observing that "there could be complete insurance of the price change that is due to aggregate market conditions and coinsurance for the deviation of the home price from the price change inferred by the index").

13. See Caplin et al., *Housing Partnerships*, 137 (incorporating a right of first refusal with a premium and a time limit into the housing partnership model to protect investors without discouraging buyers).

14. For a discussion of some of these issues, see, e.g., Shiller, *Macro Markets*.

15. Fennell, "Homeownership 2.0," provides a more detailed treatment of the topic that touches on some of the points omitted here.

16. I am grateful to Noah Zatz for discussions on this point. Cf. McAdams, "Focal Point Theory" (discussing the idea that law itself can offer a focal point capable of solving private coordination problems).

17. Rose, "What Government Can Do for Property," 213; see also Davidson, "Standardization and Pluralism," 1644–50 (suggesting that standardized property forms can serve as "regulatory platforms").

18. See, e.g., Eskridge, "One Hundred Years of Ineptitude," 1178–86 (detailing the benefits of standardization in home mortgages); Bostic and Lee, "Mortgages, Risk," 314 (suggesting that extending standardization to subprime mortgage products would be beneficial).

19. See, e.g., Rose, "What Government Can Do for Property," 213–14; Davidson, "Standardization and Pluralism," 1605–10 (listing standard property forms, which include possessory estates, security interests, and servitudes); Nelson, *Private Neighborhoods*, xiii (observing that the growing prevalence of private communities "represents a radical new development in the history of American local government" and one that is "significantly altering the way tens of millions of Americans obtain housing").

20. See Merrill and Smith, "Optimal Standardization," 35–38 (analogizing property rights to language in that a relatively small set of standardized elements make up a "lexicon" or "vocabulary" that can be flexibly combined in virtually limitless ways).

21. See, e.g., Kahneman, Knetch, and Thaler, "Endowment Effect," 199–203.

22. See, e.g., Shiller, *Macro Markets*, 17–30; Shiller, *New Financial Order*, 82–98.

23. See, e.g., Weinstein, "Unrealistic Optimism," 810 tbl. 1; Jolls, "Behavioral Economic Analysis," 1659–61.

24. Streitfeld, "Economic Fears Exclude Home Values" (reporting on the results of a Los Angeles Times/Bloomberg poll).

25. See, e.g., Fischel, "Why Are There NIMBYs?" 144–45 (relating an incident at a zoning board meeting in which homeowner opposition to a development plan was apparently based on risk aversion, rather than negative expected value).

26. See Shiller, *Macro Markets*, 24 ("Research on gambling behavior has stressed that most gamblers have preferences for activities that offer them some sense of control and mastery.").

27. See, e.g., Loomes and Sugden, "Regret Theory"; Shiller, "Derivatives Markets," 17–20 (focusing on the regret that a homeowner might experience if she spent money to hedge her home and it failed to lose value).

28. See, e.g., Scott, "Error and Rationality," 340; Thaler, *Winner's Curse*, 73; Kahneman, "Varieties of Counterfactual Thinking," 388–92.

29. Kahneman and Tversky, "Psychology of Preferences," 173.

30. See, e.g., Ritov and Baron, "Outcome Knowledge"; Ritov, "Probability of Regret"; van Dijk and Zeelenberg, "On the Psychology of 'If Only.'"

31. See, e.g., van Dijk and Zeelenberg, "Psychology of 'If Only,'" 156, 159.

32. As Shiller has discussed, the name "insurance" may carry positive connotations that produce a particular framing effect. Shiller, *New Financial Order*, 83–84.

33. See van Dijk and Zeelenberg, "Psychology of 'If Only,'" 154.

34. See ibid., 154–55 and tbl. 2.

35. See, e.g., Kahneman and Tversky, "Prospect Theory," 274, 278–79.

36. See, e.g., Choi et al., "Passive Decisions and Potent Defaults"; Thaler and Sunstein, *Nudge*, 83–87.

37. See Choi et al., "Passive Decisions and Potent Defaults," 3.

38. The tendency toward inertia might be amplified if the default is viewed as "implicit advice." Ibid., 3, 18–19; see Thaler and Sunstein, *Nudge*, 83. However, Choi et al.'s suggestion that "[e]mployees may treat a zero default as weaker implicit advice than a non-zero default" might also translate over to H2.0, if zero defaults were used for off-site risks. See Choi et al., "Passive Decisions and Potent Defaults," 19 n. 9.

39. Indeed, one company offering funding to homeowners in exchange for a share of the home's appreciation potential has suggested that realtors view the agreement as their "secret weapon." See REX Holdings, "REX & Co.: Realtors."

40. See, e.g., Baron, *Thinking and Deciding*, 474, 479.

41. See Laibson, "Golden Eggs and Hyperbolic Discounting," 444–45 (discussing purchases of illiquid assets, such as homes, as precommitment strategies); see also Davidoff, "Illiquid Housing as Self-Insurance" (suggesting that older people may use their homes as a form of self-insurance against long-term care needs).

42. See Banks et al., "Downsizing in Later Life," 11 ("Holding a risky asset such as housing when prices are highly volatile may be a dubious strategy when one faces additional health risk").

43. See Laibson, "Golden Eggs and Hyperbolic Discounting," 465–66.

44. See Friedman, *Theory of the Consumption Function*, 26–31 (presenting the permanent income hypothesis); Modigliani and Brumberg, "Utility Analysis and the Consumption Function" (presenting the life-cycle hypothesis).

45. See, e.g., Fennell and Stark, "Taxation over Time," 16–21, and sources cited therein.

46. See Friedman, *Theory of the Consumption Function*, 16 ("It is in general far easier to borrow on the basis of a tangible physical asset, or a claim to one, than on the basis of future earning power.").

47. See, e.g., Baron, *Thinking and Deciding*, 479–80 (noting these considerations and discussing Derek Parfit's work).

48. See, e.g., ibid., 475–78 (discussing dynamic inconsistency).

49. See Elster, *Ulysses Unbound*, 29–34 (explaining how precommitment responds to inconsistent time preferences).

50. See Shiller and Weiss, "Home Equity Insurance," 29 (suggesting limiting the purchase of hedging instruments to the time of home purchase, sale, or refinancing, noting that "[a]t these times, the homeowner has legal counsel and advice of others that would naturally be used to help make an informed decision about risk-management contracts as well").

51. See, e.g., Shiller, *Macro Markets*, 171.

52. Genesove and Mayer, "Loss Aversion and Seller Behavior."

53. See ibid. It is not clear that holding out for a better price is always irrational, however. See Cauley and Pavlov, "Rational Delays" (suggesting that holding out during down markets can be rational, if the option value of doing so exceeds the carrying costs of the home).

54. See Thaler and Johnson, "Gambling with the House Money," 657–58; see also Shiller, "Derivatives Markets," 18–20.

55. See Shiller, *Macro Markets*, 207–8 (characterizing financial innovations as public goods); Caplin et al., "Home Equity Insurance," 28 (noting the potential social benefits of Syracuse's home equity insurance pilot program for those not enrolled in it).

56. See Fischel, *Homevoter Hypothesis*, 74–75 (suggesting the pain that homeowners would experience in selling at a loss constrains "exit" and encourages "voice" in the local political process); Hirschman, *Exit, Voice, and Loyalty*.

57. See Caplin et al., "Home Equity Insurance," 28 (suggesting that home equity protection programs might have "confidence-building effects" even if not many households purchase the protection); Schelling, "Neighborhood Tipping," 174 (exploring how speculation about future neighborhood changes might affect a homeowner's decision whether to stay or leave, and observing that "[i]f capital losses are involved, the whole process can be aggravated by the attempt to get rid of one's house a little sooner than everyone else").

58. See Caplin et al., "Shared-Equity Mortgages," 237–38 (presenting rough calculations that suggest shared-equity mortgages could increase homeownership by more than 1 percent).

59. See U.S. Bureau of the Census, *Geographic Mobility: 2004 to 2005*, tbl. 17 (reflecting moves by 29 percent of renter households and 6.34 percent of owner-occupant households).

60. See Frank, *Luxury Fever*, 159–60.

61. Caplin et al., "Shared-Equity Mortgages," 226–27, tbl. 6 (explaining that "at some point, borrowers achieve an income level that makes it possible to pay regular mortgage interest on the most valuable house that their assets will permit them to purchase").

62. See Frank, *Luxury Fever,* 79–81 (discussing adaptation effects in the context of housing); Kahneman and Varey, "Psychology of Utility," 136–47 (analyzing the impact of adaptation and comparison on subjective well-being).

63. Cf. Merrill, "Constitutional Rights as Public Goods," 870–72 (observing that bargains to cede constitutional rights that produce positive externalities impact people other than the individual rights-holders engaged in those bargains).

64. See, e.g., Fennell, "Contracting Communities," 849–90 (discussing a variety of reasons why the restrictions in private communities may not adequately serve the interests of residents of those communities).

65. Cf. Caplin et al., "Shared-Equity Mortgages," 211 (observing that shared-equity mortgages "are not a panacea for housing affordability problems and the associated constraints on building wealth").

BIBLIOGRAPHY

Articles and Books

Abramowicz, Michael. "The Law-and-Markets Movement." *American University Law Review* 49 (1999): 327–431.

Abramowicz, Michael, and John F. Duffy. "Intellectual Property for Market Experimentation." *New York University Law Review* 83 (2008): 337–410.

Abramowicz, Michael, and M. Todd Henderson. "Prediction Markets for Corporate Governance." *Notre Dame Law Review* 82 (2007): 1343–1414.

Acker, Frederick W. "Performance Zoning." *Notre Dame Law Review* 67 (1991): 363–401.

Akerlof, George A. "The Market for 'Lemons': Quality, Uncertainty and the Market Mechanism." *Quarterly Journal of Economics* 84 (1970): 488–500.

Alexander, Gregory S. "Freedom, Coercion, and the Law of Servitudes." *Cornell Law Review* 73 (1988): 883–905.

Alpern, Andrew, and Seymour Durst. *Holdouts!* New York: McGraw-Hill, 1984.

Anderson, Terry L., and Fred S. McChesney. "Introduction: The Economic Approach to Property Rights." In *Property Rights: Cooperation, Conflict, and Law,* edited by Terry L. Anderson and Fred S. McChesney, 1–11. Princeton: Princeton University Press, 2003.

Arrow, Kenneth J. "The Property Rights Doctrine and Demand Revelation under Incomplete Information." In *Economics and Human Welfare,* edited by Michael J. Boskin, 23–39. New York: Academic Press, 1979.

———. "The Theory of Discrimination." In *Discrimination in Labor Markets,* edited by Orley Ashenfelter and Albert Rees, 3–33. Princeton: Princeton University Press, 1973.

Atwood, James R. "An Economic Analysis of Land Use Conflicts." *Stanford Law Review* 21 (1969): 293–315.

Ayres, Ian. *Optional Law: The Structure of Legal Entitlements.* Chicago: University of Chicago Press, 2005.

————. "Protecting Property with Puts." *Valparaiso University Law Review* 32 (1998): 793–831.

Ayres, Ian, and J. M. Balkin. "Legal Entitlements as Auctions: Property Rules, Liability Rules, and Beyond." *Yale Law Journal* 106 (1996): 703–51.

Ayres, Ian, and Paul M. Goldbart. "Optimal Delegation and Decoupling in the Design of Liability Rules." *Michigan Law Review* 100 (2001): 1–79.

Ayres, Ian, and Barry Nalebuff. "An Equity Kicker." *Forbes*, May 19, 2008.

————. "Why Not? Price-Protect Your Home." *Forbes*, August 29, 2002. http://www.forbes.com/business/2002/08/28/0829whynot.html.

Ayres, Ian, and Eric Talley. "Solomonic Bargaining: Dividing a Legal Entitlement to Facilitate Coasean Trade." *Yale Law Journal* 104 (1995): 1027–1117.

Babcock, Linda, and George Loewenstein. "Explaining Bargaining Impasse: The Role of Self-Serving Biases." *Journal of Economic Perspectives* 11 (1997): 109–26.

Baird, Douglas G., Robert H. Gertner, and Randal C. Picker. *Game Theory and the Law.* Cambridge, MA: Harvard University Press, 1994.

Banks, James, Richard Blundell, Zoë Oldfield, and James P. Smith. "House Price Volatility and Housing Ownership over the Life Cycle." University College London Discussion Papers in Economics No. 04-09, 2004. http://www.econ.ucl.ac.uk/papers/working_paper_series/0409.pdf.

————. "Housing Price Volatility and Downsizing in Later Life." NBER Working Paper No. 13496, October 2007. http://www.nber.org/papers/w13496.

Baron, Jonathan. *Thinking and Deciding.* 3rd ed. Cambridge: Cambridge University Press, 2000.

Barzel, Yoram. *Economic Analysis of Property Rights.* 2nd ed. Cambridge: Cambridge University Press, 1997.

Barzel, Yoram, and Tim R. Sass. "The Allocation of Resources by Voting." *Quarterly Journal of Economics* 105 (1990): 745–71.

Baumol, William J. *Superfairness: Applications and Theory.* Cambridge, MA: MIT Press, 1986.

Baumol, William J., and Wallace E. Oates. *The Theory of Environmental Policy.* 2nd ed. Cambridge: Cambridge University Press, 1988.

Becker, Gary S. "A Note on Restaurant Pricing and Other Examples of Social Influences on Prices." *Journal of Political Economy* 99 (1991): 1109–16.

Becker, Gary S., and Kevin M. Murphy. 2000. *Social Economics: Market Behavior in a Social Environment.* Cambridge, MA: Belknap Press, 2000.

Been, Vicki. "'Exit' as a Constraint on Land Use Exactions: Rethinking the Unconstitutional Conditions Doctrine." *Columbia Law Review* 91 (1991): 473–545.

————. "What's Fairness Got to Do With It? Environmental Justice and the Siting of Locally Undesirable Land Uses." *Cornell Law Review* 78 (1993): 1001–1085.

Bell, Abraham, and Gideon Parchomovsky. "The Integration Game." *Columbia Law Review* 100 (2000): 1965–2029.

————. "Of Property and Antiproperty." *Michigan Law Review* 102 (2003): 1–70.

————. "Pliability Rules." *Michigan Law Review* 101 (2002): 1–79.

————. "Taking Compensation Private." *Stanford Law Review* 59 (2007): 871–906.

———. "Takings Reassessed." *Virginia Law Review* 87 (2001): 277–318.

Bénabou, Roland. "Equity and Efficiency in Human Capital Investment: The Local Connection." *Review of Economic Studies* 63 (1996): 237–64.

Bergstrom, Theodore, and John H. Miller. *Experiments with Economic Principles: Microeconomics*. 2nd ed. Boston: McGraw-Hill, 2000.

Black, Charles L., Jr. "The Lawfulness of the Segregation Decisions." *Yale Law Journal* 69 (1960): 421–30.

Blackstone, William. *Commentaries on the Laws of England*. Vol. 2. Oxford: Clarendon Press, 1766.

Blinder, Alan S. "A Modest Proposal: Eco-Friendly Stimulus." *New York Times*, July 27, 2008. http://www.nytimes.com/2008/07/27/business/27view.html.

Bogart, William T. "'What Big Teeth You Have!': Identifying the Motivations for Exclusionary Zoning." *Urban Studies* 30 (1993): 1669–81.

Bostic, Raphael W., and Kwan Ok Lee. "Mortgages, Risk, and Homeownership among Low- and Moderate-Income Families." *American Economic Review* 98, no. 2 (2008): 310–14.

Bounds, Gwendolyn. "'Green' Lawns Spur Neighborhood Wars." Real Estate Journal. *Wall Street Journal*, July 12, 2007. http://www.realestatejournal.com/home-garden/20070712-bounds.html.

Boyle, Phelim, and Feidhlim Boyle. *Derivatives: The Tools that Changed Finance*. London: Risk Books, 2001.

Brams, Steven J., and Alan D. Taylor. *Fair Divison: From Cake-Cutting to Dispute Resolution*. Cambridge: Cambridge University Press, 1996.

Brealey, Richard A., and Stewart C. Myers. *Principles of Corporate Finance*. 7th ed. New York: McGraw-Hill, 2003.

Brekke, Kjell Arne, Karine Nyborg, and Mari Rege. "The Fear of Exclusion: Individual Effort When Group Formation Is Endogenous." *Scandinavian Journal of Economics* 109 (2007): 531–50.

Brooks, Richard R. W., and Kathryn E. Spier. "Trigger Happy or Gun Shy? Dissolving Common Value Partnerships with Texas Shootouts." Yale Law and Economics Research Paper No. 298, June 2004. http://www.ssrn.com/abstract=556164.

Brower, Todd. "Communities within the Community: Consent, Constitutionalism, and Other Failures of Legal Theory in Residential Associations." *Journal of Land Use and Environmental Law* 7 (1992): 203–73.

Brueckner, Jan K. "Consumption and Investment Motives and the Portfolio Choices of Homeowners." *Journal of Real Estate Finance and Economics* 15, no. 2 (1997): 159–80.

Brueckner, Jan K., and Man-Soo Joo. "Voting with Capitalization." *Regional Science and Urban Economics* 21 (1991): 453–67.

Bruegmann, Robert. "Urban Density and Sprawl: An Historical Perspective." In *Smarter Growth: Market-Based Strategies for Land-Use Planning in the 21st Century*, edited by Randall G. Holcombe and Samuel R. Staley, 155–77. Westport, CT: Greenwood Press, 2001.

Buchanan, James M. "The Institutional Structure of Externality." *Public Choice* 14 (1973): 69–82.

———. "Principles of Urban Fiscal Strategy." *Public Choice* 11 (1971): 1–16.

Buchanan, James M., and Marilyn R. Flowers. *The Public Finances: An Introductory Textbook.* 4th ed. Homewood, IL: Richard D. Irwin, 1975.

Buchanan, James M., and William C. Stubblebine. "Externality." *Economica* 29 (1962): 371–84.

Buchanan, James M., and Gordon Tullock. *The Calculus of Consent: Logical Foundations of Constitutional Democracy.* Ann Arbor: University of Michigan Press, 1962.

Buchanan, James M., and Yong J. Yoon. "Symmetric Tragedies: Commons and Anticommons." *Journal of Law and Economics* 43 (2000): 1–13.

Bucks, Brian K., Arthur B. Kennickell, and Kevin B. Moore. "Recent Changes in U.S. Family Finances: Evidence from the 2001 and 2004 Survey of Consumer Finances." *Federal Reserve Bulletin,* 2006. http://www.federalreserve.gov/pubs/oss/oss2/2004/bull0206.pdf.

Byrne, J. Peter, and Michael Diamond. "Affordable Housing, Land Tenure, and Urban Policy: The Matrix Revealed." *Fordham Urban Law Journal* 34 (2007): 527–93.

Calabresi, Guido. *The Costs of Accidents.* New Haven: Yale University Press, 1970.

———. "Remarks: The Simple Virtues of *The Cathedral.*" *Yale Law Journal* 106 (1997): 2201–7.

Calabresi, Guido, and A. Douglas Melamed. "Property Rules, Liability Rules, and Inalienability: One View of the Cathedral." *Harvard Law Review* 85 (1972): 1089–128.

Callies, David L., Robert H. Freilich, and Thomas E. Roberts. *Cases and Materials on Land Use.* 4th ed. St. Paul, MN: Thomson/West, 2004.

Cane, Peter. *The Anatomy of Tort Law.* Oxford: Hart, 1997.

Caplin, Andrew, James H. Carr, Frederick Pollock, Zhong Yi Tong, Kheng Mei Tan, and Trivikraman Thampy. "Shared-Equity Mortgages, Housing Affordability, and Homeownership." *Housing Policy Debate* 18 (2007): 209–42.

Caplin, Andrew, Sewin Chan, Charles Freeman, and Joseph Tracy. *Housing Partnerships: A New Approach to a Market at a Crossroads.* Cambridge, MA: MIT Press, 1997.

Caplin, Andrew, Noël Cunningham, Mitchell Engler, and Frederick Pollock. "Facilitating Shared Appreciation Mortgages to Prevent Housing Crashes and Affordability Crises." The Hamilton Project, Discussion Paper 2008-12. The Brookings Institution, September 2008. http://www.brookings.edu/papers/2008/09_mortgages_caplin.aspx.

Caplin, Andrew, Christopher Joye, Peter Butt, Edward Glaeser, and Michael Kuczynski. "Innovative Approaches to Reducing the Costs of Home Ownership." A Report Commissioned by the Menzies Research Centre for the Prime Minister's Home Ownership Task Force, vol. 1, June 2003. http://www.mrcltd.org.au/research/home-ownership/volume_1.pdf.

Caplin, Andrew, William N. Goetzmann, Eric Hangen, Barry J. Nalebuff, Elisabeth

Prentice, John Rodkin, Matthew I. Spiegel, and Tom Skinner. "Home Equity Insurance: A Pilot Project." Yale International Center for Finance, Working Paper No. 03-12, May 2003. http://ssrn.comabstract_id=410141.

Case, Anne C., and Lawrence F. Katz. "The Company You Keep: The Effects of Family and Neighborhood on Disadvantaged Youths." National Bureau of Economic Research, Working Paper No. 3705, May 1991. http://www.nber.org/papers/w3705.

Case, Karl E., Jr., and Robert J. Shiller. "Mortgage Default Risk and Real Estate Prices: The Use of Index-Based Futures and Options in Real Estate." *Journal of Housing Research* 7, no. 2 (1996): 243–58.

Case, Karl E., Jr., Robert J. Shiller, and Allan N. Weiss. "Index-Based Futures and Options in Real Estate." *Journal of Portfolio Management* 19, no. 2 (1993): 83–92.

Cauley, Stephen Day, and Andrey D. Pavlov. "Rational Delays." *Journal of Real Estate Finance and Economics* 24, nos. 1/2 (2002): 143–66.

Cauley, Stephen Day, Andrey Pavlov, and Eduardo Schwartz. "Homeownership as a Constraint on Asset Allocation." *Journal of Real Estate Finance and Economics* 34, no. 3 (2007): 283–311.

Chang, Yun-chien. "A Framework of Just Compensation Assessment." New York University Law and Economics Working Paper No. 140, 2008. http://lsr.nellco.org/nyu/lewp/papers/141.

———. "Self-Assessment of Takings Compensation: An Empirical Study." New York University Law and Economics Working Paper No. 140, 2008. http://lsr.nellco.org/nyu/lewp/papers/140.

Charness, Gary and Chun-Lei Yang. "Endogenous Group Formation and Public Goods Provision: Exclusion, Exit, Mergers, and Redemption," April 2008. http://ssrn.com/abstract=932251.

Chatterjee, Satyajit. "Taxes, Homeownership, and the Allocation of Residential Real Estate." *Business Review,* Federal Reserve Bank of Philadelphia, September/October 1996. http://www.philadelphiafed.org/research-and-data/publications/business-review/1996/september-october/real-estate-risks.cfm.

Chau, Derek K. Y., Michael Firth, and Bin Srinidhi. "Leases with Purchase Options and Double Moral Hazard." *Journal of Business Finance and Accounting* 33 (2006): 1390–401.

Choi, James J., David Laibson, Brigitte Madrian, and Andrew Metrick. "Passive Decisions and Potent Defaults." NBER Working Paper No. 9917, August 2003. http://www.nber.org/papers/w9917.

Christie, Les. "New Way to Bet on Real Estate." *CNN.money.com,* March 22, 2006. http://money.cnn.com/2006/03/22/real_estate/playing_the_home_price_market/.

Christman, John. *The Myth of Property: Toward an Egalitarian Theory of Ownership.* New York: Oxford University Press, 1994.

Chubb, John E., and Terry M. Moe. *Politics, Markets, and America's Schools.* Washington, DC: Brookings Institution, 1990.

Cinyabuguma, Matthias, Talbot Page, and Louis Putterman. "Cooperation under the

Threat of Expulsion in a Public Goods Experiment." *Journal of Public Economics* 89 (2005): 1421–35.

Ciriacy-Wantrup, S. V., and Richard C. Bishop. "'Common Property' as a Concept in Natural Resources Policy." *Natural Resources Journal* 15 (1975): 713–27.

Clawson, Marion. "Why Not Sell Zoning and Rezoning? (Legally, That Is)." *Cry California* (1966–67): 9.

Clotfelter, Charles. "The Private Life of Public Economics." *Southern Economic Journal* 59 (1993): 579–96.

CME Group. "S&P/Case-Shiller Home Price Indices Futures and Options: Introductory Guide." http://www.cme.com/files/cmehousing_brochure.pdf.

Coase, R. H. "The Problem of Social Cost." *Journal of Law and Economics* 3 (1960): 1–44.

Cohen, Lloyd. "Holdouts and Free Riders." *Journal of Legal Studies* 20 (1991): 351–62.

Cole, Daniel H. "Why *Kelo* Is Not Good News for Local Planners and Developers." *Georgia State University Law Review* 22 (2006): 803–56.

Coleman, Jules L., and Jody Kraus. "Rethinking the Theory of Legal Rights." *Yale Law Journal* 95 (1986): 1335–71.

Cook, Philip J., and Jens Ludwig, "Assigning Deviant Youths to Minimize Total Harm." National Bureau of Economic Research Working Paper No. 11390, June 2005. http://www.nber.org/papers/w11390.pdf.

Cooter, Robert. "The Cost of Coase." *Journal of Legal Studies* 11 (1982): 11–33.

———. "Unity in Tort, Contract, and Property: The Model of Precaution." *California Law Review* 73 (1985): 1–51.

Cooter, Robert, and Thomas Ulen. *Law and Economics.* 4th ed. Boston: Pearson/Addison-Wesley, 2004.

Cornes, Richard, and Todd Sandler. *The Theory of Externalities, Public Goods, and Club Goods.* Cambridge: Cambridge University Press, 1986.

Coy, Peter. "Ralph Liu's Clever Idea: SwapRent." *Business Week: Hot Property Blog.* October 11, 2007. http://www.businessweek.com/the_thread/hotproperty/archives/2007/10/ralph_lius_clev.html.

Crittenden, Michael, and Jessica Holzer. "Relief Nears for 3 Million Strapped Homeowners." *Wall Street Journal,* October 30, 2008. http://online.wsj.com/article/SB122531677860781723.html.

Cropper, Maureen L., and Wallace E. Oates. "Environmental Economics: A Survey." *Journal of Economic Literature* 30 (1992): 675–740.

Dagan, Hanoch, and Michael A. Heller. "The Liberal Commons." *Yale Law Journal* 110 (2001): 549–623.

Dana, David A. "Land Use Regulation in an Age of Heightened Scrutiny." *North Carolina Law Review* 75 (1997): 1243–303.

Davidoff, Thomas. "Illiquid Housing as Self-Insurance: The Case of Long-Term Care." January 2008. http://ssrn.com/abstract=1009738.

Davidson, Nestor. "Standardization and Pluralism in Property Law." *Vanderbilt Law Review* 61 (2008): 1597–1663.

Davis, John Emmeus. "Shared Equity Homeownership: The Changing Landscape of

Resale-Restricted, Owner-Occupied Housing." National Housing Institute Paper, 2006. http://www.nhi.org/policy/SharedEquity.html.

De Alessi, Louis. "Gains from Private Property." *In Property Rights: Cooperation, Conflict, and Law,* edited by Terry L. Anderson and Fred S. McChesney, 90–112. Princeton: Princeton University Press, 2003.

Delafons, John. *Land-Use Controls in the United States.* 2nd ed. Cambridge, MA: MIT Press, 1969.

Demsetz, Harold. "Toward a Theory of Property Rights." *American Economic Review* 57, no. 2 (1967): 347–59.

Depoorter, Ben, and Sven Vanneste. "Putting Humpty Dumpty Back Together: Experimental Evidence of Anticommons Tragedies." *Journal of Law, Economics and Policy* 3 (2006): 1–23.

Diamond, Douglas B., Jr., and George S. Tolley. "The Economic Roles of Urban Amenities." In *The Economics of Urban Amenities,* edited by Douglas B. Diamond Jr. and George S. Tolley, 3–44. New York: Academic Press, 1982.

Dibadj, Reza. "Regulatory Givings and the Anticommons." *Ohio State Law Journal* 64 (2003): 1041–1124.

Dickerson, A. Mechele. "Caught in the Trap: Pricing Racial Housing Preferences." Review of *The Two Income Trap,* by Elizabeth Warren and Amelia Warren Tyagi. *Michigan Law Review* 103 (2005): 1273–94.

Dietderich, Andrew G. "An Egalitarian's Market: The Economics of Inclusionary Zoning Reclaimed." *Fordham Urban Law Journal* 43 (1996): 23–104.

Dietz, Robert D., and Donald R. Haurin. "The Social and Micro-Level Consequences of Homeownership." *Journal of Urban Economics* 54 (2003): 401–50.

DiPasquale, Denise, and Edward L. Glaeser. "Incentives and Social Capital: Are Homeowners Better Citizens?" *Journal of Urban Economics* 45 (1999): 354–84.

Downs, Anthony. *Opening up the Suburbs: An Urban Strategy for America.* New Haven: Yale University Press, 1973.

Dukeminier, Jesse, James E. Krier, Gregory S. Alexander, and Michael H. Schill. *Property.* 6th ed. New York: Aspen, 2006.

Dynarski, Mark, Robert Schwab, and Ernest Zampelli. "Local Characteristics and Public Production: The Case of Education." *Journal of Urban Economics* 26 (1989): 250–63.

Economist, "Come Rain or Come Shine." Feb. 8, 2007.

Eggertsson, Thráinn. "Open Access versus Common Property." In *Property Rights: Cooperation, Conflict, and Law,* edited by Terry L. Anderson and Fred S. McChesney, 73–89. Princeton: Princeton University Press, 2003.

Elberg, Amos B. "Remedies for Common Interest Development Rule Violations." *Columbia Law Review* 101 (2001): 1958–97.

Ellickson, Bryan. "Jurisdictional Fragmentation and Residential Choice." *American Economic Review* 61, no. 2 (1971): 334–39.

Ellickson, Robert C. "Adverse Possession and Perpetuities Law: Two Dents in the Libertarian Model of Property Rights." *Washington University Law Quarterly* 6 (1986): 723–37.

———. "Alternatives to Zoning: Covenants, Nuisance Rules, and Fines as Land Use Controls." *University of Chicago Law Review* 40 (1973): 681–781.

———. "Cities and Homeowners Associations." *University of Pennsylvania Law Review* 130 (1982): 1519–80.

———. *The Household: Informal Order around the Hearth.* Princeton: Princeton University Press, 2008.

———. *Order without Law: How Neighbors Settle Disputes.* Cambridge, MA: Harvard University Press, 1991.

———. "Property in Land." *Yale Law Journal* 102 (1993): 1315–1400.

———. "Suburban Growth Controls: An Economic and Legal Analysis." *Yale Law Journal* 86 (1977): 385–511.

———. "Unpacking the Household: Informal Property Rights around the Hearth." *Yale Law Journal* 116 (2006): 226–328.

Ellickson, Robert C., and Vicki L. Been. *Land Use Controls: Cases and Materials.* 3rd ed. New York: Aspen, 2005.

Elster, Jon. *The Cement of Society: A Study of Social Order.* Cambridge: Cambridge University Press, 1989.

———. *Ulysses Unbound: Studies in Rationality, Precommitment, and Constraints.* Cambridge: Cambridge University Press, 2000.

Emerson, Thomas I. "Freedom of Association and Freedom of Expression." *Yale Law Journal* 74 (1964): 1–35.

Epple, Dennis, Thomas Romer, and Radu Filimon. "Community Development with Endogenous Land Use Controls." *Journal of Public Economics* 35 (1988): 133–62.

Epstein, Richard A. "A Clear View of *The Cathedral:* The Dominance of Property Rules." *Yale Law Journal* 106 (1997): 2091–2120.

———. "Covenants and Constitutions." *Cornell Law Review* 73 (1988): 906–27.

———. "Holdouts, Externalities, and the Single Owner: One More Salute to Ronald Coase." *Journal of Law and Economics* 36 (1993): 553–86.

———. "On the Optimal Mix of Private and Common Property." In *Property Rights,* edited by Ellen Frankel Paul, Fred D. Miller Jr., and Jeffrey Paul, 17–41. Cambridge: Cambridge University Press, 1994.

———. "Protecting Property Rights with Legal Remedies: A Common Sense Reply to Professor Ayres." *Valparaiso University Law Review* 32 (1998): 833–53.

Eskridge, William N., Jr. "One Hundred Years of Ineptitude: The Need for Mortgage Rules Consonant with the Economic and Psychological Dynamics of the Home Sale and Loan Transaction." *Virginia Law Review* 70 (1984): 1083–1218.

Farber, Daniel A. "Public Choice and Just Compensation." *Constitutional Commentary* 9 (1992): 279–308.

Farnsworth, Ward. *The Legal Analyst: A Toolkit for Thinking about the Law.* Chicago: University of Chicago Press, 2007.

Farrell, Joseph. "Information and the Coase Theorem." *Journal of Economic Perspectives* 1, no. 2 (1987): 113–29.

Fennell, Lee Anne. "Beyond Exit and Voice: User Participation in the Production of Local Public Goods." *Texas Law Review* 80 (2001): 1–87.

———. "Common Interest Tragedies." *Northwestern University Law Review* 98 (2004): 907–90.

———. "Contracting Communities." *University of Illinois Law Review* 2004 (2004): 829–98.

———. "Exclusion's Attraction: Land Use Controls in Tieboutian Perspective." In *The Tiebout Model at Fifty: Essays in Public Economics in Honor of Wallace Oates,* edited by William A. Fischel, 163–98. Cambridge, MA: Lincoln Institute of Land Policy, 2006.

———. "Hard Bargains and Real Steals: Land Use Exactions Revisited." *Iowa Law Review* 86 (2000): 1–85.

———. "Homeownership 2.0." *Northwestern University Law Review* 102, no. 3 (2008): 1047–1118.

———. "Homes Rule." Review of *The Homevoter Hypothesis: How Home Values Influence Local Government Taxation, School Finance, and Land-Use Policies,* by William A. Fischel. *Yale Law Journal* 112 (2002): 617–64.

———. "Properties of Concentration." *University of Chicago Law Review* 73 (2006): 1227–97.

———. "Property and Half-Torts." *Yale Law Journal* 116 (2007): 1400–1471.

———. "Revealing Options." *Harvard Law Review* 118 (2005): 1399–1488.

———. "Slices and Lumps," University of Chicago Law and Economics, Olin Working Paper No. 395, March 2008. http://ssrn.com/abstract=1106421.

———. "Taking Eminent Domain Apart." *Michigan State Law Review* 2004 (2004): 957–1004.

Fennell, Lee Anne, and Kirk J. Stark. "Taxation over Time." *Tax Law Review* 59 (2005): 1–64.

Fenster, Mark. "Community by Covenant, Process, and Design: Cohousing and the Contemporary Common Interest Community." *Journal of Land Use and Environmental Law* 15 (1999): 3–54.

———. "Regulating Land Use in a Constitutional Shadow: The Institutional Contexts of Exactions." *Hastings Law Journal* 58 (2007): 729–75.

Field, Patrick, Jennifer Gilbert, and Michael Wheeler. "Trading the Poor: Intermunicipal Housing Negotiation in New Jersey." *Harvard Negotiation Law Review* 2 (1997): 1–33.

Fischel, William A. "An Economic History of Zoning and a Cure for Its Exclusionary Effects." *Urban Studies* 41 (2004): 317–40.

———. "The Economics of Land Use Exactions: A Property Rights Analysis." *Law and Contemporary Problems* 50, no. 1 (1987): 101–13.

———. "Equity and Efficiency Aspects of Zoning Reform." *Public Policy* 27 (1979): 301–32.

———. *The Homevoter Hypothesis: How Home Values Influence Local Government Taxation, School Finance, and Land-Use Policies.* Cambridge, MA: Harvard University Press, 2001.

———. *Regulatory Takings: Law, Economics, and Politics.* Cambridge, MA: Harvard University Press, 1995.

———. "Voting, Risk Aversion, and the NIMBY Syndrome: A Comment on Robert Nelson's *Privatizing the Neighborhood.*" *George Mason Law Review* 7 (1999): 881–903.

———. "Why Are There NIMBYs?" *Land Economics* 77 (2001): 144–53.

Follain, James R., and Lisa Sturman Melamed. "The False Messiah of Tax Policy: What Elimination of the Home Mortgage Interest Deduction Promises and a Careful Look at What It Delivers." *Journal of Housing Research* 9 (1998): 179–99.

Ford, Richard Thompson. "The Boundaries of Race: Political Geography in Legal Analysis." *Harvard Law Review* 107 (1994): 1843–1921.

———. "Geography and Sovereignty: Jurisdictional Formation and Racial Segregation." *Stanford Law Review* 49 (1997): 1365–1445.

Foster, Sheila R. "The City as an Ecological Space: Social Capital and Urban Land Use." *Notre Dame Law Review* 82 (2006): 527–82.

Fox, Lorna. *Conceptualising Home: Theories, Laws, and Policies.* Oxford: Hart, 2007.

Frank, Robert H. *Choosing the Right Pond: Human Behavior and the Quest for Status.* New York: Oxford University Press, 1985.

———. "The Demand for Unobservable and Other Nonpositional Goods." *American Economic Review* 75, no. 1 (1985): 101–16.

———. *Falling Behind: How Rising Inequality Harms the Middle Class.* Berkeley: University of California Press, 2007.

———. *Luxury Fever: Why Money Fails to Satisfy in an Era of Excess.* New York: Free Press, 1999.

Franzese, Paula A. "Does It Take a Village? Privatization, Patterns of Restrictiveness and the Demise of Community." *Villanova Law Review* 47 (2002): 553–93.

Friedman, Milton. *A Theory of the Consumption Function.* Princeton: Princeton University Press, 1957.

Frey, Bruno. *Not Just for the Money: An Economic Theory of Personal Motivation.* Cheltenham, U.K.: Edward Elgar, 1997.

Frug, Gerald E. "City Services." *New York University Law Review* 73 (1998): 23–96.

Fryer, Roland G., Jr., Jacob K. Goeree, and Charles A. Holt. "Experience-Based Discrimination: Classroom Games." *Journal of Economic Education* 36 (2005): 160–70.

Gale, William G., Jonathan Gruber, and Seth Stephens-Davidowitz. "Encouraging Homeownership through the Tax Code." *Tax Notes* 115 (2007): 1171–89.

Garnett, Nicole Stelle. "Ordering the City." Unpublished book manuscript. New Haven: Yale University Press (forthcoming).

———. "Suburbs as Exit, Suburbs as Entrance." *Michigan Law Review* 106 (2007): 277–304.

Genesove, David, and Christopher Mayer. "Loss Aversion and Seller Behavior: Evidence from the Housing Market." *Quarterly Journal of Economics* 116 (2001): 1233–60.

Gewirtz, Paul. "Remedies and Resistance." *Yale Law Journal* 92 (1983): 585–681.

Gillette, Clayton P. "Courts, Covenants, and Communities." *University of Chicago Law Review* 61 (1994): 1375–441.

———. "Opting Out of Public Provision." *Denver University Law Review* 73 (1996): 1185–219.

———. "Regionalization and Interlocal Bargains." *New York University Law Review* 76 (2001): 190–271.

Glaeser, Edward L., Jed Kolko, and Albert Saiz. "Consumers and Cities." In *The City as an Entertainment Machine,* edited by Terry Nichols Clark, 177–83. Amsterdam: Elsevier Science, 2004.

Glaeser, Edward L., and Andrei Shleifer, "The Curley Effect: The Economics of Shaping the Electorate." *Journal of Law, Economics, and Organization* 21 (2005): 1–19.

Gneezy, Uri, and Aldo Rustichini. "A Fine Is a Price." *Journal of Legal Studies* 29 (2000): 1–17.

Godsil, Rachel D. "Viewing the Cathedral from behind the Color Line: Property Rules, Liability Rules, and Environmental Racism." *Emory Law Journal* 53 (2004): 1807–85.

Godsil, Rachel D., and David Simunovich. "Just Compensation in an Ownership Society." In *Private Property, Community Development, and Eminent Domain,* edited by Robin Paul Malloy, 133–47. Aldershot, U.K.: Ashgate, 2008.

Goetz, Charles J. *Cases and Materials on Law and Economics.* St. Paul, MN: West, 1984.

Goldberg, Victor P. *Framing Contract Law: An Economic Perspective.* Cambridge, MA: Harvard University Press, 2006.

Gramlich, Edward M. *Subprime Mortgages: America's Latest Boom and Bust.* Washington, DC: Urban Institute Press, 2007.

Grey, Thomas C. "The Disintegration of Property." In *Property: Nomos XXII,* edited by J. Roland Pennock and John W. Chapman, 69–85. New York: New York University Press, 1980.

Haddock, David D. "Irrelevant Externality Angst." *Journal of Interdisciplinary Economics* 19 (2007): 3–18.

Hagerty, James R. "Mortgage Woes Force Banks to Take Hits to Sell Homes." *Wall Street Journal,* May 14, 2007, A2.

———. "Product Taps Home Equity without Taking Out Loan." *Real Estate Journal. Wall Street Journal,* May 11, 2007. http://www.realestatejournal.com/buysell/mortgages/20070511-hagerty.html.

Hamilton, Bruce W. "Capitalization of Intrajurisdictional Differences in Local Tax Prices." *American Economic Review* 66, no. 4 (1976): 742–53.

———. "A Review: Is the Property Tax a Benefit Tax?" In *Local Provision of Public Services: The Tiebout Model after Twenty-five Years,* edited by George R. Zodrow, 85–108. New York: Academic Press, 1983.

———. "Zoning and Property Taxation in a System of Local Governments." *Urban Studies* 12 (1975): 205–11.

Hansmann, Henry. "A Theory of Status Organizations." *Journal of Law, Economics and Organization* 2 (1986): 119–30.

Hardin, Garrett. "The Tragedy of the Commons." *Science* 162 (1968): 1243–48.

Hardin, Russell. *Collective Action*. Baltimore: Johns Hopkins University Press, 1982.

Harris, J. W. *Property and Justice*. Oxford: Clarendon Press, 1996.

Hauk, Esther. "Leaving the Prison: Permitting Partner Choice and Refusal in Prisoner's Dilemma Games." *Computational Economics* 18 (2001): 65–87.

Hauk, Esther, and Rosemarie Nagel. "Choice of Partners in Multiple Two-Person Prisoner's Dilemma Games: An Experimental Study." *Journal of Conflict Resolution* 45, no. 6 (2001): 770–93.

Haurin, Donald R., Robert Dietz, and Bruce Weinberg. "The Impact of Neighborhood Homeownership Rates: A Review of the Theoretical and Empirical Literature." *Journal of Housing Research* 13 (2003): 119–51.

Heck, Katherine, and James H. Fowler. "Friends, Trust, and Civic Engagement," October 2007. http://ssrn.com/abstract=1024985.

Heilbrun, James. "Poverty and Public Finance in the Older Central Cities." In *Readings in Urban Economics,* edited by Matthew Edel and Jerome Rothenberg, 523–45. New York: Macmillan, 1972.

Heller, Michael. "The Boundaries of Private Property." *Yale Law Journal* 108 (1999): 1163–1223.

———. *The Gridlock Economy: How Too Much Ownership Wrecks Markets, Stops Innovation, and Costs Lives*. New York: Basic Books, 2008.

———. "The Tragedy of the Anticommons: Property in the Transition from Marx to Markets." *Harvard Law Review* 111 (1998): 621–88.

Heller, Michael, and Rebecca S. Eisenberg. "Can Patents Deter Innovation? The Anticommons in Biomedical Research." *Science* 280 (1998): 698–701.

Heller, Michael, and Rick Hills. "Land Assembly Districts." *Harvard Law Review* 121 (2008): 1465–1527.

Henderson, J. Vernon, and Y. M. Ioannides. "A Model of Housing Tenure Choice." *American Economic Review* 73, no. 1 (1983): 98–113.

Henderson, J. Vernon, Peter Mieszkowski, and Yvon Sauvageau. "Peer Effects and Educational Production Functions." *Journal of Public Economics* 10 (1978): 97–106.

Hersey, Pala. "*Moore v. City of East Cleveland:* The Supreme Court's Fractured Paean to the Extended Family." *Journal of Contemporary Legal Issues* 14 (2004): 57–64.

Heymann, Philip B. "The Problem of Coordination: Bargaining and Rules." *Harvard Law Review* 86 (1973): 797–877.

Hilber, Christian A. L. "Neighborhood Externality Risk and the Homeownership Status of Properties." *Journal of Urban Economics* 57, no. 2 (2005): 213–41.

Hills, Roderick M., Jr. "The Constitutional Rights of Private Governments." *New York University Law Review* 78 (2003): 144–238.

Hirsch, Fred. *Social Limits to Growth*. Cambridge, MA: Harvard University Press, 1976.

Hirschman, Albert O. *Exit, Voice, and Loyalty: Responses to Declines in Firms, Organizations, and States*. Cambridge, MA: Harvard University Press, 1970.

Hohfeld, Wesley Newcomb. *Fundamental Legal Conceptions as Applied in Judicial*

Reasoning and Other Legal Essays. Edited by Walter Wheeler Cook. New Haven: Yale University Press, 1923.

Holland, Daniel M., and William M. Vaughn. "An Evaluation of Self-Assessment under a Property Tax." In *The Property Tax and Its Administration,* edited by Arthur D. Lynn Jr., 79–118. Madison: University of Wisconsin Press, 1969.

Homans, George Caspar. *English Villagers of the Thirteenth Century.* Cambridge, MA: Harvard University Press, 1941.

Honoré, Tony. "Ownership." In *Making Law Bind,* 161–92. Oxford: Clarendon Press, 1987.

Hoxby, Caroline. "Peer Effects in the Classroom: Learning from Gender and Race Variation." National Bureau of Economic Research, Working Paper No. 7867, August 2000. http://www.nber.org/papers/w7867.

Hsu, Shi-Ling. "A Two-Dimensional Framework for Analyzing Property Rights Regimes." *U.C. Davis Law Review* 36 (2003): 813–93.

Hughes, Mark Alan, and Therese J. McGuire. "A Market for Exclusion: Trading Low-Income Housing Obligations under Mount Laurel III." *Journal of Urban Economics* 29 (1991): 207–17.

Hunter, Albert. *Symbolic Communities: The Persistence and Change of Chicago's Local Communities.* Chicago: University of Chicago Press, 1974.

Hyatt, Wayne S. "Reinvention Redux: Continuing the Evolution of Master-Planned Communities." *Real Property Probate and Trust Journal* 38 (2003): 45–72.

Hyatt, Wayne S., and Susan F. French. *Community Association Law: Cases and Materials on Common Interest Communities.* Durham, NC: Carolina Academic Press, 1998.

Inhaber, Herbert. "Market-Based Solution to the Problem of Nuclear and Toxic Waste Disposal." *Journal of the Air and Waste Management Association* 41 (1991): 808–16.

Innes, Robert. "Enforcement Costs, Optimal Sanctions, and the Choice between Ex-Post Liability and Ex-Ante Regulation." *International Review of Law and Economics* 24 (2004): 29–48.

Jackson, John E. "Public Needs, Private Behavior, and Metropolitan Governance: A Summary Essay." In *Public Needs and Private Behavior in Metropolitan Areas,* edited by John E. Jackson, 1–29. Cambridge, MA: Ballinger, 1975.

Jacobs, Jane. *Dark Age Ahead.* New York: Random House, 2004.

———. *The Death and Life of Great American Cities.* New York: Random House, 1961.

Jencks, Christopher, and Susan E. Mayer. 1990. "The Social Consequences of Growing Up in a Poor Neighborhood." In *Inner-City Poverty in the United States,* edited by Laurence E. Lynn Jr. and Michael G. H. McGeary, 111–86. Washington, DC: National Academy Press, 1990.

Jolls, Christine. "Behavioral Economic Analysis of Redistributive Legal Rules." *Vanderbilt Law Review* 51 (1998): 1653–77.

Jolls, Christine, Cass R. Sunstein, and Richard H. Thaler. "A Behavioral Approach to Law and Economics." In *Behavioral Law and Economics,* edited by Cass R. Sunstein, 13–58. Cambridge: Cambridge University Press, 2000.

Kahneman, Daniel. "Varieties of Counterfactual Thinking." In *What Might Have Been: The Social Psychology of Counterfactual Thinking*, edited by Neal J. Roese and James M. Olson, 375–96. Mahwah, NJ: Lawrence Erlbaum, 1995.

Kahneman, Daniel, Jack L. Knetsch, and Richard H. Thaler. "Anomalies: The Endowment Effect, Loss Aversion, and Status Quo Bias." *Journal of Economic Perspectives* 5 (1991): 193–206.

Kahneman, Daniel, and Amos Tversky. "Prospect Theory: An Analysis of Decision under Risk." *Econometrica* 47 (1979): 263–92.

———. "The Psychology of Preferences." *Scientific American* 246 (1982): 160–73.

Kahneman, Daniel, and Carol Varey. "Notes on the Psychology of Utility." In *Interpersonal Comparisons of Well-Being*, edited by Jon Elster and John E. Roemer, 127–59. Cambridge: Cambridge University Press, 1991.

Karkkainen, Bradley C. "Zoning: A Reply to Critics." *Journal of Land Use and Environmental Law* 10 (1994): 1–46.

Kelman, Mark. *A Guide to Critical Legal Studies*. Cambridge, MA: Harvard University Press, 1987.

Kendig, Lane. *Performance Zoning*. With Susan Connor, Cranston Byrd, and Judy Heyman. Washington, DC: Planners Press, American Planning Association, 1980.

Kennedy, Duncan. "The Limited Equity Coop as a Vehicle for Affordable Housing in a Race and Class Divided Society." *Howard Law Journal* 46 (2002): 85–125.

Kennedy, Duncan, and Frank Michelman. "Are Property and Contract Efficient?" *Hofstra Law Review* 8 (1980): 711–70.

Keser, Claudia, and Frans van Winden. "Conditional Cooperation and Voluntary Contributions to Public Goods." *Scandinavian Journal of Economics* 102 (2000): 23–29.

Kling, Jeffrey R., Jeffrey B. Liebman, and Lawrence F. Katz. "Experimental Analysis of Neighborhood Effects." *Econometrica* 75 (2007): 83–119.

Knysh, Sergey I., Paul M. Goldbart, and Ian Ayres. "Instantaneous Liability Rule Auctions: The Continuous Extension of Higher-Order Liability Rules." Unpublished manuscript, 2004. On file with author.

Kollman, Ken, John H. Miller, and Scott E. Page. "Political Institutions and Sorting in a Tiebout Model." *American Economic Review* 87, no. 5 (1997): 977–92.

Korobkin, Russell B. "Bounded Rationality, Standard Form Contracts, and Unconscionability." *University of Chicago Law Review* 70 (2003): 1203–95.

Krier, James E. "Marketable Pollution Allowances." *University of Toledo Law Review* 25 (1994): 449–55.

———. "The Tragedy of the Commons, Part Two." *Harvard Journal of Law and Public Policy* 15 (1992): 325–47.

Krier, James E., and Stewart J. Schwab. "Property Rules and Liability Rules: The Cathedral in Another Light." *New York University Law Review* 70 (1995): 440–83.

Krugman, Paul. "Home Not-So-Sweet Home." *New York Times,* June 23, 2008. http://www.nytimes.com/2008/06/23/opinion/23krugman.html.

Ladd, Helen F., and John Yinger. *America's Ailing Cities: Fiscal Health and the Design of Urban Policy*. Baltimore: Johns Hopkins University Press, 1989.

Laibson, David. "Golden Eggs and Hyberbolic Discounting." *Quarterly Journal of Economics* 112 (1997): 443–77.

Landes, William M., and Richard A. Posner. "Indefinitely Renewable Copyright." *University of Chicago Law Review* 70 (2003): 471–518.

Leland, John. "Facing Default, Some Abandon Homes to Banks." *New York Times,* February 29, 2008, A1.

Leovy, Jill. "Community Struggles in Anonymity; Without a Name to Anchor It, the Area L.A. Once Called South Central Has Become All But Invisible." *Los Angeles Times,* July 7, 2008, B1.

Levine, Jonathan. *Zoned Out: Regulation, Markets, and Choices in Transportation and Metropolitan Land-Use.* Washington, DC: Resources for the Future, 2006.

Levine, Peter. "Building the Electronic Commons." *The Good Society* 11, no. 3 (2002): 1–9.

Levinson, Daryl J. "Empire-Building Government in Constitutional Law." *Harvard Law Review* 118 (2005): 915–72.

Levmore, Saul. "Carrots and Torts." In *Chicago Lectures in Law and Economics,* edited by Eric A. Posner, 203–22. New York: Foundation Press, 2000.

———. "Self-Assessed Valuation Systems for Tort and Other Law." *Virginia Law Review* 68 (1982): 771–861.

———. "Unifying Remedies: Property Rules, Liability Rules, and Startling Rules." *Yale Law Journal* 106 (1997): 2149–73.

———. "Voting with Intensity." *Stanford Law Review* 53 (2000): 111–61.

Lewinsohn-Zamir, Daphna. "The Choice between Property Rules and Liability Rules Revisited: Critical Observations from Behavioral Studies." *Texas Law Review* 80 (2001): 219–60.

———. "Consumer Preferences, Citizen Preferences, and the Provision of Public Goods." *Yale Law Journal* 108 (1998): 377–406.

Libecap, Gary D. *Contracting for Property Rights.* Cambridge: Cambridge University Press, 1989.

Libecap, Gary D., and James L. Smith. "The Economic Evolution of Petroleum Property Rights in the United States." *Journal of Legal Studies* 31 (2002): s589–608.

Logan, John R., and Harvey L. Molotch. *Urban Fortunes: The Political Economy of Place.* 20th anniversary edition. Berkeley: University of California Press, 2007.

Loomes, Graham, and Robert Sugden. "Regret Theory: An Alternative Theory of Rational Choice under Uncertainty." *Economic Journal* 92 (1982): 805–24.

Ludwig, Jens, and Jeffrey R. Kling. "Is Crime Contagious?" *Journal of Law and Economics* 50 (2007): 491–518.

Mahoney, Julia D. "Perpetual Restrictions on Land and the Problem of the Future." *Virginia Law Review* 88 (2002): 739–87.

Malani, Anup. "Valuing Laws as Local Amenities." *Harvard Law Review* 121 (2008): 1273–1331.

Malhotra, Naresh K. "Information Load and Consumer Decision Making." *Journal of Consumer Research* 8 (1982): 419–30.

Manski, Charles F. "Educational Choice (Vouchers) and Social Mobility." *Economics of Education Review* 11 (1992): 351–69.

Marcus, Matityahu, and Michael K. Taussig. "A Proposal for Government Insurance of Home Values against Locational Risks." *Land Economics* 46 (1970): 404–13.

Markby, William. *Elements of Law: Considered with Reference to Principles of General Jurisprudence.* 6th ed. Oxford: Clarendon Press, 1905.

Markovits, Daniel. "Quarantines and Distributive Justice." *Journal of Law, Medicine and Ethics* 33 (2005): 323–44.

Marwell, Gerald, and Pamela Oliver. *The Critical Mass in Collective Action: A Micro-Social Theory.* Cambridge: Cambridge University Press, 1993.

McAdams, Richard H. "A Focal Point Theory of Expressive Law." *Virginia Law Review* 86 (2000): 1649–1729.

———. "The Origin, Development, and Regulation of Norms." *Michigan Law Review* 96 (1997): 338–433.

McAdams, Richard H., and Eric B. Rasmusen. "Norms and the Law." In *The Handbook of Law and Economics,* vol. 2, edited by A. Mitchell Polinsky and Steven M. Shavell, 1573–1618. Amsterdam: Elsevier, 2007.

McDonald, John F. "What Is Public Use? Eminent Domain and the Kelo Decision." *Cornell Real Estate Review* 5, no. 1 (2007): 10–25.

McDougall, Harold A. "Regional Contribution Agreements: Compensation for Exclusionary Zoning." *Temple Law Quarterly* 60 (1987): 665–95.

McKenzie, Evan. *Privatopia: Homeowner Associations and the Rise of Residential Private Government.* New Haven: Yale University Press, 1994.

McKinnon, John D., and Martin Vaughan. "White House Rethinks Tax Hikes." *Wall Street Journal,* Mar. 5, 2009, A3.

McNamara, Maureen A. "The Legacy and Efficacy of Homeowner's Equity Assurance: A Study of Oak Park, Illinois." *Northwestern Law Review* 78 (1984): 1463–84.

Merges, Robert P. "Contracting into Liability Rules: Intellectual Property Rights and Collective Rights Organizations." *California Law Review* 84 (1996): 1293–1393.

Merrill, Thomas W. "*Dolan v. City of Tigard:* Constitutional Rights as Public Goods." *Denver University Law Review* 72 (1995): 859–88.

———. "The Economics of Public Use." *Cornell Law Review* 72 (1986): 61–116.

———. "Property and the Right to Exclude." *Nebraska Law Review* 77 (1998): 730–55.

Merrill, Thomas W., and Henry E. Smith. "Optimal Standardization in the Law of Property: The *Numerus Clausus* Principle." *Yale Law Journal* 110 (2000): 1–70.

———. *Property: Principles and Policies.* New York: Foundation Press, 2007.

———. "What Happened to Property in Law and Economics?" *Yale Law Journal* 111 (2001): 357–98.

Michelman, Frank I. "Ethics, Economics and the Law of Property." In *Ethics, Economics and the Law: Nomos XXIV,* edited by J. Roland Pennock and John W. Chapman, 3–40. New York: New York University Press, 1982.

———. "There Have To Be Four." *Maryland Law Review* 64 (2005): 136–58.

Mihalopoulos, Dan, Robert Becker, and Darnell Little. "How Cash, Clout Transform Chicago Neighborhoods." *Chicago Tribune,* January 27, 2008, 1.

Miller, John H., and Scott E. Page. *Complex Adaptive Systems: An Introduction to Computational Models of Social Life.* Princeton: Princeton University Press, 2007.

Mills, Edwin S. "Economic Analysis of Urban Land-Use Controls." In *Current Issues in Urban Economics,* edited by Peter Mieszkowski and Mahlon Straszheim, 511–41. Baltimore: Johns Hopkins University Press, 1979.

Mishan, Ezra J. *The Costs of Economic Growth.* New York: F. A. Praeger, 1967.

———. "Pareto Optimality and the Law." *Oxford Economic Papers* 19, no. 3 (1967): 255–87.

Modigliani, Franco, and Richard Brumberg. "Utility Analysis and the Consumption Function: An Interpretation of Cross-Section Data." In *Post-Keynesian Economics,* edited by Kenneth K. Kurihara, 388–436. London: Allen and Unwin, 1954.

Moe, Terry M. *Schools, Vouchers, and the American Public.* Washington, DC: Brookings Institution Press, 2001.

Morris, Madeline. "The Structure of Entitlements." *Cornell Law Review* 78 (1993): 822–98.

Musgrave, Richard A. *Fiscal Systems.* New Haven: Yale University Press, 1969.

Nadler, Janice, and Shari Seidman Diamond. "Eminent Domain and the Psychology of Property Rights: Proposed Use, Subjective Attachment, and Taker Identity." *Journal of Empirical Legal Studies* 5 (2008): 713–49.

Nash, Jonathan Remy. "Trading Species: A New Direction for Habitat Trading Programs." *Columbia Journal of Environmental Law* 32 (2007): 1–40.

Nash, Jonathan Remy, and Richard L. Revesz. "Markets and Geography: Designing Marketable Permit Schemes to Control Local and Regional Pollutants." *Ecology Law Quarterly* 28 (2001): 569–661.

Nechyba, Thomas J. "Public and Private School Competition and U.S. Fiscal Federalism." In *Fiscal Decentralization and Land Policies,* edited by Gregory K. Ingram and Yu-Hung Hong, 305–27. Cambridge, MA: Lincoln Institute of Land Policy, 2008.

Nelson, Robert H. *Private Neighborhoods and the Transformation of Local Government.* Washington, DC: Urban Institute Press, 2005.

———. "Privatizing the Neighborhood: A Proposal to Replace Zoning with Private Collective Property Rights to Existing Neighborhoods." *George Mason Law Review* 7 (1999): 827–80.

———. "The Puzzle of Local Double Taxation: Why Do Private Community Associations Exist?" *Independent Review* 13 (2008): 345–65.

———. *Zoning and Property Rights: An Analysis of the American System of Land-Use Regulation.* Cambridge, MA: MIT Press, 1977.

Nolon, John R. "*Golden* and Its Emanations: The Surprising Origins of Smart Growth." *Urban Lawyer* 35 (2003): 15–73.

Oakerson, Ronald J. *Governing Local Public Economies: Creating the Civic Metropolis.* Oakland, CA: Institute for Contemporary Studies Press, 1999.

Oates, Wallace E. "From Research to Policy: The Case of Environmental Economics." *University of Illinois Law Review* 2000 (2000): 135–53.

———. "On Local Finance and the Tiebout Model." *American Economic Review* 71, no. 2 (1981): 93–98.

———. "The Use of Local Zoning Ordinances to Regulate Population Flows and the Quality of Local Services." In *Essays in Labor Market Analysis,* edited by Orley C. Ashenfelter and Wallace E. Oates, 201–19. New York: Halstead Press, 1977.

O'Flaherty, Brendan. *City Economics.* Cambridge, MA: Harvard University Press, 2005.

O'Hare, Michael. "'Not on *My* Block You Don't': Facility Siting and the Strategic Importance of Compensation." *Public Policy* 25 (1977): 407–58.

Oliver, Pamela, Gerald Marwell, and Ruy Teixeira. "A Theory of the Critical Mass I: Interdependence, Group Heterogeneity, and the Production of Collective Action." *American Journal of Sociology* 91 (1985): 522–56.

Ostrom, Elinor. *Governing the Commons: The Evolution of Institutions for Collective Action.* Cambridge: Cambridge University Press, 1990.

Ostrom, Elinor, Roy Gardner, and James Walker. *Rules, Games, and Common-Pool Resources.* Ann Arbor: University of Michigan Press, 1994.

Parchomovsky, Gideon, and Peter Siegelman. "Selling Mayberry: Communities and Individuals in Law and Economics." *California Law Review* 92 (2004): 75–146.

Parisi, Francesco, Norbert Schulz, and Ben Depoorter. "Duality in Property: Commons and Anticommons." *International Review of Law and Economics* 25 (2005): 578–91.

Peñalver, Eduardo M. "Property as Entrance." *Virginia Law Review* 91 (2005): 1889–1972.

Penner, J. E. "The 'Bundle of Rights' Picture of Property." *UCLA Law Review* 43 (1996): 711–820.

———. *The Idea of Property in Law.* Oxford: Clarendon Press, 1997.

———. "Misled by 'Property.'" *Canadian Journal of Law and Jurisprudence* 18 (2005): 75–93.

Perin, Constance. *Everything in Its Place: Social Order and Land Use in America.* Princeton: Princeton University Press, 1977.

Pestoff, Victor. "Beyond Exit and Voice in Social Services: Citizens as Coproducers." In *Delivering Welfare,* edited by Perri 6 and Isabel Vidal, 151–68. Barcelona: Centre d'Iniciatives de l'Economia Social, 1994.

Phillips, Michael M., and Ruth Simon. "Mortgage Bailout to Aid 1 in 9 U.S. Homeowners." *Wall Street Journal,* March 5, 2009, A1.

Pigou, A. C. *The Economics of Welfare.* 4th ed. New York: Macmillan, 1962.

Plassmann, Florenz, and T. Nicolaus Tideman. "Accurate Valuation in the Absence of Markets." *Public Finance Review* 36 (2008): 334–58.

Pogodzinski, J. Michael, and Tim R. Sass. "The Economic Theory of Zoning: A Critical Review." *Land Economics* 66 (1990): 294–314.

Poindexter, Georgette C. "Towards a Legal Framework for Regional Redistribution of

Poverty-Related Expenses." *Washington University Journal of Urban and Contemporary Law* 47 (1995): 3–50.

Polinsky, A. Mitchell. "On the Choice between Property Rules and Liability Rules." *Economic Inquiry* 18 (1980): 233–46.

———. "Resolving Nuisance Disputes: The Simple Economics of Injunctive and Damage Remedies." *Stanford Law Review* 32 (1980): 1075–1112.

Porat, Ariel, and Alex Stein. *Tort Liability under Uncertainty.* Oxford: Oxford University Press, 2001.

Posner, Richard A. *Economic Analysis of Law.* 7th ed. New York: Aspen Publishers, 2007.

Pozdena, Randall Johnston. *The Modern Economics of Housing: A Guide to Theory and Policy for Finance and Real Estate Professionals.* New York: Quorum Books, 1988.

Pritchett, Wendell E. "The 'Public Menace' of Blight: Urban Renewal and the Private Uses of Eminent Domain." *Yale Law and Policy Review* 21 (2003): 1–52.

Putnam, Robert D. *Bowling Alone: The Collapse and Revival of American Community.* New York: Simon and Schuster, 2000.

———. "*E Pluribus Unum:* Diversity and Community in the Twenty-first Century." *Scandinavian Political Studies* 30 (2007): 137–74.

Qadeer, M. A. "The Nature of Urban Land." *American Journal of Economics and Sociology* 40 (1981): 165–82.

Radin, Margaret Jane. "Residential Rent Control." *Philosophy and Public Affairs* 15 (1986): 350–80.

Randolph, Patrick A., Jr. "Changing the Rules: Should Courts Limit the Power of Common Interest Communities to Alter Unit Owners' Privileges in the Face of Vested Expectations?" *Santa Clara Law Review* 38 (1998): 1081–1133.

Rawling, Zach. "Reevaluating Leasing Restrictions in Common Interest Developments: Rejecting Reasonableness in Favor of Consent." 2007. http://works.bepress.com/zach_rawling/3.

Rawls, John. *A Theory of Justice.* Cambridge, MA: Belknap Press, 1971.

Réaume, Denise. "Individuals, Groups, and Rights to Public Goods." *University of Toronto Law Journal* 38 (1988): 1–27.

Reich, Charles A. "The New Property." *Yale Law Journal* 73 (1965): 733–87.

Reichman, Uriel. "Judicial Supervision of Servitudes." *Journal of Legal Studies* 7 (1978): 139–64.

Riccardi, Nicholas. "Leveling Restrictions on Houses' Big Growth; Communities Target McMansions, Hoping to Preserve Character." *Los Angeles Times,* July 23, 2007, A12.

Rich, Motoko. "Homeowner Boards Blur Line of Just Who Rules the Roost." *New York Times,* July 27, 2003, A1.

Ritov, Ilana. "Probability of Regret: Anticipation of Uncertainty Resolution in Choice." *Organizational Behavior and Human Decision Processes* 66 (1996): 228–36.

Ritov, Ilana, and Jonathan Baron. "Outcome Knowledge, Regret, and Omission Bias." *Organizational Behavior and Human Decision Processes* 64 (1995): 119–27.

Roisman, Florence Wagman. "The Right to Remain: Common Law Protections for Security of Tenure: An Essay in Honor of John Otis Calmore." *North Carolina Law Review* 86 (2008): 817–57.

Rose, Carol M. "Expanding the Choices for the Global Commons: Comparing Newfangled Tradable Allowance Schemes to Old-Fashioned Common Property Regimes." *Duke Environmental Law and Policy Forum* 10 (1999): 45–72.

———. "Planning and Dealing: Piecemeal Land Controls as a Problem of Local Legitimacy." *California Law Review* 71 (1983): 839–912.

———. "Servitudes, Security, and Assent: Some Comments on Professors French and Reichman." *Southern California Law Review* 55 (1982): 1403–16.

———. "The Several Futures of Property: Of Cyberspace and Folk Tales, Emission Trades and Ecosystems." *Minnesota Law Review* 83 (1998): 129–82.

———. "The Shadow of *The Cathedral*." *Yale Law Journal* 106 (1997): 2175–2200.

———. "What Government Can Do for Property (and Vice Versa)." In *The Fundamental Interrelationships Between Government and Property*, edited by Nicholas Mercuro and Warren J. Samuels, 209–22. New York: Routledge, 1999.

Rose-Ackerman, Susan. "Beyond Tiebout: Modeling the Political Economy of Local Government." In *Local Provision of Public Services: The Tiebout Model after Twenty-five Years*, edited by George R. Zodrow, 55–83. New York: Academic Press, 1983.

Rosenberry, Katharine N. "Home Businesses, Llamas and Aluminum Siding: Trends in Covenant Enforcement." *John Marshall Law Review* 31 (1998): 443–87.

Rosenblum, Nancy L. *Membership and Morals: The Personal Uses of Pluralism in America.* Princeton: Princeton University Press, 1998.

Ross, Stephen, and John Yinger. "Sorting and Voting: A Review of the Literature on Urban Public Finance." In *Handbook of Regional and Urban Economics,* vol. 3, edited by Paul Cheshire and Edwin S. Mills, 2001–2060. Amsterdam: North-Holland, 1999.

Rothenberg, Jerome. "The Nature of Redevelopment Benefits." In *Readings in Urban Economics,* edited by Matthew Edel and Jerome Rothenberg, 215–26. New York: Macmillan, 1972.

Rothschild, Michael, and Lawrence J. White. "The Analytics of the Pricing of Higher Education and Other Services in Which the Customers Are Inputs." *Journal of Political Economy* 103 (1995): 573–86.

Rousseau, Jean-Jacques. *On the Origin of Inequality.* Translated by G. D. H. Cole. Great Books of the Western World, Encyclopedia Britannica. London, 1952.

Rubinfeld, Daniel L. "The Economics of the Local Public Sector." In *Handbook of Public Economics,* vol. 2, edited by Alan J. Auerbach and Martin Feldstein, 571–645. Amsterdam: North-Holland, 1985.

Ryan, James E., and Michael Heise. "The Political Economy of School Choice." *Yale Law Journal* 111 (2002): 2043–2136.

Salzman, James, and J. B. Ruhl. "Currencies and the Commodification of Environmental Law." *Stanford Law Review* 53 (2000): 607–94.

Sampson, Robert J., and Stephen W. Raudenbush. "Systematic Social Observation of

Public Spaces: A New Look at Disorder in Urban Neighborhoods." *American Journal of Sociology* 105 (1999): 603–51.

Schelling, Thomas C. "Dynamic Models of Segregation." *Journal of Mathematical Sociology* 1 (1971): 143–86.

———. *Micromotives and Macrobehavior.* New York: Norton, 1978.

———. "A Process of Residential Segregation: Neighborhood Tipping." In *Racial Discrimination in Economic Life,* edited by Anthony H. Pascal, 157–84. Lexington, MA: Lexington Books, 1972.

Schlager, Edella, and Elinor Ostrom. "Property-Rights Regimes and Coastal Fisheries: An Empirical Analysis." In *The Political Economy of Customs and Culture: Informal Solutions to the Commons Problem,* edited by Terry L. Anderson and Randy T. Simmons, 13–41. Lanham, MD: Rowman and Littlefield, 1993.

Schorr, David B. "How Blackstone Became a Blackstonian." *Theoretical Inquiries in Law* 10, no. 1 (2009): 103–26. http://www.bepress.com/til/default/vol10/iss1/art5.

Schragger, Richard C. "The Limits of Localism." *Michigan Law Review* 100 (2001): 371–472.

———. "Paying for Our Localism: Internalizing the Costs of Exclusion." Unpublished draft, February 4, 2000, on file with author.

Schuck, Peter H. *Diversity in America: Keeping Government at a Safe Distance.* Cambridge, MA: Belknap Press, 2003.

Schuetz, Jenny, Vicki Been, and Ingrid Gould Ellen. "Neighborhood Effects of Concentrated Mortgage Foreclosures." NYU Law and Economics Research Paper No. 08-41, September 2008. http://ssrn.com/abstract=1270121.

Schwab, Robert M., and Wallace E. Oates. "Community Composition and the Provision of Local Public Goods: A Normative Analysis." *Journal of Public Economics* 44 (1991): 217–37.

Schwab, Robert M., and Ernest M. Zampelli. "Disentangling the Demand Function from the Production Function for Local Public Services: The Case of Public Safety." *Journal of Public Economics* 33 (1987): 245–60.

Schwemm, Robert G. "Discriminatory Housing Statements and 3604(c): A New Look at the Fair Housing Act's Most Intriguing Provision." *Fordham Urban Law Journal* 29 (2001): 187–316.

Scott, Robert E. "Error and Rationality in Individual Decisionmaking: An Essay on the Relationship between Cognitive Illusions and the Management of Choices." *Southern California Law Review* 59 (1986): 329–62.

Selmi, Michael. "Was the Disparate Impact Theory a Mistake?" *UCLA Law Review* 53 (2006): 701–82.

Sen, Amartya K. "Isolation, Assurance and the Social Rate of Discount." *Quarterly Journal of Economics* 81 (1967): 112–24.

Shavell, Steven. "Liability for Harm versus Regulation of Safety." *Journal of Legal Studies* 13 (1984): 357–74.

Shiller, Robert J. "Derivatives Markets for Home Prices." NBER Working Paper No. 13962, April 2008. http://www.nber.org/papers/w13962.

———. *Macro Markets: Creating Institutions for Managing Society's Largest Economic Risks.* Oxford: Clarendon Press, 1993.

———. *The New Financial Order.* Princeton: Princeton University Press, 2003.

———. "Radical Financial Innovation." In *Entrepreneurship, Innovation, and the Growth Mechanism of the Free-Enterprise Economies,* edited by Eytan Sheshinski, Robert J. Strom, and William J. Baumol, 306–23. Princeton: Princeton University Press, 2007.

Shiller, Robert J., and Allan N. Weiss. "Home Equity Insurance." *Journal of Real Estate Finance and Economics* 19 (1999): 21–47.

———. "Moral Hazard in Home Equity Conversion." *Real Estate Economics* 28 (2000): 1–31.

Siegan, Bernard H. *Land Use without Zoning.* Lexington, MA: Lexington Books, 1972.

Silverman, Ronald H. "Subsidizing Tolerance for Open Communities." *Wisconsin Law Review* 1977 (1977): 375–501.

Sinai, Todd, and Nicholas S. Souleles. "Owner-Occupied Housing as a Hedge against Rent Risk." *Quarterly Journal of Economics* 120 (2005): 763–89.

Singer, Joseph William. *Entitlement: The Paradoxes of Property.* New Haven: Yale University Press, 2000.

———. "The Ownership Society and Takings of Property: Castles, Investments, and Just Obligations." *Harvard Environmental Law Review* 30 (2006): 309–38.

Smith, Henry E. "Exclusion and Property Rules in the Law of Nuisance." *Virginia Law Review* 90 (2004): 965–1049.

———. "Exclusion versus Governance: Two Strategies for Delineating Property Rights." *Journal of Legal Studies* 31 (2002): S453–87.

———. "Property and Property Rules." *New York University Law Review* 79 (2004): 1719–98.

———. "Semicommon Property Rights and Scattering in the Open Fields." *Journal of Legal Studies* 29 (2000): 131–69.

Smithsimon, Greg. "Rent Regulation: The Right Tool for the Right Job." *Planetizen,* May 14, 2007. http://planetizen.com/node/24451.

Sommer, Robert. *Personal Space: The Behavioral Basis of Design.* Englewood Cliffs, NJ: Prentice Hall, 1969.

Span, Henry A. "How the Courts Should Fight Exclusionary Zoning." *Seton Hall Law Review* 32 (2001): 1–107.

Speight, Alan E. H. *Consumption, Rational Expectations, and Liquidity: Theory and Evidence.* New York: St. Martin's Press, 1989.

Stabile, Donald R. *Community Associations: The Emergence and Acceptance of a Quiet Innovation in Housing.* Westport, CT: Greenwood Press, 2000.

Stake, Jeffrey E. "Toward an Economic Understanding of Touch and Concern." *Duke Law Journal* 1988 (1988): 925–74.

Stiglitz, Joseph E. "The Theory of Local Public Goods Twenty-five Years after Tiebout: A Perspective." In *Local Provision of Public Services: The Tiebout Model after Twenty-five Years,* edited by George R. Zodrow, 17–53. New York: Academic Press, 1983.

Stoll, Robert R. *Sets, Logic, and Axiomatic Theories.* San Francisco: W. H. Freeman, 1961.

Stolzenberg, Nomi Maya. "'He Drew a Circle That Shut Me Out': Assimilation, Indoctrination, and the Paradox of a Liberal Education." *Harvard Law Review* 106 (1993): 581–667.

Stone, Michael E. "Social Ownership." In *A Right to Housing: Foundation for a New Social Agenda,* edited by Rachel G. Bratt, Michael E. Stone, and Chester Hartman, 240–78. Philadelphia: Temple University Press, 2006.

Strahilevitz, Lior Jacob. "Exclusionary Amenities in Residential Communities." *Virginia Law Review* 92 (2006): 437–99.

———. "Information Asymmetries and the Rights to Exclude." *Michigan Law Review* 104 (2006): 1835–98.

Streitfeld, David. "Economic Fears Exclude Home Values." *Chicago Tribune,* April 12, 2007, business section, 1.

Streitfeld, David, and Gretchen Morgenson. "Building Flawed American Dreams." *New York Times,* October 19, 2008. http://www.nytimes.com/2008/10/19/business/19cisneros.html.

Stretton, Hugh, and Lionel Orchard. *Public Goods, Public Enterprise, Public Choice: Theoretical Foundations of the Contemporary Attack on Government.* New York: St. Martin's Press, 1994.

Sugden, Robert. "Reciprocity: The Supply of Public Goods through Voluntary Contributions." *Economic Journal* 94 (1984): 772–87.

Sunstein, Cass R. "Social Norms and Social Roles." *Columbia Law Review* 96 (1996): 903–68.

Sunstein, Cass R., and Edna Ullmann-Margalit. "Solidarity Goods." *Journal of Political Philosophy* 9, no. 2 (2001): 129–49.

Swarns, Rachel L. "Rise in Renters is Erasing Gains for Ownership." *New York Times,* June 21, 2008, A1.

Syz, Juerg, Paolo Vanini, and Marco Salvi. "Property Derivatives and Index-Linked Mortgages." *Journal of Real Estate Finance and Economics* 36 (2008): 23–35.

Taylor, Ralph B., Barbara A. Koons, Ellen M. Kurtz, Jack B. Greene, and Douglas D. Perkins. "Street Blocks with More Nonresidential Land Use Have More Physical Deterioration: Evidence from Baltimore and Philadelphia." *Urban Affairs Review* 31 (1995): 120–36.

Tergesen, Anne. "Trading on the Future: 'Equity Release' Is the Newest Way to Turn Your Home Into a Piggy Bank; But the Risks Can Be Sizable." *Wall Street Journal,* September 13, 2008, R6.

Thaler, Richard H. *The Winner's Curse: Paradoxes and Anomalies of Economic Life.* New York: Free Press, 1992.

Thaler, Richard H., and Eric J. Johnson. "Gambling with the House Money and Trying to Break Even: The Effects of Prior Outcomes on Risky Choice." *Management Science* 36 (1990): 643–60.

Thaler, Richard H., and Cass R. Sunstein. *Nudge: Improving Decisions about Health, Wealth, and Happiness.* New Haven: Yale University Press, 2008.

Thompson, Barton H., Jr. "Tragically Difficult: The Obstacles to Governing the Commons." *Environmental Law* 30 (2000): 241–78.

Tideman, T. Nicolaus. "Three Approaches to Improving Urban Land Use." Ph.D. dissertation, University of Chicago, 1969.

Tideman, T. Nicolaus, and Gordon Tullock. "A New and Superior Process for Making Social Choices." *Journal of Political Economy* 84 (1976): 1145–59.

Tiebout, Charles M. "A Pure Theory of Local Expenditures." *Journal of Political Economy* 64 (1956): 416–24.

Tilly, Chris, Philip Moss, Joleen Kirschenman, and Ivy Kennelly. "Space as a Signal: How Employers Perceive Neighborhoods in Four Metropolitan Labor Markets." In *Urban Inequality: Evidence from Four Cities,* edited by Alice O'Connor, Chris Tilly, and Lawrence D. Bobo, 304–38. New York: Russell Sage Foundation, 2001.

Ulen, Thomas S. "The Public Use of Private Property: A Dual-Constraint Theory of Efficient Governmental Takings." In *Taking Property and Just Compensation: Law and Economics Perspectives of the Takings Issue,* edited by Nicholas Mercuro, 163–98. Norwell, MA: Kluwer Academic, 1992.

Ullmann-Margalit, Edna. *The Emergence of Norms.* Oxford: Clarendon Press, 1977.

van Dijk, Eric, and Marcel Zeelenberg. "On the Psychology of 'If Only': Regret and the Comparison Between Factual and Counterfactual Outcomes." *Organizational Behavior and Human Decision Processes* 97 (2005): 152–60.

Van Hemert, James. "Time to Update the Zoning Code." *Rocky Mountain News,* June 23, 2007, news section, 29.

Venkatesh, Sudhir Alladi. *American Project: The Rise and Fall of a Modern Ghetto.* Cambridge, MA: Harvard University Press, 2000.

Walters, Alan A. *Noise and Prices.* Oxford: Clarendon Press, 1975.

Walzer, Michael. *Politics and Passion: Toward a More Egalitarian Liberalism.* New Haven: Yale University Press, 2004.

Wax, Amy L. "Bargaining in the Shadow of the Market: Is There a Future for Egalitarian Marriage?" *Virginia Law Review* 84 (1998): 509–672.

Webber, Melvin M. "Order in Diversity: Community without Propinquity." In *Cities and Space: The Future Use of Urban Land,* edited by Lowdon Wingo Jr., 23–54. Baltimore: Johns Hopkins University Press, 1963.

Wechsler, Herbert. "Toward Neutral Principles of Constitutional Law." *Harvard Law Review* 73 (1959): 1–35.

Weinstein, Neil D. "Unrealistic Optimism about Future Life Events." *Journal of Personality and Social Psychology* 39 (1980): 806–20.

Weiser, Jay. "The Real Estate Covenant as Commons: Incomplete Contract Remedies over Time." *Southern California Interdisciplinary Law Journal* 13 (2004): 269–330.

Weiss, Marc A., and John W. Watts, "Community Builders and Community Associations: The Role of Real Estate Developers in Private Residential Governance." In *Residential Community Associations: Private Government in the Intergovernmental System?* edited by Advisory Commission on Intergovernmental Relations, 95–104. Washington, DC: Advisory Commission on Intergovernmental Relations, 1989.

White, Michelle J. "Fiscal Zoning in Fragmented Metropolitan Areas." In *Fiscal Zoning and Land Use Controls,* edited by Edwin S. Mills and Wallace E. Oates, 31–100. Lexington, MA: Lexington Books, 1975.

———. "Suburban Growth Controls: Liability Rules and Pigovian Taxes." *Journal of Legal Studies* 8 (1979): 207–30.

Wilcox, Pamela, and Neil Quisenberry, Debra T. Cabrera, and Shayne Jones. "Busy Places and Broken Windows? Toward Defining the Role of Physical Structure and Process in Community Crime Models." *Sociological Quarterly* 45 (2004): 185–207.

Wilmot, Ben. "Radical Thinking to Shake Up the Mortgage Market." *Australian Financial Review,* September 22, 2005. http://w4.stern.nyu.edu/news/news.cfm?doc_id=4889.

Winokur, James L. "Choice, Consent, and Citizenship in *Common Interest Communities.*" In *Common Interest Communities: Private Governments and the Public Interest,* edited by Stephen E. Barton and Carol J. Silverman, 87–124. Berkeley: Institute of Governmental Studies Press, 1994.

Wittman, Donald. "Prior Regulation versus Post Liability: The Choice between Input and Output Monitoring." *Journal of Legal Studies* 6 (1977): 193–211.

Yinger, John. "Capitalization and the Median Voter." *American Economic Review* 71, no. 2 (1981): 99–103.

———. "Prejudice and Discrimination in the Urban Housing Market." In *Current Issues in Urban Economics,* edited by Peter Mieszkowski and Mahlon Straszheim, 430–68. Baltimore: Johns Hopkins University Press, 1979.

Young, Iris Marion. *Justice and the Politics of Difference.* Princeton: Princeton University Press, 1990.

"Zoning for the Regional Welfare." Student Note. *Yale Law Journal* 89 (1980): 748–68.

Cases

Amphitheaters, Inc. v. Portland Meadows, 198 P.2d 847 (Or. 1948).

Barnard v. Adams, 51 U.S. 270 (1850).

Boomer v. Atlantic Cement Co., 257 N.E.2d 870 (N.Y. 1970).

Chicago Lawyers' Committee for Civil Rights Under Law v. Craigslist, 519 F.3d 666 (7th Cir. 2007).

Dolan v. City of Tigard, 512 U.S. 374 (1994).

Euclid v. Ambler Realty, 272 U.S. 365 (1926).

Evangelical Lutheran Church of the Ascension of Snyder, N.Y. v. Sahlem, 172 N.E. 455 (N.Y. 1930).

Hills Dev. Co. v. Township of Bernards, 510 A.2d 621 (N.J. 1986).

Huntington Branch NAACP v. Town of Huntington, 844 F.2d 926 (2d Cir 1988), aff'd 488 U.S. 15 (1988) (per curiam).

Jacque v. Steenberg Homes, 563 N.W.2d 154 (Wis. 1997).

Jones v. Alfred H. Mayer Co., 392 U.S. 409 (1968).

Kelo v. City of New London, 545 U.S. 469 (2005).

Korematsu v. United States, 323 U.S. 214 (1944).

Licker v. Harkleroad, 558 S.E.2d 31 (Ga. Ct. App. 2001).

Moore v. City of East Cleveland, 431 U.S. 494 (1977).

Nollan v. Cal. Coastal Comm'n, 483 U.S. 825 (1987).

Rick v. West, 228 N.Y.S.2d 195 (Sup. Ct. 1962).

Shelley v. Kraemer, 334 U.S. 1 (1948).

S. Burlington County NAACP v. Township of Mt. Laurel, 336 A.2d 713 (N.J. 1975) (Mount Laurel I).

S. Burlington County NAACP v. Township of Mt. Laurel, 456 A.2d 390 (N.J. 1983) (Mount Laurel II).

Spur Indus. v. Del E. Webb Dev. Co., 494 P.2d 700 (Ariz. 1972).

United States v. Causby, 328 U.S. 256 (1946).

United States v. Hunter, 459 F.2d 205 (4th Cir. 1972).

Wasserman's v. Township of Middletown, 645 A.2d 100 (N.J. 1994).

Statutory, Executive, and Administrative Materials

City of Coral Gables. "So You Want to Paint Your House." http://www.coralgables .com/CGWeb/documents/bnz_docs/brochures/So_You_Want_to_Paint_ v2.pdf.

Internal Revenue Service. *Summary of the Credit for Qualified Hybrid Vehicles.* http://www.irs.gov/newsroom/article/0,,id=157557,00.html.

The Kaiser Committee. "A Decent Home: Report of the President's Committee on Urban Housing." Washington, DC: U.S. Government Printing Office, 1969. Reprint in *Readings in Urban Economics,* edited by Matthew Edel and Jerome Rothenberg, 178–93. New York: Macmillan, 1972.

Model Penal Code. Washington, D.C.: American Law Institute, 1962.

New Jersey Department of Community Affairs, Council on Affordable Housing. "Reports and Quick Facts." http://www.state.nj.us/dca/affiliates/coah/reports/.

New Jersey Legislature. Fair Housing Act. *New Jersey Statutes Annotated* 52:27D-301 et seq.

Restatement (Third) of Property: Servitudes. Washington, DC: American Law Institute, 2000.

Roosevelt, Franklin D. Executive Order no. 9066, "Authorizing the Secretary of War to Prescribe Military Areas." February 19, 1942. *Code of Federal Regulations,* title 3, 1093 (1938 cumulative supplement, 1943).

U.S. Bureau of the Census. *American Housing Survey for the United States, 2005.* Table 1A1, Introductory Characteristics, All Housing Units. http://www.census .gov/hhes/www/housing/ahs/ahs05/tab1a=1.pdf.

———. "Census Bureau Reports on Residential Vacancies and Homeownership." *U.S. Census Bureau News,* October 28, 2008. http://www.census.gov/hhes/ www/housing/hvs/qtr308/files/q308press.pdf.

————. *Geographic Mobility: 2004 to 2005.* Table 17, General Mobility of Householders, by Tenure, Age, and Household Income in 2004: 2004 to 2005. http://www .census.gov/population/www/socdemo/migrate/cps2005.html.

————. *Historical Census of Housing Tables: Homeownership.* http://www.census.gov/ hhes/www/housing/census/historic/owner.html.

————. *Housing Vacancies and Homeownership, Annual Statistics: 2007.* Table 12, Home-ownership Rates by Area: 1960 to 2007. http://www.census.gov/hhes/www/ housing/hvs/annual07/ann07t12.html.

————. *Population: 1790 to 1990.* Table 4, United States, Urban and Rural. http://www .census.gov/population/censusdata/table-4.pdf.

————. *Urban/Rural and Metropolitan/Nonmetropolitan Population: 2000. Data Set: Census 2000* Summary File 1 (SF1) 100-Percent Data.

U.S. Congress. Civil Rights Act of 1866. *U.S. Code* 42, sec. 1982.

————. Civil Rights Act of 1964, Title VII. *U.S. Code* 42, sec. 2000e et seq.

————. Elementary and Secondary Education Act of 1965, Title I. *U.S. Code* 20, sec. 6333.

————. Fair Housing Act. *U.S. Code* 42, sec. 3601 et seq.

————. Housing and Economic Recovery Act of 2008, Public Law 110-289, *U.S. Statutes at Large* 122: 265 (2008).

————. Internal Revenue Code. *U.S. Code* 26. §§ 163(h); 164; 121.

Web Sites

Alamo Drafthouse Cinema. http://www.drafthouse.com/lakecreek/shows.php?id=88.

CME Weather Products. http://www.cme.com/trading/weather/.

Community Associations Institute. "Industry Data: National Statistics." http://www .caionline.org/.

Kling, Jeffrey. "Moving to Opportunity Research." http://www.nber.org/~kling/ mto/index.html.

Macro Markets. "S&P/Case-Shiller Home Price Indices." http://www.macro markets.com/csi_housing/sp_caseshiller.asp.

National Housing Institute/Shelterforce, nhi_press@nhi.org. Posting to colist@comm org.wisc.edu (May 4, 2007). http://comm-org.wisc.edu/pipermail/colist/2007-May/ 004667.html.

REX Holdings. "REX & Co.: Realtors." http://www.rexagreement.com/index.php/ rex/who_we_serve_realtors_why_rex/.

INDEX